Giant Book of
Challenging
THINKING
PUZZLES

MICHAEL A. DISPEZIO

The Main Street Press

10 9 8 7 6 5 4 3 2

Published In 1999 by Sterling Publishing Company, Inc.
387 Park Avenue South, New York, N.Y. 10016

Material in this collection was adapted from
Critical Thinking Puzzles
Great Critical Thinking Puzzles
and
Challenging Critical Thinking Puzzles
© Michael A. DiSpezio

Distributed in Canada by Sterling Publishing
c/o Canadian Manda Group
One Atlantic Avenue, Suite 105
Toronto, Ontario, Canada M6K 3E7

Distributed in Great Britain and Europe by Cassell PLC
Wellington House, 125 Strand
London WC2R 0BB, United Kingdom

Distibuted in Australia by Capricorn Link (Australia) Pty Ltd.
P.O. Box 6651, Baulkham Hills, Business Centre,
NSW 2153, Australia

CONTENTS

SECTION 1

SECTION 2

SECTION 3

Section 1
Critical Thinking
PUZZLES

Introduction

When we think critically we are engaging in intellectual strategies to probe the basic nature of a problem, situation, or puzzle. By these strategies, we mean making observations, predictions, generalizations, reasonings by assumptions, comparisons and contrasts, uncovering relationships between the parts to the whole, and looking for sequences. It sounds like a lot, but everyone has these skills and the puzzles in this book are designed to challenge, exercise, and stretch the way you interpret the world.

Some of the puzzles here are old favorites that have entertained people for years. Several of them are presented in their time-tested way. Most of the standards, however, have a new twist or updated story added. Other puzzles require some inventive solutions, so don't be afraid to be creative. Most of them can be done with a pencil or pen.

Some require inexpensive materials that can probably be found around the house: a pair of scissors, markers, tape, toothpicks, and a yardstick. Even though some puzzles can be solved using algebra, they were selected for their ability to be visualized and figured out this way. Therefore, in addition to being fun to do, they offer an arena to practice thinking skills.

Statements such as "I want you to memorize this list" or "That's a good answer, but it wasn't the one I expected" help to extinguish critical thought. Although you'll never have to measure an ant's path or alter a flag, the process of creating and evaluating a reasonable answer is a worthwhile experience. By the time you finish this section, those powerful skills will be back on track, probing your everyday experiences for a more thorough and deeper understanding.

Ready to start? Great, because the fun is about to begin.

—Michael

Pyramid Passage

Ancient Egyptian pyramids were built as royal tombs. Within these massive stone structures were rooms, halls and connecting passageways. Look at the figure below. Can you draw four paths that connect the matching symbols? The paths may not cross, they may not enter a non-matching pyramid, nor may they go outside the large pyramid boundary.

Magic Pyramid

For this pyramid, can you place the numbers 1,2,3,4,5, and 6 in the circles shown below? Only one number may be placed in a circle and all numbers must be used. When the final arrangement is complete, the sum of each side's three numbers must all be the same number.

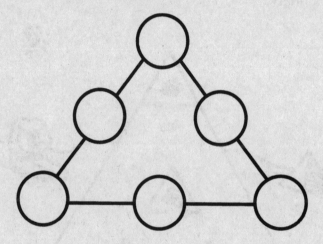

Pyramid Builders

The Egyptian pyramids at Giza are incredible structures that took many years to complete. They were constructed out of large rectangular stone blocks, each weighing about as much as a car. The two largest pyramids contain over two million of these blocks!

Now, it's your turn to work. Can you build a three dimensional pyramid using two odd-shaped blocks?

Copy the figure below onto two pieces of stiff paper. Fold along the inner lines as shown and use tape to secure the edges.

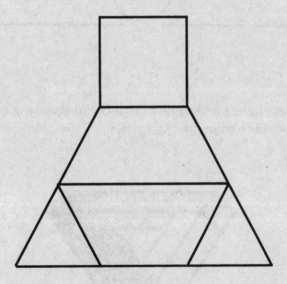

Now arrange the blocks to form a pyramid with four sides.

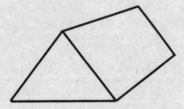

Trial by Triangle

Take a look at these two identical triangles. They are made with six sticks.

Can you rearrange the sticks so that they form four triangles? All of the new triangles must be the same size as these original two!

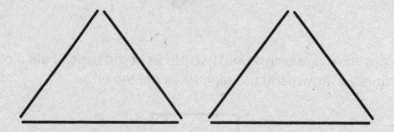

By the way, here's a triangle that you can draw but can't build. It's called an impossible triangle. See why?

Before you go on to the next puzzle, take a look at these strange objects. Do you think that they can also be built? Or do you think there may be some sort of trick?

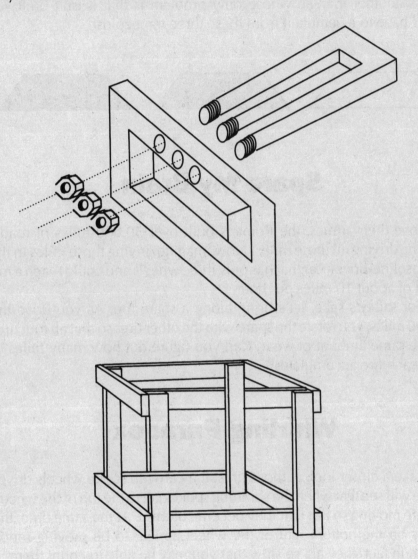

Trapezoid 2 Triangle

Here's another triangle whose only problem is that it isn't built yet. You'll have to assemble it from these three trapezoids!

Spare My Brain

To move their armies, the Romans built over 50,000 miles of roads. Imagine driving all those miles! Now imagine driving those miles in the first gasoline-driven car that has only three wheels and could reach a top speed of about 10 miles per hour.

For safety's sake, let's bring along a spare tire. As you drive the 50,000 miles, you rotate the spare with the other tires so that all four tires get the same amount of wear. Can you figure out how many miles of wear each tire accumulates?

Whirling Paradox

Let's take a closer look at those tires. If a car with spoke wheels drives by, we will see that when the spinning spokes get to the top of the wheel, they are moving so fast that they become blurred. At the same time, the spokes on the bottom half of the wheel appear to be moving much slower. In fact, they are so slow that you may be able to count them. If the spokes are connected to the same wheel, how can this be?

HINT: There may be a connection between this observation and the sound of a speeding car as it zooms by.

Lost?

Now we're on foot. Imagine that you and several friends have hiked into a remote region of the countryside. Your final destination is the land of Ultima. After leaving the village of Skullara, you continue following the trail and come across an important intersection. There is, however, one slight problem.

The sign showing which way to go has been knocked down. How can you figure out what is the right direction you need to go?

Sand Traps

As you continue on your hike, you're handed a map of the terrain ahead. This is not a safe place. In fact, the entire region is filled with quicksand, which is shown on the map as black splotches. Contrary to belief, quicksand does not suck or pull you under. Instead, it's your weight that makes you sink in this water and fine sand mixture.

Your challenge is to discover a path from any point on the bottom edge of the map to any point on the top edge without running into quicksand (black splotches). To make it more challenging, the path must consist of only two straight lines.

To start, place your pencil anywhere on the bottom border of the map. Then draw a straight line. When you stop, don't lift the pencil. Complete your trip using one more straight line.

Which Mountain?

Now that you've made it past the quicksand, it's time to do some climbing. You have a choice of climbing one of three geometrically shaped mountains, which are all 10,000 feet high. One of the mountains is a perfect cylinder, another is in the shape of a cone, and the third looks like the top half of a sphere. Several out-of-work math teachers have constructed roads that go from the base to the summit of each mountain. All three roads are built so that you climb 1 vertical foot every 20 horizontal feet. If you wish to walk the shortest distance from base to summit, which mountain would you choose?

Compass Caper

A compass is a reliable tool that always point north—or does it? There are many reports of compass needles that unexpectedly turn away from north. The strangest natural cause for this disturbance may be a shooting star. As the meteor streaks across the sky, it upsets the electrical balance of the air and produces a magnetic force that some believe affects the compass reading.

We, however, will work with a compass that always gives a true heading. Suppose you start a hike by traveling directly south for 500 paces. Then, you turn and go due east for another 100 paces. You turn once more and go due north for 500 paces. You are now in the exact same spot where you started from, but in front of you is a bear. What color is it?

A Cut Above

With all that hiking, you've probably now worked up an appetite. So how about some pizza?

Suppose this is the early 1900's and you're in New York City's Little Italy getting a Pizza Margherita, named in honor of a pizza-loving Italian princess. Can you divide the pie into eight equal slices in only three straight cuts? All the pieces must be identical: each with an upper surface covered with sauce, lower baked crust, and a crusty edge.

HINT: Don't worry about the mess. You won't have to clean it.

Kitchen Cups

Have you ever seen the written form of the Sanskrit language? If so, you probably are amazed at how different this ancient language from India looks from ours. Some English words, however, are based on Sanskrit. For example, cup comes from the Sanskrit word *kupa*, which means water well. This puzzle requires several water wells.

Suppose you need to measure exactly 1 cup of water. All that you have in your kitchen are two containers. The smaller container holds 3 cups and the larger holds 5 cups. How can you use these two containers to measure exactly 1 cup of water?

NOW, IGOR, ALL WE NEED IS ONE CUP OF WATER!

Moldy Math

Now let's talk about something else that you might have, but not want, in your kitchen. While you are raiding the refrigerator, you look behind the stove and discover a slice of bread that you misplaced several weeks ago. Needless to say, it is covered with mold. Since the mold started growing, the area it has covered has doubled each day. By the end of the eighth day, the entire surface of the bread is covered. When was the bread half-covered with mold?

And a Cut Below

Have you ever heard of the cheesemobile? It's a giant refrigerated truck that was built to carry a piece of Cheddar cheese. Why, then, all the fuss? Simple. The cheese weighed over 40,000 pounds!

Take a look a the smaller barrel of cheese below. If you make these three complete and straight cuts, how many pieces of cheese will you have?

Egg Exactly

Suppose you have only two egg timers, a 5-minute and a 3-minute. Can you use these two measuring devices to time an egg that must be boiled for exactly 2 minutes?

WHY AGAIN DID YOU SAY YOU WANTED TO KNOW THIS?

Losing Marbles?

Marbles have been around for a long time. In fact, archaeologists have discovered marbles buried alongside an Egyptian child who died over 4000 years ago! The word "marble," however, comes from the Greek word *marmaros*, which is a white polished stone made from the mineral agate.

Now it's your turn to play with them. Place a marble in a cup and carry it to the opposite side of the room. Too easy, huh? To make this more challenging, the cup must be turned upside down. This may take a little bit of creative problem solving, but it can be done.

A Puzzle of Portions

Did you know that 3 ounces plus 3 ounces doesn't always equal 6 ounces? As illogical as this may sound, its true because of the behavior of the small particles (and spaces) that make up liquids. When different liquids are mixed, the particles tend to fill in some of the open spaces. As a result, the liquid becomes more compact and occupies less volume. It's only a small difference, but it is measurable.

Let's try mixing something whose volume does not change. Your challenge is to split some apple juice into three equal portions. The juice comes in a 24-ounce container. You have only three other containers, each holding 5, 11, and 13 ounces. How can you divide the juice into three equal portions?

HINT: At the very least, it will take four steps.

Mixed Up?

Root beer, not cola, is the oldest-marketed soft drink in America. Before it was sold in the United States, root beer was brewed in many colonial homes. It contained many ingredients including molasses, licorice, vanilla, and the bark from birch trees. It was going to be called root tea but was later changed to root beer to attract the tavern crowd.

Here is one 8-ounce cup filled with root beer and another 8-ounce cup filled with cola. Take 1 tablespoon of root beer and add it to the cola. Stir the mixture. Now take 1 tablespoon of the mixture and add it to the root beer. Is there more root beer in the cola or cola in the root beer?

Toothpick Teasers

For the puzzles in this group, you can also use pieces of straws or small sticks if you don't have toothpicks.

These six toothpicks are arranged in a hexagon. Starting with this arrangement, can you form two identical diamonds by moving only two toothpicks and adding just one more?

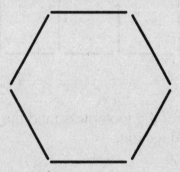

These sixteen toothpicks form eight identical triangles. Can you remove four toothpicks so that four of these triangles are left? All of the toothpicks that remain must be a side of the triangles with no loose ends sticking out.

Form four (and only four) identical squares by removing eight toothpicks.

Move only three of the toothpicks (and the eye) to make the fish swim in the opposite direction.

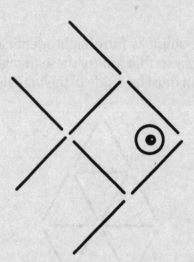

Going to the Movies

Let's take a break from these puzzles and go to the movies. The map below shows an assortment of routes from your home (H) to the movie theater (M). If you can only travel in a north, east, or northeast direction, how many possible routes are there from your home to the theater?

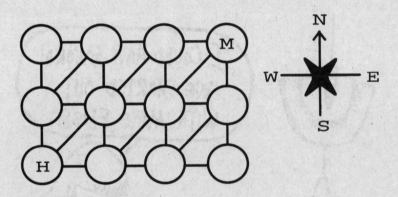

Now Seating?

Suppose two boys and three girls go to the movie theater and they all sit in the same row. If the row has only 5 seats:

1. How many different ways can the two boys and three girls be seated in this row?
2. What are the chances that the two children at the ends of the row are both boys?
3. What are the chances that the two children at the ends of the row are both girls?

Weighing In...

The movie playing in the theater is about a scientist who changes into a fly. Before she transforms herself, she carefully weighs a jar of sleeping flies. Then, she shakes the jar to wake them up. While they are flying, the scientist weighs the jar again. Does the jar full of flies weigh less when the insects are flying?

The Strangest Eyes

The scientist has transformed herself into a fly. One of her eyes is made up of one loop coiled into a spiral-like design. The other eye is made up of two separate loops shaped into a similar design. Can you tell which eye is the single loop and which one is the double without tracing the lines with a pencil?

Monkey Business

The theater shows a double feature. The second movie is about Tarzan going into the moving business.

For his first job, Tarzan must raise a 35-pound crate into his neighbor's tree house. To do this, he first attaches a pulley to a tree branch. He then passes a rope through the pulley and ties it to the crate. Just as he is about to lift the crate, he is called away to help a nearby elephant.

A passing chimp observes the situation and decides to help. The chimp also weighs 35 pounds. As the chimp pulls down on the rope what happens to the crate?

Head Count

In the final scene, a pet store owner is counting the birds and lizards that Tarzan has delivered to her store. For some odd reason, she decides to tally only the heads and scaly legs of these animals. When she has finished, she has counted thirty heads and seventy legs. How many birds and how many lizards are there?

Möbius Strip

Here is one of the strangest loops you'll ever see. It's called a Möbius strip in honor of the German mathematician who first investigated its properties.

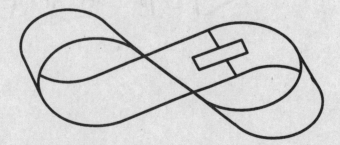

To build a Möbius strip, you need a strip of paper about 1 inch wide and 10 inches long. Coil the paper into a simple loop. Then put a single twist in the loop before securing the ends together with a piece of tape. Use a marker to color one side of the strip red and the other side blue. You'll soon discover that this loop has only one side!

Möbius strips are used in manufacturing. Many machines have belts that are used to connect different spinning parts. By using a belt sewn into a Möbius strip, the belt wears evenly on both sides.

Suppose you divide right down the middle of the Möbius strip. What shape would you get? Make a guess; then use a pair of scissors to carefully divide the strip.

Aunt Möbius?

THINK ABOUT IT! If we place two ants side by side on a Möbius strip and start them off in opposite directions, they will first pass each other on opposite sides of the paper. Then one ant will be walking on the top side of the strip, while the other will be on the bottom side!

Ant Walk

Let's pick up an ant from the strip and place it on one corner of a sugar cube. This cube has sides all measuring 1 centimeter. If the ant can only walk along the edges of the cube, what is the total distance it can travel without retracing any part of its path?

Cubic Quandaries

A wooden cube is painted red. Suppose it is divided with six equal cuts into the smaller cubes as shown.

1. How many smaller cubes are there?
2. How many of these smaller cubes
   a. have only one side that is painted red?
   b. have two sides that are painted red?
   c. have three sides that are painted red?
   d. have no sides that are red?

Squaring Off

Make a copy of these four rectangles. Cut out the shapes and then arrange them to form a perfect square.

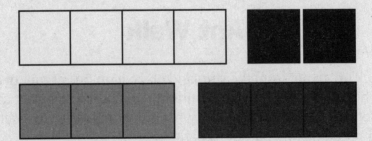

Saving Face

How good are you at visualizing things? These next few puzzles test your ability to rotate and construct objects in your mind.

These blocks below represent the same block. What figure is missing on the upper face of the last block?

Which of the four cubes below can be created by folding this design?

Finally, if you fold up this flat sheet along the inner lines, which figure represents the result?

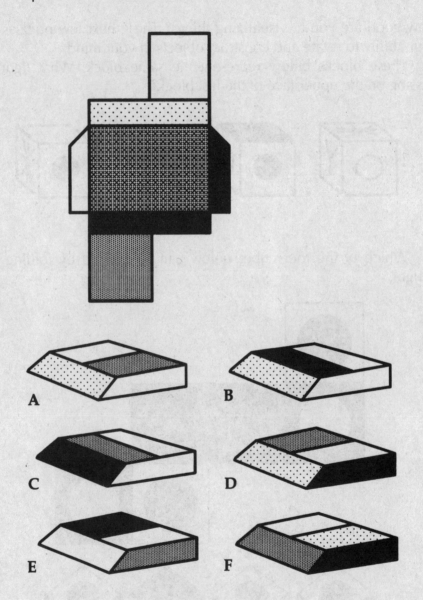

Cut the Cards

Have you ever played cards and wished you had a different hand? Suppose you need a heart instead of a spade. Well, here's your chance to change one suit into another.

Photocopy the spade below. Then use a pair of scissors to cut it into three pieces so that the pieces can be fitted together to form a heart. Can you do it?

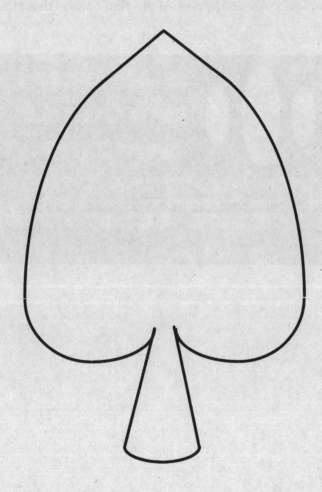

Stripped Stripe

There is a legend about a king who had six brothers and six sisters. His country's flag reflected this family structure with twelve bold stripes. When two of his brothers moved out of the kingdom, the king had two of the stripes removed.

Can you figure out how to cut the flag into as few pieces as possible so that the pieces can be put back together to make the same type of flag, but with two less stripes? No part of the flag can be discarded.

Missing Square

Count the number of blocks that make up this pattern. If you don't want to count each block, you can multiply the number of rows by the number of columns to get a total of sixty-four blocks.

Now photocopy the pattern.

Using a pair of scissors, separate the checkerboard along the inner lines. Reassemble the pieces as shown below.

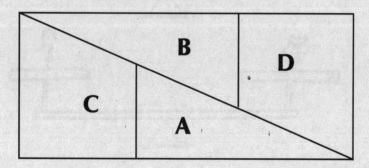

Now count the blocks, or, if you'd rather, just multiply again. The new figure is thirteen blocks long and five blocks high. That gives us sixty-five blocks. Where did the extra block come from?

Tipping the Scales

What whole animal(s) must be added to balance the fourth scale?

Snake Spread

These hungry snakes are swallowing each other. Since they began this odd dining experience, the circle they formed has gotten smaller. If they continue to swallow each other, what will eventually happen to the circle of snakes?

Falcon Flight

Two bicyclists are situated 60 miles apart. One has a falcon on his shoulder. The bicyclists start riding toward each other at the same time, both maintaining a constant speed of 30 mph. The moment they begin, the falcon flies off the first cyclist's shoulder and toward the other. The falcon flies at a constant ground speed of 45 mph. When the falcon meets the other rider, he reverses direction and flies back to the first cyclist (who is now considerably closer). The falcon continues this back and forth pattern until the riders finally meet. How far did the falcon fly?

A Question of Balance

Place two fingers at the ends of a yardstick. Slowly move the fingers toward each other. As you'll discover, your fingers always meet in the middle of the yardstick.

 Now place both fingers in the middle of the stick. Slowly try moving the two of them out to the opposite ends. This time you'll find that one finger remains in the middle while the other moves to the end. Can you explain this behavior?

Well-Balanced Plate

Here's a game that you are guaranteed to win as long as you let your opponent go first. Start with a plate on the exact center of a table. Your opponent must place another plate on the table. Then, it's your turn. During each turn, both of you must continue placing plates until no more plates will fit, but, don't worry, you'll win. Can you figure out the secret?

DOUBLE OR NOTHING ON YOUR ALLOWANCE? OKAY. BUT, YOU GO FIRST.

Robot Walkers

Have you ever seen a robot walker? It is designed to move over various types of terrain so that scientists can use it to explore nearby planets. Our robot walkers are positioned at the corners of a square plot of land. Each robot is programmed to follow the robot directly ahead of it. If all the robots move at the same speed, what will happen to the square pattern? Will the robots ever meet?

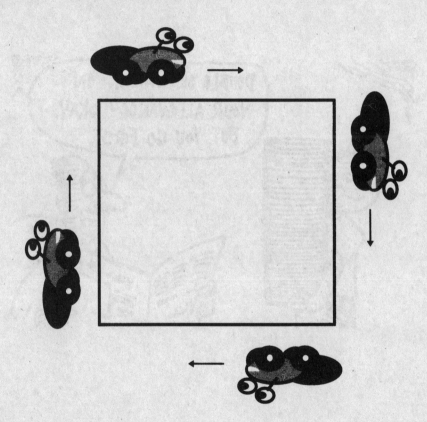

Chain Links

Suppose you own four pieces of chain. One chain has 5 links, two chains have 4 links, and one chain has 3 links.

You go to the jeweler and ask her to make a bracelet using all of these chains. She says it would cost $.50 to break a link and $1.00 to weld a link together. You calculate that it would cost $6.00 to build the bracelet. The jeweler, however, says that it would only cost $4.50. Can you figure out how she can assemble your bracelet for less?

Rope Ruse

There is an old legend about an ancient magician who could tie a rope into a knot while holding on to each end of the rope. Can you?

Money Magic

Look at the picture below. Can you guess what will happen when the bill is pulled from both ends?

After you've made your prediction, use a dollar bill and two paper clips to assemble this puzzle. Make sure that each paper clip grips only two of the three side-by-side sections. Slowly pull the bill apart. What happens to the clips? How is it possible?

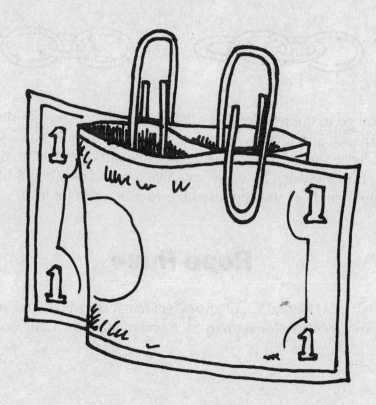

Revolutionary Thoughts

Different things orbit the earth at various speeds and distances. For example, satellites and space instruments released by the space shuttle are only several hundred miles away from the earth, while communications satellites circle at a distance of about 22,300 miles!

In this puzzle, Satellite X-1 orbits our planet once every 9 hours, Satellite Beta once every 4½ hours, and Satellite Parking once every 3 hours.

At time zero, the satellites are positioned in a straight line. How long will it take for all three objects to position themselves again in a straight line?

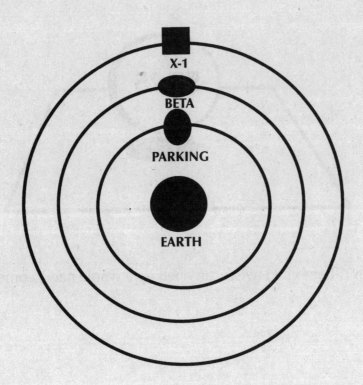

Baffling Holes

Black holes are celestial objects created by collapsed stars. These holes have tremendous concentration of matter and produce such a strong gravitational field that even light can't escape from it. If a black hole was placed on the surface of the earth, our entire planet would be sucked into it!

The hole in this puzzle is not as large as a black hole, but finding its solution can be a big challenge. Do you think a quarter can pass through a hole that is the size of a nickel? You can't tear, cut, or rip the hole. Impossible, you say? Trace the outline of a nickel onto an index card. Carefully cut out this outline.

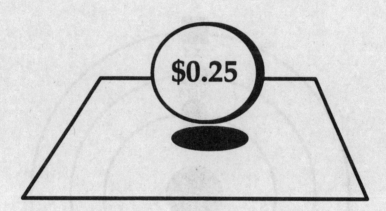

HINT: Bends and twists can open up a whole new geometry.

A Giant Step

Passing a quarter through a nickel-sized hole is nothing when you can step through an index card.

Carefully use a pair of scissors or a modeling knife to cut out the pattern of slots shown here. When you are finished, the hole will open in an accordian-like style and allow you to step through it!

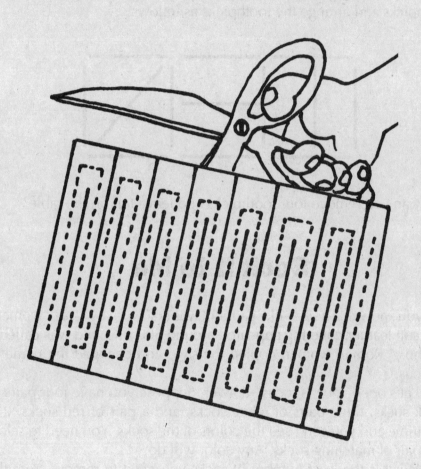

A Fair Solution

Two teenagers are deciding how to share the last piece of pizza. One of them must divide the slice. Both are afraid that the other will cut the slice unfairly and take the larger piece. Can this conflict be resolved by these teenagers so that both will be satisfied by the other one's cut?

After finishing their pizza, the happy teenagers bring out a box of toothpicks and arrange the toothpicks as follows:

Can you remove four toothpicks and leave ten on the table?

Sock It to Me

Did you know that a sock-like garment was first worn by Greek women? This soft leather covering appeared around 600 B.C. and was called a "sykhos." Roman women copied the style and changed the name to "soccus."

Let's open your "soccus" drawer. Suppose you have four pairs of black socks, three pairs of white socks, and a pair of red socks. It is nighttime and you can't see the colors of the socks. You need to select one pair of matching socks. Any color will do.

What is the least number of socks you need to remove from the drawer to ensure that you have at least one matching pair?

Nuts!

When you rotate a bolt clockwise, it travels into the threads of a nut. When that same bolt is rotated counterclockwise, the nut and bolt will separate.

Suppose you have two bolts aligned within each other's threads. If both bolts are rotated clockwise, will they move together, separate, or remain the same distance apart?

Here's something else to think about. In many large cities, the light bulbs used in places such as subway stations are unique. Instead of screwing into the socket with a clockwise motion, they require counterclockwise turns. What sense does it make to have these different from most other bulbs?

Doubtful Dimensions

John want to ship a baseball bat to his sister. The bat is 4 feet, 11 inches long. He places it in a rectangular box that is 5 feet long. When he takes it to the shipper, they can't send the package because it is too long. All dimensions of the package must be 4 feet or less in order to be shipped.

When John returns home, he figures out how he can repack the bat. What does he do?

Machine Madness

The identical wheels of this machine are connected by a series of belts. The outer rim of each wheel has a circumference of 8 centimeters. The rim of each wheel's inner shaft has a circumference of 4 centimeters. If the crank is rotated up one-quarter turn, what hour would the clock's hand point to?

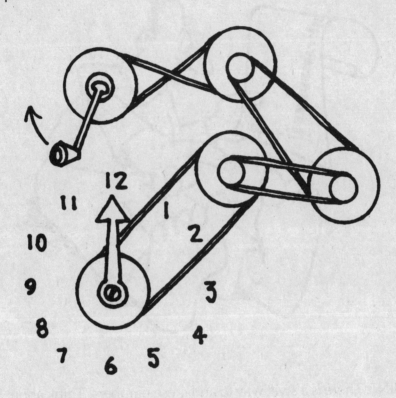

Putting It Together

Suppose you have a list of numbers from one to one hundred. How quickly can you add them all up without using a calculator?

HINT: There is a swift way to add these numbers. Think about how the numbers at the opposite ends of the list relate to each other.

The Heat Is On

The next time you drive under a highway bridge, take a close look at its ends. It is most likely that one end of the bridge will be attached directly to the road. The other end, however, will probably have a small gap. The gap is there on purpose. When the temperature rises, the bridge expands. If the gap wasn't there, the expanding metal bridge might shatter the roadway!

How about holes? Do they also expand when heated? Suppose a metal washer is placed in a flame. What happens to the size of its hole?

City Pipes

Beneath almost every city is an intricate system of large water-carrying pipes. These pipes transport runoff that falls through sewer openings and keep the city streets from flooding when there'a a rainstorm.

The pipes are connected to the surface through manhole openings. Manhole covers fit over the openings. How does their shape prevent them from falling into the hole?

HINT: Think of how the bat from the "Doubtful Dimensions" puzzle on page 48 was packaged!

Magic Square

Take a look a the grid below. Like the "Magic Pyramid" puzzle presented on page 8 of this book, the Magic Square is created when the right numbers are placed in the empty boxes.

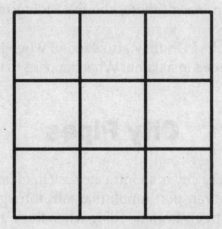

Place a number from 1 to 9 in each of the boxes . Don't repeat any of the numbers. Their arrangement must result in any row of three numbers (vertical, horizontal, or diagonal) adding up to 15.

Anti-Magic Square

Like the Magic Square, the Anti-Magic Square uses the same grid as above, except you have to place the numbers 1 to 9 to create a square where each row's sum is *different*.

Think that's easy? Give it a try. Remember, you can't repeat any of the numbers.

Numbers Game

Here's another game that you're bound to win as long as you let your opponent go first.

The object of the game is simple. The first one to reach 100 wins!

Each round involves adding a number from 1 to 10 to the previous number. Your opponent goes first and identifies a number from 1 to 10. You add to that number and announce the sum. The turns continue until 100 is reached.

The winning strategy is for you to always produce the key numbers, which are 12, 23, 34, 45, 56, 67, 78, 89, and the winning 100.

So if your opponent says 8, you add 4 to get to the first key number 12. You continue adding to the keys, and within nine rounds you'll be a winner.

Now suppose you can only add a number from 1 to 5 to your opponent's number until you reach 50.

What would the key numbers now be?

What's Next?

Take a look at the pattern below. These symbols have a logical order. Can you draw the next symbol in the sequence?

HINT: A little reflection with your thinking skills may help you solve this puzzle.

Connect the Dots

Starting at the top center dot, can you connect all of the other nine dots with only four straight lines? The four lines must all be connected and your pencil can't leave the paper while drawing the answer.

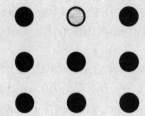

Another Ant Walk

A queen ant finds herself climbing onto the metal framework of a bridge at the spot marked by the arrow.

Can you trace the path she'd need to follow in order to walk across every piece of frame only once and end up at the top of the bridge (marked by an X)?

Her path must be a continuous line.

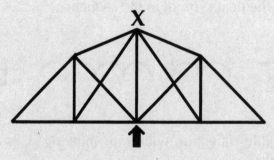

In Order

Examine the set of pictures on the next page. Can you place them in their most logical order?

Tangrams

In Asia, tangrams are known as "the seven plates of wisdom." No wonder, since this Chinese puzzle, probably one of the most famous dissection games, has been around for at least several hundred years.

A tangram consists of five triangles, a square, and a rhomboid.

To get these shapes, copy the lines shown below onto a square sheet of heavy stock paper. Use a pair of scissors to cut out each of the seven sections.

Another way you can make the seven shapes is to start with a square sheet of paper.

1. Cut the square in half to make two large triangles.

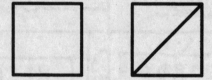

2. Cut one of the triangles in half to make two equal triangles (Sections I and II).

3. Fold back the corner of the other triangle and cut along this fold to get another triangle (Section III).

4. Cut the remaining piece into two equal halves.

5. Fold and cut one of the pieces to get a square and right triangle (Sections IV and V).

6. Fold and cut the other piece like this (Sections VI and VII).

With your seven pieces, try and create these figures.

Fractured Farmland

While flying over farmland, a pilot notices the rectangular shape of the fields below. She sketches the lines that divide the fields.

When she returns to the airport, she wonders how many different rectangles can be formed by the lines drawn below?

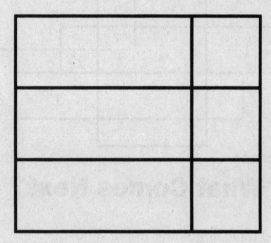

HINT: Don't forget that a square is also a rectangle.

Number Sense

The number symbols we use are called Arabic numerals. Logically, they originated in the Middle East. Right? Wrong. They were created in India. Europeans learned these symbols from Arabic scholars and, inadvertently, the name Arabic numeral stuck.

Now try not to get stuck on this number problem. Can you uncover the logic used to place each of the numbers below? If so, what number should be placed at the question mark?

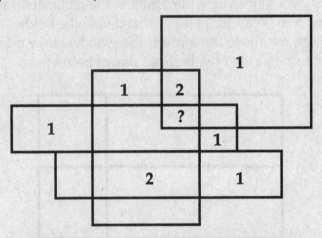

What Comes Next?

Choose the next logical member of the sequence.

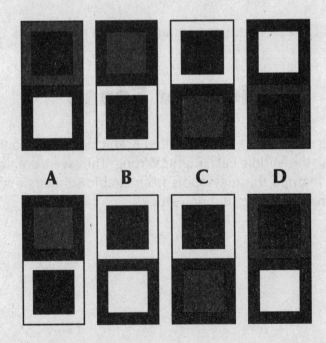

A   B   C   D

The Marked Park

Jethro's custom racer has two different-sized tires. The smaller front tire has a circumference of 7 feet. The larger rear tire has a circumference of 9 feet.

Rita, the meter maid, sees Jethro's racer parked in a 10-minute zone and decides to mark the curbside tires with a spot of paint. She places a mark on the front and rear tires exactly where each tire touches the ground.

Twenty minutes later, Rita returns. She sees both marks still touching the ground. As she begins writing a parking ticket, Jethro returns and explains that he did move his racer. In fact, he moved it the exact distance required to rotate the marks back into their same relative position. Assuming Jethro is telling the truth, what is the shortest distance that the racer was moved?

Pattern Path

All fo the numbers below form a sequence. Can you figure out the logic of the sequence? If so, begin at the point marked start and trace a path from box to box. The boxes can be connected horizontally, vertically, or diagonally. Double and triple digit numbers can be made by grouping the numbers this way. You can go through a box only once. Your mission is to finish at the stop sign located in the bottom right corner.

START

2	1	6	4	2	4
8	4	3	2	0	8
6	2	6	1	0	4
1	4	5	5	2	0
2	8	2	1	9	6

Pile Puzzler

Cards can be arranged in many different orders. Don't try all of them unless you have time to count 80,660,000,000,000,000,000,000,000,000, 000,000,000,000,000,000,000,000, 000,000,000,000,000,000.

 Here's a card challenge that has fewer solutions. Exchange one card from each of the piles to form three piles with equal sums.

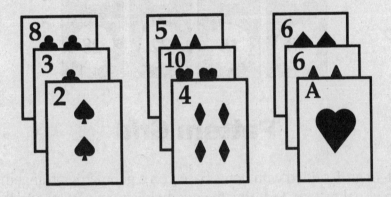

 In this puzzle, the Ace only counts as one. Only one card can be exchanged from each pile.

Pattern Puzzler

The five numbers within each circle represent a mathematical relationship. This same relationship is displayed in each of the four circles.

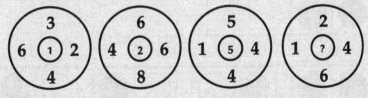

 Using this pattern, what is the most likely value for the question mark in the last circle?

Titillating Tiles

There's a tile below that doesn't fit with the other four in the group.
Can you figure out the relationship of the tiles and find the one that is different?

Pattern Grid

A pattern grid is filled with items based on a geometric arrangement to form a visual pattern. Examine the grid below for a pattern and then try to select the section that completes it.

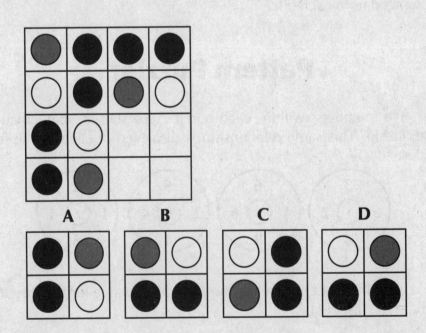

ANSWERS

Pyramid Passage

Magic Pyramid

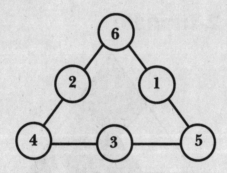

Pyramid Builders

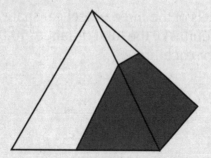

Trial by Triangle

1.   In order to create these four equal triangles, you'll have to use all three dimensions. By constructing a three-dimensional pyramid shape, you'll create same-sized triangles on the structure's three sides and bottom.

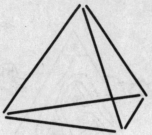

2.   Like the impossible triangle, these two objects are optical illusions and cannot be built.

Trapezoids 2 Triangle

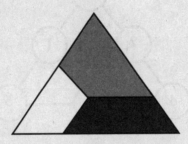

Spare My Brain

Since the four wheels of the three-wheel car share the journey equally, simply take three-fourths of the total distance (50,000 miles) and you'll get 37,500 miles for each tire.

Whirling Paradox

Relative to a stationary observer, the top of the wheel is moving faster than the bottom of the wheel. It all has to do with the forward motion of the car. Since the top half of the wheel is moving in the same direction as the car, their speeds are added together to obtain the relative speed of the moving upper spoke.

However, the lower spokes are moving in the opposite direction as the car. In this case, subtraction of the speeds results in a much slower relative speed—slow enough to count the individual spokes.

Lost?

To find out which way to go, you need to stand the sign back up.

Since you came from Skullara, align the sign so that the Skullara arrow points back to it. All the other arrows will then be pointed to the correct directions.

Sand Traps

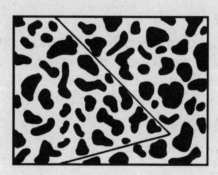

Which Mountain?

It doesn't matter which mountain you climb. All three paths will be the same length. The length of the path is not determined by the shape of the mountain but the slope of the road.

Since all three mountain paths have the same slope, you'd have to walk the same distance in order to climb each 10,000 foot summit.

Compass Caper

White. The bear must be a polar bear. To conform to the given pattern, the hiker must begin the trek at the magnetic North Pole.

A Cut Above

Make two cuts to divide the pizza along its diameter into 4 equal parts. Then stack the quarters on top of each other. Make another cut down the middle of the stack.

Although it might be messy, you'll have eight equal slices.

Kitchen Cups

Fill the three-cup container with water. Pour it into the five-cup container. Fill the three-cup container again, and fill up the five-cup container. This will leave you with exactly one cup of water in the three-cup container.

Moldy Math

This is simpler than it may seem. Since the mold doubles in size every day, it covered half as much area one day before!

And a Cut Below

Eight pieces as shown below:

Egg Exactly

Simultaneously turn over the five- and three-minute timers when you begin to boil the water.

When the three-minute timer runs out, put the egg into the boiling water. When the five-minute timer runs out, the egg is done. Two minutes have elapsed.

Losing Marbles?

Start spinning the marble along the bottom of the cup so that it pushes against the inner wall.

When the spin is fast enough, the force overcomes the pull of gravity and the cup can be turned upside down.

A Puzzle of Portions

There are several ways to divide the juice. Here's one of the quickest:

Vessel Size	24	13	11	5
To start	24	0	0	0
First	8	0	11	5
Second	8	13	3	0
Third	8	8	3	5
Fourth	8	8	8	0

Mixed Up?

There is the same amount of root beer in the cola as there is cola in the root beer.

For every drop of root beer that is in the cola cup, a drop of cola has been displaced and is in the root beer cup.

Toothpick Teasers

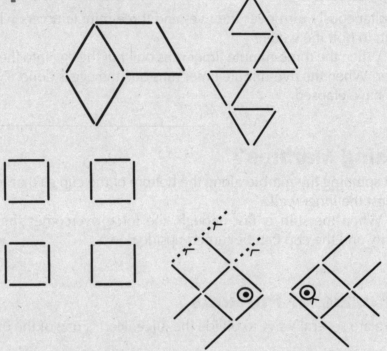

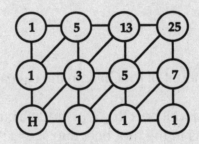

Going to the Movies

Tracing, counting, and remembering each step would drive you crazy. To make things easier, just write down the possible paths to each circle. The number of paths to the next circle is equal to the sum of the paths that connect it.

Now Seating?

1. There are ten possible combinations: BBGGG, BGBGG, BGGBG, BGGGB, GBBGG, GBGBG, GBGGB, GGBBG, GGBGB, GGGBB.
2. The chances for two boys being on the ends are 1 in 10.
3. The chances for two girls being on the ends are 3 in 10.

Weighing In...

The weight of the jar doesn't change. In order to fly, the insects must produce downward air currents that are equal in force to their weight. Therefore, whether standing or in flight, the insects push down with the same force.

The Strangest Eyes

Unfortunately, you will need to check this one by tracing over the pattern. As you do, you'll discover a single loop on the left and a double loop on the right.

Monkey Business

Both the crate and the chimp go up.

Head Count

Although this type of problem is perfect for algebra, let's do it visually. If all of the thirty heads belonged to two-legged birds, then there'd be only sixty legs. If one of the animals has four legs, then there'd be sixty-two legs. If two animals are four-legged, there'd be sixty-four legs.

By continuing in this pattern until we reach seventy legs, we will get a combination of twenty-five birds and five lizards.

Möbius Strip

The shape you get from dividing the Möbius strip is one large continuous loop with four twists.

Ant Walk

Nine centimeters. One basic pattern is illustrated below.

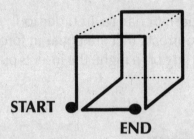

START

END

Although there are other turns, they cover the same total length.

Cubic Quandaries

There is a total of 27 cubes. There are six cubes with one red side, twelve cubes with two red sides, eight cubes with three red sides, and one cube with no red sides.

Squaring Off

Saving Face

1. The face should have a circle design.

2. The pattern folds into a cube that looks like this:

3. Folding the creases would produce this final version:

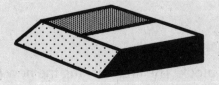

Cut the Cards

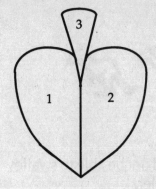 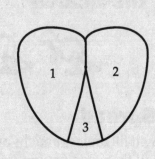

Stripped Stripe

Here is the cut pattern....

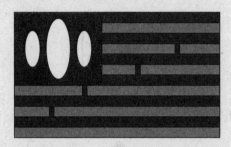

and here is the reassembly.

Missing Square

There isn't an extra block. The area making the new block was "shaved off" from some of the other blocks. The loss of each block's area is so small that it's not easy to observe.

Tipping the Scales

Snake Spread

The snakes will fill their stomachs and not be able to swallow anymore. The circle will then stop getting smaller.

Falcon Flight

The falcon's total distance is determined by the amount of time he was aloft and the speed he maintained.

The speed is given. The time is derived from the two cyclists. Since the cyclists are 60 miles apart and drive toward each other at 30 mph, the total time elapsed is 2 hours. The bird flying at 45 miles per hour will cover 90 miles in this 2-hour time period.

A Question of Balance

It has to do with friction, balance, and the weight of the yardstick.

As you move your fingers toward the middle of the yardstick, the balance of the yardstick shifts. The finger that is closer to the middle will support more weight, making it easier for the other, more distant finger to "catch up" and move closer to the middle as well. This "catching up" flip-flops between the two fingers until they both arrive at the middle of the yardstick.

The finger that moves first from the middle immediately bears less of the ruler's weight, which makes it easier for this finger to keep moving. The farther it moves, the easier sliding becomes.

Well-Balanced Plate

You must mirror your opponent's placement of the plate. This way, as long as he has a place for his plate, you have a place for yours.

Robot Walkers

The robots follow a path that forms a continually shrinking and rotating square. Eventually, the robots will meet in the middle of the square.

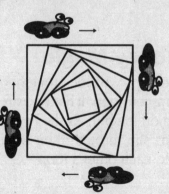

Chain Links

Select the chain with three links. Break open one of the links and use it to connect any two of the other sections. Break another of its links and use it to connect two other sections. Break the third and final link and use it to make a complete loop.

Rope Ruse

Fold your arms as shown below. Then, pick up the free end of the rope while your arms are already crossed. As you uncross your arms, the rope will automatically knot itself.

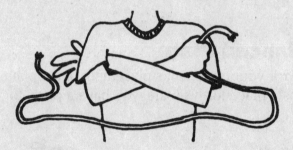

Money Magic

The clips will lock together and drop off the bill. A paper clip isn't a complete loop. It has two stretched openings through which the clip can slip off the bill. As the two sections of the bill move by each other, the clips slip through their openings and are pushed together to "reclip" onto each other's loop.

Revolutionary Thoughts

Four and a half hours. In order to be in a straight line the satellites must travel either one full revolution or one-half revolution. In 4½ hours, they'll look like this:

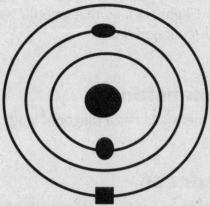

Baffling Holes

Fold the card in half so that the circular hole is also folded in half. Then slightly twist the paper as you pass the quarter snugly through the hole.

A Fair Solution

1. Either teenager can cut the slice, but the other person selects who gets which slice.
2. The four removed toothpicks leave the word "TEN."

Sock It to Me

Four socks. In a worst case scenario, if you draw three socks, each of a different color, the next sock you draw guarantees a matching color.

Nuts!

1. As you rotate each screw in a clockwise direction, they come together.
2. City-owned bulbs have opposite threads so that they won't screw into the standard light sockets that people have in their homes. Therefore, this discourages theft.

Doubtful Dimensions

A box with 3 X 4 dimensions has a diagonal length of 5 feet.

Machine Madness

Midway between 10 and 11 o'clock. The rotation decreases from one-quarter turn to one-eighth turn between the second and third wheel.

As the smaller hub of the second wheel rotates one-quarter turn, it moves the attached belt by only one foot. The 1-foot belt movement spins the larger third wheel only one-eighth of a revolution. This one-eighth turn remains the same for the fourth and fifth wheel. The belt twist between the first and second wheel changes the spin from clockwise to counterclockwise.

Putting It Together

The list contains fifty pairs of numbers that add to 100 (100+0, 99+1, 98+2, 97+3, etc.) with the number 50 as the unpaired leftover. 50 X 100 + 50 = 5,050.

The Heat Is On

As the washer expands, so does the hole it forms. Think of the washer as an image being stretched on a graphics program. Both the washer and its encircled hole will enlarge.

City Pipes

It is impossible for the round sewer cover to fall into the round pipe.

If the cover and tube had rectangular dimensions, the cover would be able to slip into the tube by being tilted in diagonally. But no matter how you tilt the circular cover, it can't fit through a hole of the same dimension.

Magic Square

8	3	4
1	5	9
6	7	2

Anti-Magic Square

5	1	3
4	2	6
8	7	9

Numbers Game

The trick to figuring out the key numbers is to keep subtracting the maximum you can add plus one beginning with the starting number.

For instance, because you can only use the numbers 1-5, if you work in increments 6 down from 50, you will get your key numbers: 8, 14, 20, 26, 32, 38, 44.

What's Next?

The symbols are the mirror images of the numbers 1 to 4 rotated on their sides. The next image is a 5, modified in the same way.

Connect the Dots

The trick to this challenge is that the line can go out of the grid. Otherwise, it is impossible to complete.

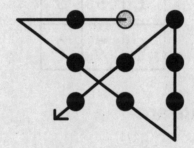

Another Ant Walk

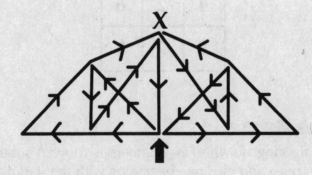

In Order

1. Girl walks to right wearing raingear and umbrella, passes grocery store, in the heavy rain.
2. Girl walks to right, passes record store, wearing raingear and umbrella, in less rain.
3. Girl stops, umbrella up, she holds out hand to feel rain. There is no rain.
4. Girl has stopped, folds up umbrella. There is no rain.
5. Girl walks to left, holds folded umbrella, passes record store. There is no rain.
6. Girl walks to left, holds folded umbrella, passes grocery store. There is no rain.
7. Girl walks to right holding baseball bat, passes grocery store. It is sunny.
8. Girl walks to right, passes record store, holds baseball bat. It is sunny.

Tangrams

Fractured Farmland

Eighteen: one whole composite block (1,2,3,4,5,6); six separate blocks (1) (2) (3) (4) (5) (6); three horizontal pairs (1&4) (2&5) (3&6); four vertical pairs (1&2) (2&3) (4&5) (5&6); two vertical triplets (1,2,3) (4,5,6); two large blocks (1,4,2&5) (2,5,3&6)

1	4
2	5
3	6

Number Sense

Three. Each number identifies the numbers of overlapping rectangles that cover that space.

What Comes Next?

D. During each step, the colors advance from outside top to inside top to inside bottom to ouside bottom to outside top.

The Marked Park

Sixty-three feet. The lowest common multiple between the small wheel (7 feet) and large wheel (9 feet) is obtained by multiplying seven and nine.

Pattern Path

The sequence of the path is made by multiplying the digits by two: 2, 4, 8,16, 32, 64,128, etc. Here's a small part of that path:

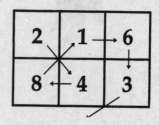

Pile Puzzler

To make things easy, first find the total value for each pile by adding up all the card values. Divide the sum (forty-five) by three to get the value for each pile (fifteen).

10	6	6
2	5	A
3	4	8

Pattern Puzzler

Three. The central number (E) is obtained by dividing the product of the top (A) and bottom (B) numbers by the product of the right (D) and left (C) numbers. A X B/C X D = E.

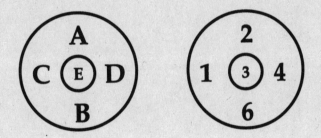

Titillating Tiles

54/22. With the other tiles, when you multiply the individual digits of the top number, you arrive at the bottom number. For example, 4 X 8 = 32.

Pattern Grid

D. The grid is divided into four 4 X 4 tiles. As you go in a "Z" pattern from the top left tile to right to bottom left to right, you'll see that the tile rotates one-quarter turn.

Section 2

GREAT
Critical Thinking
PUZZLES

Introduction

Hang on to your brains because here we go again!

In this section, I present more of the best puzzles for stimulating your critical thinking skills. From mental paths to army ants, you'll encounter an assortment of challenges that are designed to pump up your brain power.

Psychologists and educators refer to critical thinking skills as a variety of higher-level thinking strategies that can be used to analyze, solve, and evaluate all sorts of things, such as facts, theories, statements, and, of course, puzzles. The array of brain-bending puzzles presented in this section should engage many of these skills.

You will have to uncover assumptions, solve by analogy, sequence events, generalize, and discover all sorts of patterns. You will also find yourself digging deeper into your brain to come up with some creative possibilities. Once generated, novel possibilities need to be analyzed in order to determine if they work.

As in section one, there are old-time favorite puzzles with a new twist. For centuries, they have challenged and entertained people. But unbeknownst to the puzzled, these conundrums were also producing new thought channels that had been etched into the cells, chemicals, and electrical patterns of the brain.

Most of the puzzles here can be done with a pencil or pen. Others require simple items, such as loose change or matchsticks, that can be found around the house. But what they all need is for you to be creative and inventive in solving them.

So why wait? Just jump right in and you will be on your way to boosting your critical thinking skills again!

—Michael

Brain Net

Your brain is an incredible piece of machinery. About the size of a squished softball, it contains billions of brain cells. These cells make more connections than all of the phones in the world. It's this huge network that produces your brain power! Want to feel the "brain net" in action?

Take a look at the drawing below. Your job is to figure out how many different paths can get you across from start to finish.

You can only move to the right. You can't go back. When you arrive at a "fork," take either the top or bottom route. Start counting.

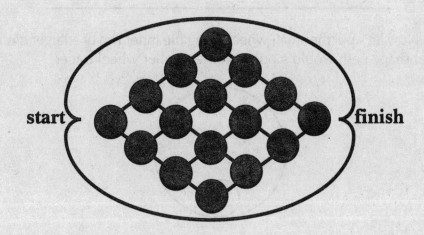

Predicting Paths

One of your brain's most powerful capabilities is the ability to think visually. When we think in this way, we construct a mind's eye image of a shape, scene, or concept. This image can be rotated, changed, moved, and analyzed. How good are you at visual thinking? Here's your first chance to find out.

Suppose we roll the wheel along the flat surface. Draw the shape that would be traced by the point within the wheel.

Now let's put the small wheel along the inner rim of a larger circle. What shape path would a point on the smaller wheel trace?

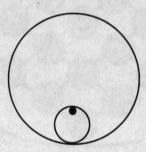

Finally, suppose the inner wheel remains stationary. What pattern would be traced out by a point on the larger rim as it rolls around (and remains in contact with) the inner wheel?

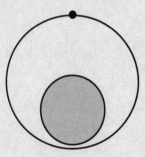

Who's That?

Look into a mirror and who do you see? You? Perhaps, but it's not the same you that everyone else sees. Its a right-left reversed image. The ear that appears on your left side is seen by others on your right side.

Suppose you want to see yourself exactly as others see you. How can you set up two small mirrors so that your reflection isn't reversed?

Leftovers Again?

Your brain is divided into two halves. The left half is more number-oriented, rational, and concrete. Your right half is more creative, playful, and artistic. To solve this next puzzle, you'll have to borrow a little from both sides of your brain.

In an art class, students are taught how to shape a 1-ounce bag of clay into a small statue. During this process, some clay remains unused (actually, it falls to the floor). For every five statues that are made, there is enough extra clay to make one more statue. Suppose a student is presented with 25 ounces of clay. What is the maximum number of statues he can sculpt?

Brownie Cut

Now that art class is over, it's time for cooking class.

A chocolate brownie emerges from the oven. Karen cuts the square brownie in half. She then divides one of the halves into two smaller but equal parts.

Before she can eat the larger piece, two of her friends unexpectedly arrive. Karen wants everyone to have the same amount of dessert. In the fewest number of cuts, how can she produce three equal portions?

Balancing Gold

A gold bar balances with nine-tenths of 1 pound and nine-tenths of a similar gold bar. How much does each gold bar weigh?

Thrifty Technique

Don't put that balance away! You'll need it along with a few pounds of brain cells to help solve this next problem.

By the way, did you know that Albert Einstein's brain was "normal" in weight? For the most part, it resembled an ordinary brain. There was, however, a slight difference. He had extra "cleanup" cells (called neuroglial cells). These cells move around the brain to get rid of dead or injured nerve cells. Perhaps his "well-swept" brain supercharged his intelligence?

You have nine gold coins. One of the coins is counterfeit and is filled with a lighter-than-gold substance. Using a balance, what strategy can you use to uncover the counterfeit coin?

To make things a little more difficult, you must identify the fake coin with only two uses of the balance.

Tricky Tide

In the Bay of Fundy, the tides can vary in height by almost 50 feet. The bay in our puzzle has a tidal range of only 6 feet. A boat moors in the middle of this bay. A ladder hangs down from the deck of the boat and touches the flat sea surface. The rungs are 1 foot apart.

At low tide, ten rungs of the ladder are exposed. At high tide, the water level rises 6 feet. How many of the rungs will remain exposed?

Breaking Up Is Hard to Do

How fast can you think? Faster than a speeding bullet? Faster than electricity? For most of us, thoughts race around our brains between 3 to 300 mph. Who knows, this puzzle may break your brain's speed record.

The square encloses a 4 x 4 grid. There are five different ways this grid can be divided into identical quarters. Each way uses a different shape. Can you uncover the layout of all five patterns?

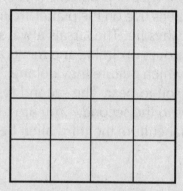

Disorder

Buildings crumble. Living things decompose. It's a scientific principle that things tend to go from order to disorder. The fancy name for this principle is entropy. There are, however, a few things that appear to go against this tendency. Crystals grow and become more complex. Living things take simple chemicals and build complex tissues.

This puzzle, however, uses entropy. Notice how neat and orderly the arrangement of numbers is. Now, let's play the entropy game and rearrange the numbers so that no two consecutive numbers touch each other. They cannot align side by side, up and down, or diagonally.

	1	
2	3	4
5	6	7
	8	

True or False?

Here's a totally different type of problem. This one is based on logic.

Two cultures of aliens live on the planet Trekia, the carpals and the tarsals. The carpals always lie. The tarsals always tell the truth.

A space traveler arrives on Trekia and meets a party of three aliens. She asks the aliens to which culture they belong. The first one murmurs something that is too soft to hear. The second replies, "It said it was a carpal." The third says to the second, "You are a liar!" From this information, figure out what culture the third alien belongs to.

Pack Up Your Troubles

A fragile item is to be shipped in a cardboard box. In order to prevent the item from hitting against the walls of the box, plastic foam cubes are used as "bumpers." There are ten of these cubes. How can you position them along the inner walls of the box so that there is an equal number of cubes along each wall?

Don't Come Back This Way Again!

The pitcher plant is a carnivorous plant that eats insects. An unfortunate insect walks into the pitcher plant's flower. When it tries to reverse direction, it can't. Tiny spines on the petals' surface face downward, which forces the insect to move in one direction—down.

Here's your chance not to go back. The shape below is made with one continuous line. Starting anywhere, can you complete the shape without lifting your pencil from the page? As you probably guessed, your path cannot cross over itself.

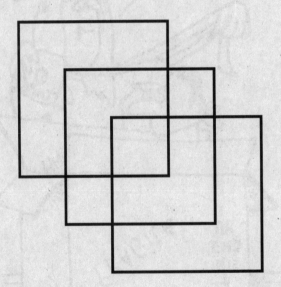

Meet Me on the Edge

Did you know that an ant can lift about fifty times its body weight? If you had that power, you'd be able to lift over 2 tons!

Suppose we position one of those powerful ants on a corner of a sugar cube. On the opposite corner, we position a fly. Suppose the two insects begin walking towards each other. If they can only walk along the edges of the cube (and never go backwards), what is the probability that their paths will cross?

Only the Shadow Knows?

A medium-size jet has a wingspan of 120 feet. An albatross is a bird with a wingspan of about 12 feet. At what altitude would each object have to fly in order to cast shadows of equal size?

More Shadow Stuff

At a certain time of day, a 25-foot telephone pole casts a 10-foot shadow. At that same time, how high would a tree have to be in order to cast a 25-foot shadow?

Trip Times

Did you know that the speed record for cars is over 700 miles per hour? To attain this supersonic speed, the cars use rocket engines. They move so quickly that if the car body had wings, the vehicle would fly!

The car in our problem is much slower. In 1 hour, traveling at 30 mph, it climbs to the top of the hill. When the car reaches the top, the driver remembers that she left her field guide to mountain life back home. She immediately turns around and drives downhill at 60 mph. Assuming that she spent no time at the top, what was her average speed?

HINT: It is not 45 mph.

Average Puzzle

How fast can you ride a bicycle? To get into the *Guinness Book of Records* for human-powered cycling, you'd need to ride faster than 60 mph.

An ordinary cyclist travels up and down a hill. Going up, she maintains a constant speed of 10 mph. It takes her 1 hour to get to the top. Assuming that the hill is symmetric, what speed must she maintain on the way going down if she wishes to average 20 mph? Before you bask in victory, the answer is not 30 mph.

Palindrome

A palindrome is a word or number that reads the same backwards as it does forward. Numbers such as 606 and 4334 are palindromes.

While driving his car, Bob (so much of a palindrome lover that he changed his name from John to Bob) observes that the odometer reading forms a palindrome. It displays the mileage 13,931.

Bob keeps driving. Two hours later, he looks at the odometer again and, to his surprise, it displays a different palindrome!

What is the most likely speed that Bob is traveling?

Stacking Up

Can you arrange these numbered blocks into three equal stacks so that the sum of the numbers displayed in each stack must be equal to any other stack.

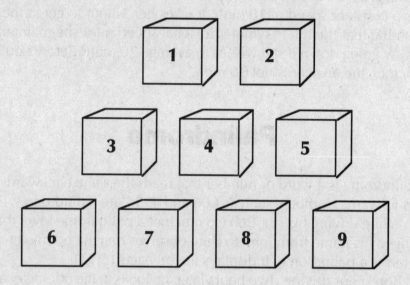

Star Birth

Trace this octagon pattern onto a separate sheet of paper. Then decide how to divide this shape into eight identical triangles that can be arranged into a star. The star will have eight points and an octagon-shaped hole in its center. When you think you've come up with an answer, trace the pattern onto the octagon. Cut out the separate parts and reassemble them into a star.

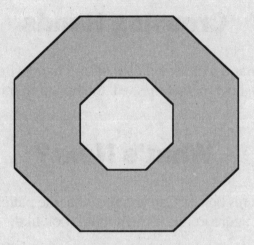

Flip Flop

Did you know that the ancient Egyptians believed that triangles had sacred qualities? This may have led to the superstition about walking under a ladder. When a ladder is placed against a wall, it forms a triangle. To walk through the triangle might provoke the wrath of the gods.

The triangle below is made up of ten disks. Can you move three of the disks to make the triangle point in the opposite direction?

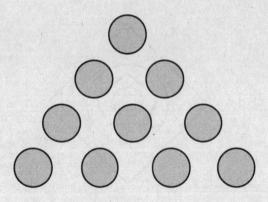

Crossing Hands

Picture in your mind a clock with a face and hands. Between the hours of 5 AM and 5 PM, how many times will the hour and minute hands cross each other?

What's Next?

Examine the figures below. Can you see what the pattern is and find out what the fourth figure in this series should look like?

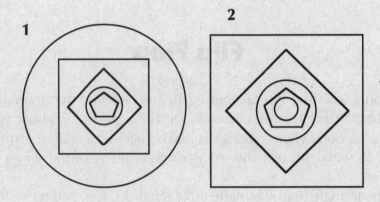

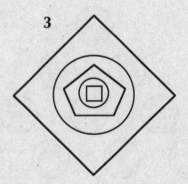

Trying Triangles

How many triangles can be found in this figure?

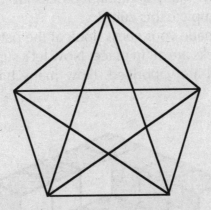

Flipping Pairs

Place three coins with their indicated side facing up as shown. In three moves, arrange the coins so that all three have the same side facing up. A move consists of flipping *two* coins over to their opposite side.

NOTE: Flipping the pair of outer coins three times doesn't count!

Missing Blocks

Examine the figure of blocks below. Let's assume that the hidden blocks are all in place. How many additional blocks are needed to fill in the empty region to complete this cube?

Once you've made your guess, look at the pattern again. Assume that the hidden blocks are all in place. Now let's suppose that all of the blocks you can see are vaporized. How many blocks would be left behind?

Matchstick Memories

Years ago, matchsticks were made from small sections of wood. These common and inexpensive objects were perfect props for after-dinner or parlor room activities. Nowadays, toothpicks offer the same advantages. So get your picks together and arrange them in the three patterns shown below.

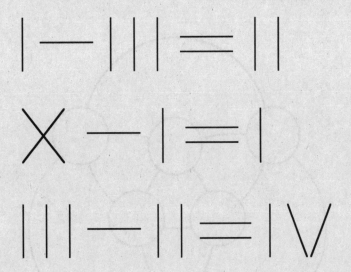

As you can see, each line of matchsticks forms an incorrect equation. The challenge is to make each one correct by changing the position of only one of the toothpicks in each row.

Sum Circle

Place the numbers one through six within the six smaller circles shown below. Each number must be used only once. The numbers must be placed so that the sum of the four numbers that fall on a circle's circumference is equal to the sum of the numbers on any other circle's circumference.

Think it's easy? Give it a try.

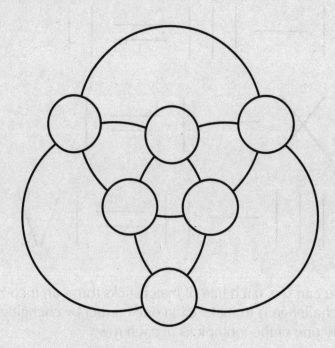

Many Rivers to Cross

Let's take a break from puzzles and go on a rowboat ride across the river. There are four adults who want to cross it. They come upon a boy and a girl playing in a rowboat. The boat can hold either two children or one adult. Can the adults succeed in crossing the river? If so, how?

Train Travel

A train travels at a constant rate of speed. It reaches a stretch of track that has fifteen poles. The poles are placed at an equal distance to each other. It takes the train 10 minutes to travel from the first pole to the tenth pole. How long will it take the train to reach the fifteenth pole?

Miles Apart

The distance from New York to Boston is 220 miles. Suppose a train leaves Boston for New York and travels at 65 mph. One hour later, a train leaves New York for Boston and travels at 55 mph. If we assume the tracks are straight paths and the trains maintain a constant speed, how far apart are the trains 1 hour before they meet?

Passing Trains

Coming from opposite directions, a freight train and a passenger train pass each other on parallel tracks. The passenger train travels at 60 mph. The freight train travels at 30 mph. A passenger observes that it takes 6 seconds to pass the freight train. How many feet long is the freight train?

HINT: There are 5,280 feet in a mile.

Souped-Up Survey

A survey agency reported their results in the local newspaper. The report states that exactly one hundred local lawyers were interviewed. Of the one hundred, seventy-five lawyers own BMWs, ninety-five lawyers own Volvos, and fifty lawyers own both a BMW and a Volvo.

Within a short time after the report, several lawyers argue that the survey results are incorrect. How can they tell?

Toasty

In order to make French toast, Ricardo must fry both sides of a bread slice for 30 seconds. His frying pan can only hold two slices of bread at once. How can he make three slices of French toast in only 1½ minutes instead of 2 minutes?

NOW, IF I CAN JUST KEEP ONE IN THE AIR AT ALL TIMES.

Circle Game

Examine the pattern of circles below. Can you place the numbers one through nine in these circles so that the sum of the three circles connected vertically, horizontally, or diagonally is equal to fifteen?

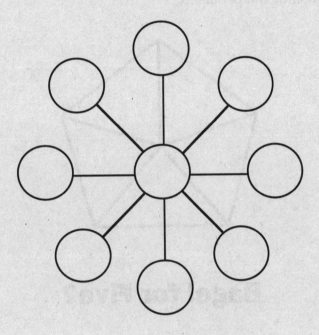

A Fare Split

Michelle rents a car to take her to the airport in the morning and return her home that evening. Halfway to the airport, she picks up a friend who accompanies her to the airport. That night, she and her friend return back to Michelle's home. The total cost is $20.00. If the amount to be paid is to be split fairly, how much money should Michelle pay?

Pentagon Parts

The pentagon below is divided into five equal parts. Suppose you color one or more parts gray. How many different and distinguishable patterns can you form? Each pattern must be unique and not be duplicated by simply rotating the pentagon.

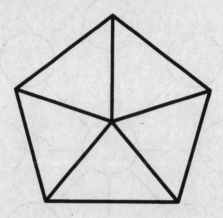

Bagel for Five?

You and four friends have decided to split a bagel for breakfast. The five of you are not fussy about the size of the piece each will receive. In other words, all the pieces don't have to be the same size.

Using two perfectly straight cuts, is it possible to divide this bagel into five pieces?

Coin Moves

Place twelve coins in the pattern shown below. Notice how they form the corners of six equal-sized squares. Can you remove three of the coins to have only three equal-sized squares remaining?

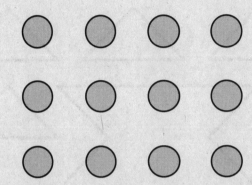

Trapezoid Trap

Divide the trapezoid below into four identical parts.

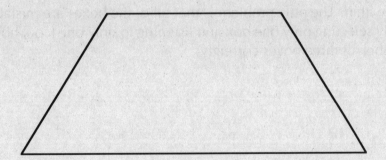

A+ Test

Here's a math challenge of a different sort. Trace these five shapes onto a sheet of stiff paper. Use a pair of scissors to carefully cut them out. Then assemble the shapes into a "plus" sign.

Mis-Marked Music

There are three boxes filled with audiocassette tapes. One box contains rap tapes, another contains jazz tapes, while the third contains both rap and jazz tapes. All three boxes have labels identifying the type of tapes within. The only problem is that all of the boxes are mislabeled.

By selecting only one box and listening to only one tape, how can you label all three boxes correctly?

Measuring Mug

Without the aid of any measuring device, how can you use a transparent 16-ounce mug to measure a volume of water that is exactly 8 ounces?

Coin Roll

Two identical coins are positioned side by side. In your mind's eye, roll the coin on the left (Coin A) over the other coin (Coin B). When Coin A reaches the opposite side of Coin B, stop. In which direction will Coin A's head be facing?

Now, let's suppose that Coin A rolls completely around Coin B. If so, how many rotations does Coin A make around its own center?

Painting on the Side

You are presented with several white cubes and a bucket of red paint. To make each of them different, you decide to paint one or more sides of each cube red. How many distinguishable cubes can you make with this painting method? Remember that any painted side must be painted completely to make it distinguishable from any other painted side.

Magic Triangle

Here's a magic triangle whose sides are formed by sets of four numbers. To solve the puzzle, place the numbers one through nine each in one of the circles. When you are finished, the sums of all three sides must be equal.

There are three different sums that can be used to reach the solution. Can you find all three?

Patterns

The arrangement of numbers below represents a pattern. This pattern is a mathematical relationship between the numbers in each square, so don't look for things like spelling, days of the week, cryptograms, or codes. Can you uncover the pattern and fill in the question mark in the last square?

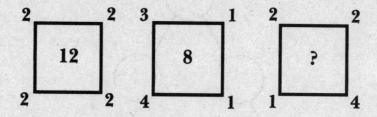

Frog Jump

A frog falls into a well that is 18 feet deep. Every day the frog jumps up a total distance of 6 feet. At night, as the frog grips the slimy well walls, it slips back down by 2 feet. At this rate, how many days will it take the frog to jump to the rim of the well?

Army Ants

Two small armies of ants meet head-on along a jungle path. Both armies would prefer to pass each other rather than fight. There is a small space along the side of the path. It is only large enough to hold one ant at a time. Is it possible for the armies to pass each other? If so, how?

No Sweat

There are six players on a coed volleyball team. After an exhausting game, each girl drinks 4 cups of water. Each boy drinks 7 cups of water. The coach drinks 9 cups.

A total of 43 cups of water is consumed by everyone. How many boys and how many girls are on the team?

Go Figure!

In a distant planet, there are four forms of life beings: zadohs, pugwigs, kahoots, and zingzags. All zadohs are pugwigs. Some pugwigs are kahoots. All kahoots are zingzags.

Which of the following statement(s) must then be true?

1. Some zadohs are zingzags.
2. Some kahoots are zadohs.
3. All kahoots are pugwigs.
4. Some zingzags are pugwigs.
5. All zingzags are zadohs.
6. Some zadohs are kahoots.

Square Pattern

Suppose you have to paint all nine squares in the grid below using one of three colors: red, blue, or green. How many different patterns can you paint if each color must be represented in every row and every column? Each pattern must be unique. In other words, a new pattern can't be made by simply rotating the grid.

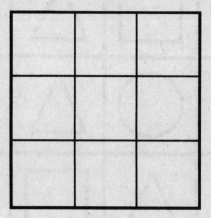

Bouncing Ball

Did you know that when a ball strikes the ground, its shape distorts? This distortion stores the energy that powers its rebound. The more its shape changes, the higher the ball will bounce.

The ball in this puzzle rebounds to half the height from which it is dropped. Suppose it is dropped from a 1-meter height. What distance would the ball travel before it comes to rest?

Complete the Pattern

Use the pattern below to determine the value for X and Y.

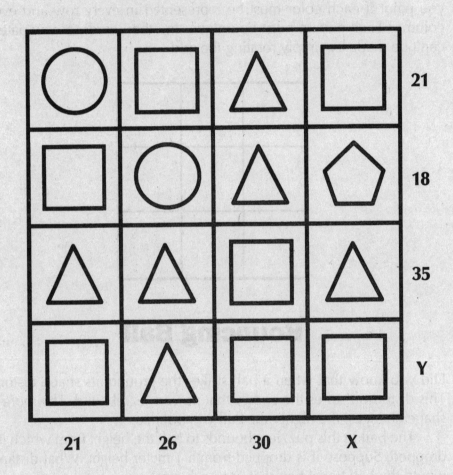

122

Checkerboard

A full-size checkerboard has eight rows and eight columns that make up its sixty-four squares. By combining the patterns of these squares, you can put together another 140 squares. The pattern below is one-fourth the area of a full size checkerboard. What is the total number of squares that are found in this smaller pattern?

Cutting Edge

Kristin wants to remodel her home. To save money, she decides to move a carpet from one hallway to another. The carpet currently fills a passage that is 3 x 12 feet. She wishes to cut the carpet into two sections that can be joined together to fit a long and narrow hallway that is 2 x 18 feet. What does her cut look like?

The Die Is Cast

Which die is unlike the other three?

Playing with Matches?

Thirty-two soccer teams enter a statewide competition. The teams are paired randomly in each round. The winning team advances to the next round. Losers are eliminated. How many matches must be played in order to crown one winner?

Competing Clicks

Let the Mouse Click Competition Begin!

Emily can click a mouse ten times in 10 seconds. Buzzy can click a mouse twenty times in 20 seconds. Anthony can click a mouse five times in 5 seconds. Assume that the timing period begins with the first mouse click and ends with the final click. Which one of these computer users would be the first to complete forty clicks?

Another Pattern

Here is another mathematical pattern that relates the four numbers of each triangle. Can you uncover the pattern and use it to complete the third triangle?

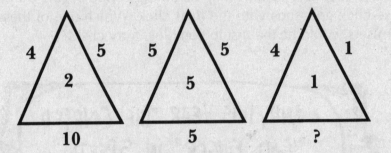

Vive le Flag

The French tricolor flag is made up of three vertical stripes: red, white, and blue. Suppose you are given four different colors of fabric and asked to create a different flag using the same tricolor design. If no two adjacent stripes can be the same color, how many different combinations of color patterns are there?

HINT: Don't forget that the flag pattern can be flipped over!

Pizza Cut

Five people want to share a square pizza. The first person (who is really hungry) removes a quarter of the pie. When the others find out, they are annoyed and try to divide the remaining three-fourths into four equal and identically shaped slices. The cuts must be straight. How must they cut the remaining pizza in order to produce four identical slices?

Slip Sliding

For this challenge, you'll need to get seven coins. Place a coin on any of the star's eight points. Then slide the coin along one of the straight lines to its endpoint. Place a second coin on another point. Slide this one down to its endpoint. Continue in this manner until all seven coins have been placed.

NOTE: It can be done—but you'll need to develop a strategy.

A, B, See?

Each letter stands for a different digit in each equation. Can you decode each one?

AB	AA	ABA	ABA
xAB	+AA	+BAB	+BAA
ABB	BBC	BBBC	CDDD

Spare Change

Jonathan has a pocket full of coins. Yet he doesn't have the right combination of coins to make change for a nickel, dime, quarter, half dollar, or dollar.

What is the largest value of coins Jonathan can have in his pocket?

Puzzling Prices

A puzzle book costs $5.00 plus one-half of its price. How much does the puzzle book cost?

HINT: It's more expensive than this book.

Gum Drop

In preparation for a party, Heather fills a large jar with gum drops. Before the party begins, Michael sees the gum drop jar. He (hoping that no one will realize) takes one-third of the drops. Soon after, Tanya takes one-third of the gum drops (she, too, hopes that no one will notice). Finally, Britt appears and, like the others, she takes one-third of the gum drops. If forty gum drops are left in the jar, how many did it originally contain?

Go-Cart Crossing

Three go-cart tracks are built as shown. Each track forms a separate one-third of a mile loop. Three go-carts begin riding at the same time from the central point where all three tracks cross. One go-cart travels at 6 mph, another at 12 mph, and the third at 15 mph. How long will it take for all three go-carts to cross paths for the fifth time?

Table Manners

Four couples enter a restaurant. How many ways can they be seated at a round table so that the men and women alternate and no husband and wife sit next to each other?

Winning Slip

A contest is fixed. Everyone knows it, including the contestants. One of the contestants, however, makes it to the final playoff level.

The master of ceremonies presents the following challenge: "This box contains two slips of paper. One slip has the word 'winner' printed on it, the other has the word 'loser.' Your task is to select the winning slip—without looking, of course."

The contestant knows that this challenge is fixed. He realizes that both slips have the word "looser." How can he select one slip and win the challenge? By the way, the contestant can't declare this contest is a fraud or he'd lose his current winnings.

Ancient Man

An ancient Greek was said to have lived one-fourth of his life as a boy, one-fifth as a youth, one-third as a man, and spent the last 13 years as an elderly gent. How old was he when he died?

Lights Out!

The total output of electrical energy from your brain is only about 20 watts. That's not an avalanche of power (especially when you consider that most household light bulbs use five times that amount). Now try powering up with this problem.

Imagine that you can't sleep because you are kept awake by the flashing neon lights that shine through a square store window. The window measures 10 x 10 feet.

A friend assures you that he can cover up half the area of the window but still leave a square section that is 10 x 10 feet. This will then satisfy both you and the storekeeper. You think your friend has lost it. Has he?

Pencil Puzzle

Can you uncover the logic used to create this layout? If so, use that same logic to determine the letter for the question mark.

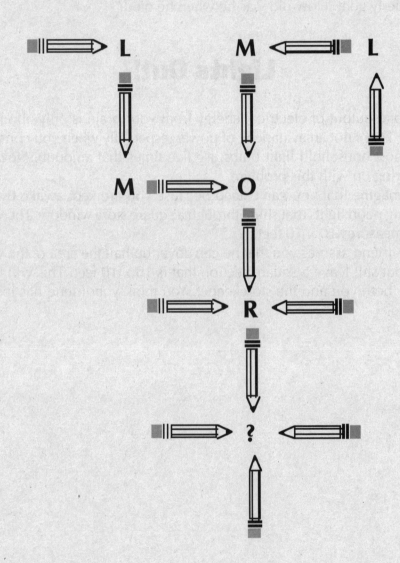

Sounds Logical?

It's the weekend! Saturdays and Sundays are the days that Sheila, Ramon, and Niko shop together for music. The CDs they purchase are either rock 'n' roll or jazz. When they visit the music store, each person will purchase one and only one CD. Here are the rules that govern their selections.

1. Either Sheila or Ramon will pick rock 'n' roll, but not both of them.
2. If Sheila picks rock 'n' roll, Niko picks jazz.
3. Niko and Ramon do not both pick jazz.

Which one of the three purchased a jazz CD on Saturday and a rock 'n' roll CD on Sunday?

Triangular Tower

Suppose ten billiard balls are placed in the standard triangular rack. If additional billiard balls are placed on top of this pattern, some balls will roll into the gullies to form a smaller, stable triangle (forget about the balls which roll off the stack). If you add more layers, you'll eventually build a billiard ball pyramid. How many billiard balls and levels would the pyramid contain?

Criss-Crossed

Place six coins in the layout as shown below. Notice that this arrangement forms two columns. The horizontal column has four coins. The vertical column has three coins. Can you move only one coin to form two columns with each containing four coins?

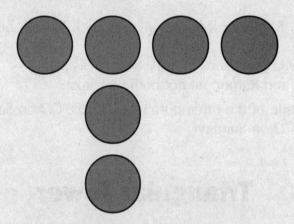

Crystal Building

Have you ever looked closely at a crystal? If so, you may have noticed that the crystal has flat sides and uniform angles. That's because a crystal is a repeating arrangement of tiny particles of matter. Often, a central particle is surrounded on all sides by other particles. Here's a puzzle that will help you visualize a crystal pattern.

Suppose you coat a tennis ball with glue. What is the maximum number of tennis balls that can attach directly to this sticky surface?

Testy Target

Ten arrows are shot at the target below. One of them misses the target completely. The others all strike it. If the total sum of points is one hundred, in which part of the target did each arrow strike?

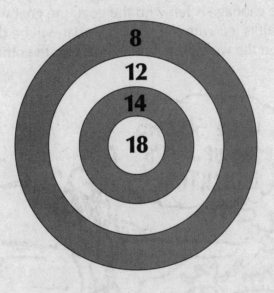

Eighth-Century Enigma

Here's a puzzle that can be traced back to the eighth century. A man has a goat, a wolf, and a head of cabbage. He comes to a river and must bring these three things across to the other side. The boat can only take the man plus either the goat, wolf, or cabbage. There is another problem. If the cabbage is left with the goat, the goat will eat the cabbage. If the wolf is left with the goat, the goat will be devoured. How can he transport the wolf, goat, and cabbage to the other side?

Planet Rotation

Our planet spins counterclockwise on its axis. It also has a counter-clockwise revolution around the sun. Suppose both motions now go clockwise. How would this affect the apparent direction of sunrise and sunset?

Shuffle

Pretend you have five cards: a ten, a jack, a queen, a king, and an ace. In your mind's eye, shuffle these five cards together and put the pile face down. If you were to select four cards, returning each card and reshuffling the deck after each pick, what kind of hand would you more likely draw: four Aces or a straight picked in sequence? Can you explain why?

Some Exchange

The first written puzzles appeared in ancient Egypt at about 1650 B.C. These puzzles were part of an 18½-foot scroll called the Rhind Papyrus. Times have changed since then, but many puzzles haven't. Just try these next ones.

Examine the two stacks of number blocks. If you exchange one block from one column with one block from the other, the number of their sums will be equal. Which blocks need to be exchanged?

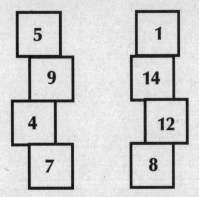

Now that you know how to balance two columns, you're ready to move up to three columns! By exchanging one block from each column, each of the three blocks' sums will be equal. Remember that all three columns must undergo only one exchange.

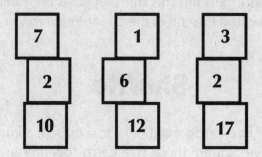

ANSWERS

Brain Net

Twenty routes. Although you can chart them all out, there is a less confusing way. Starting at the left, identify the number of routes that can get you to a circle. You can arrive at this number by adding the numbers found in the connecting circles to the left. Keep going until you get to the finish.

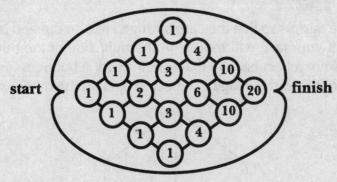

Predicting Paths

a.

b.

c.

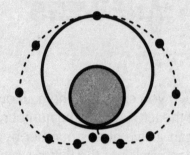

Who's That?

Position the mirrors so that they are arranged like an opened book. The right side of your face will reflect on the right side of the mirror. This image does not reflect back to that eye. Instead, it bounces to the other mirror. From there, the image is reflected back to the other eye.

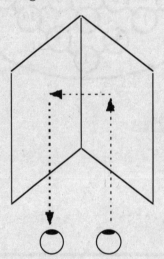

Leftovers Again?

Thirty-one statues. The 25 ounces are used directly to make twenty-five statues. During this process, 5 ounces of excess clay are produced. This extra clay is used to make five additional statues. While making these five additional statues, there is enough unused clay to make one more statue with one-fifth of the clay left over.

Brownie Cut

One cut

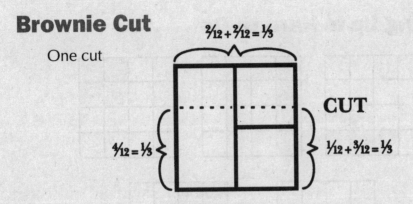

$$\frac{2}{12} + \frac{2}{12} = \frac{1}{3}$$

CUT

$$\frac{4}{12} = \frac{1}{3}$$

$$\frac{1}{12} + \frac{3}{12} = \frac{1}{3}$$

Balancing Gold

Nine pounds. Examine the objects on the right side of the balance. If we looked at the balance pan containing the two bars, we'd see that one-tenth of the gold bar is absent. In its place we have nine-tenths of a pound. From this we can infer that one-tenth of a gold bar weighs nine-tenths of a pound. Therefore, a complete gold bar would weigh ten times as much. $\frac{9}{10}$ pound x 10 = $\frac{90}{10}$, or 9 pounds.

Thrifty Technique

First, divide the coins into three groups of three. Then, balance any one group against another group. If the counterfeit is contained in either of the groups, the coins will not balance. If, however, they balance, the counterfeit coin must be in the third pile. Now that we have identified the pile with the counterfeit coin, remove one coin from the pile and balance the other two. The lighter coin will not balance. If the two coins do balance, the counterfeit coin is the one not selected.

Tricky Tide

Five rungs will still remain exposed. As the tide comes in, the boat will rise up.

Breaking Up Is Hard to Do

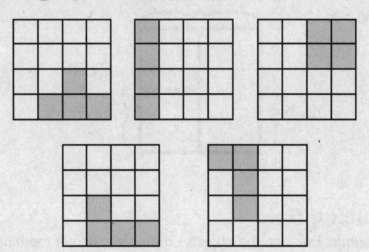

Disorder

```
              7

    3     1     4

    5     8     6

              2
```

True or False?

Tarsal. To figure this one out, we need to look at each alien's response. If the first alien was a tarsal, it would identify itself as a tarsal. If it was a carpal, it would still identify itself as a tarsal. Either way, the mumbling alien would identify itself as a "tarsal." Therefore, the second alien had to be lying. The third alien truthfully identified the carpal, making him a truth-telling tarsal.

Pack Up Your Troubles

The "trick" is using the same block in the rows of two adjacent sides.

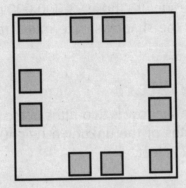

Don't Come Back This Way Again!

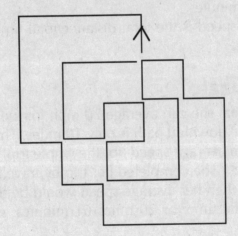

Meet Me on the Edge

One in six. The ant (or fly) can take any one of the six available routes. It doesn't matter.

Now, the other insect must select the "collision route" from its own six possible choices. Therefore, the odds are one in six.

Only the Shadow Knows?

They can never cast shadows of equal size.

Any difference in their altitude would be negligible compared to their distance from the sun. It's those 93,000,000 miles from our planet to the sun that affect the shadows' size much more than their puny distances apart.

More Shadow Stuff

At that time of day, the shadow is two-fifths of the object's height. If the tree's shadow (two-fifths of the unknown height) is 25 feet, then the height of the tree is 62½ feet.

Trip Times

Since it takes her 1 hour to reach the top (while traveling at 30 mph), the hill is a 30-mile route. Traveling at 60 mph, she'll cover that distance in only 30 minutes.

The average speed is the total distance/total time = 60 miles/1.5 hours or 40 mph.

Average Puzzle

There is no way that she can average 20 mph for the whole trip. Like the uphill path, the downhill path is only 10 miles. This distance is too short to achieve an average speed (for the whole trip) of 20 mph.

Consider this: If she completed her trip by traveling the downhill path at 600 mph, then her average speed would be the total distance divided by the total time, or 20 miles/61 minutes, or an average of about 19.6 mph.

By examining this equation, you'll see that there will be no way for her to decrease the denominator (time) below the 60 minutes she has already spent cycling up the hill.

Palindrome

55 mph. The next palindrome that the odometer can display is 14,041. To reach this value, Bob will have had to travel 110 miles. If it took him 2 hours to reach this point, his average speed will be 55 mph.

All other palindromes would have required too many miles to produce a logical speed. For example, the odometer's next palindrome is 14,141. From this, you can calculate an average speed of 105 mph—highly unlikely.

Stacking Up

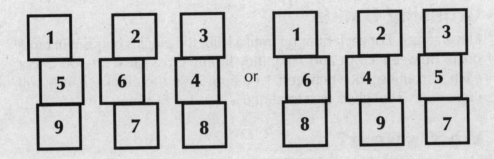

Star Birth

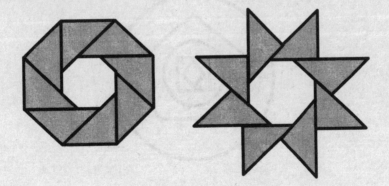

Flip Flop

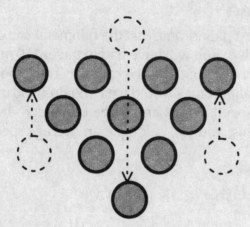

Crossing Hands

Eleven times. For each hour up until 11:00, the clock's hands will cross once. Between 11 AM and 1 PM, they'll only cross once (at noon). For each remaining hour between 1 PM and 5 PM, the clock's hands will cross once. That gives us a total of 6 + 1 + 4 = 11 times.

What's Next?

The sequence is based on the expanding geometric figures. After each figure reaches the outside perimeter, it starts again at the center.

Trying Triangles

Thirty-five triangles.

Flipping Pairs

First Move	H	H	T
Second Move	T	H	H
Third Move	T	T	T

Missing Blocks

a. Twenty-three blocks. None are missing from the bottom layer, six are missing from the second layer, eight are missing from the third layer, and nine are missing from the top layer.

b. Seventeen blocks. Eight are hidden in the bottom layer, six are hidden in the second layer, three are hidden in the third layer, and none are hidden in the top layer.

Matchstick Memories

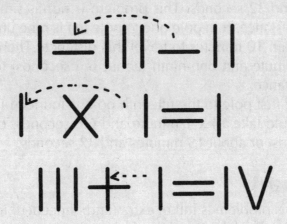

Sum Circle

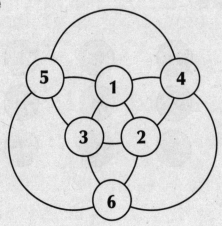

Many Rivers to Cross

First, the two children row to the far side. There, one gets out. The other child returns and gives the boat to an adult. The adult crosses the river. On the far side, the adult gets out and the child gets in the boat. The child brings the boat across the river and transports the other child back to the far side. This pattern continues until the four adults have crossed.

Train Travel

15 minutes and 32 seconds. This problem is not as simple as it may appear. The distance from pole one to pole ten is nine units. As stated, it takes the train 10 minutes to travel this distance. Therefore, it takes the train 1 minute and one-ninth (about 6.6 seconds) to travel each inter-pole distance.

From the first pole to the fifteenth pole is fourteen inter-pole distances. It should take 14 x 1 minute and 6.6 seconds, or 14 minutes and 92 seconds, or about 15 minutes and 32 seconds.

Miles Apart

120 miles. This problem is full of extra (and unneeded) information.

Think it backwards. One hour before they meet, one train is 65 miles away from the meeting point, while the other is 55 miles. Add the two distances together and you'll get 120 miles.

Passing Trains

792 feet. The length of the freight train can be calculated by knowing its relative passing speed and the time it took for it to move by. The passing speed is equal to the sum of both train speeds (60 mph +30 mph = 90 mph).

Here's where some conversion comes in. By dividing by sixty, we find that 90 mph is equal to 1.5 miles per minute. By dividing by sixty again, we find that this is equivalent to 0.025 miles per second.

The freight train takes 6 seconds to pass. Therefore, its length is 0.15 miles. To change this into feet, multiply 0.15 by the number of feet in a mile (5,280).

Souped-Up Survey

The numbers do not add up correctly. The agency stated that only one hundred people were interviewed. Yet, according to a logical breakdown of the results, they received 120 responses. You can see this by making a diagram of the data.

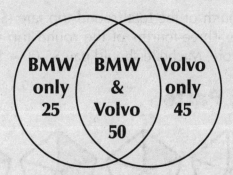

Toasty

Fry one side of two slices for 30 seconds. Flip one slice over and replace the other slice with a fresh slice of bread. At the end of 1 minute, remove the completely fried bread. Return the unfried side of the previous slice to the pan and flip the other slice over for 30 seconds.

Circle Game

When added together, the numbers at the opposite ends of this sequence equal ten (1 + 9, 2 + 8, etc.). By placing a five in the middle circle, we ensure that all the sums must equal fifteen (10 + 5).

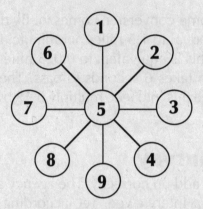

A Fare Split

$12.50. One-fourth of the total round trip fare ($5.00) was taken by Michelle alone. Three-fourths of the round trip was shared (half of $15.00). Therefore, Michelle should pay $5.00 + $7.50 or $12.50.

Pentagon Parts

Bagel for Five?

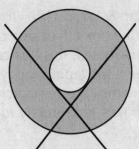

Coin Moves

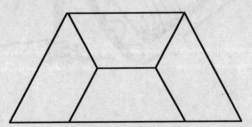

Trapezoid Trap

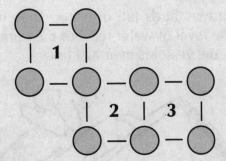

A+ Test

Mis-Marked Music

Select the box labeled "Rap & Jazz." Listen to one tape. If the marble is jazz, then you must have the box full of jazz cassettes. (Remember that since all the boxes are mislabeled, this box could not contain the mix of rap and jazz.) Likewise, if the tape is rap, you have selected the all-rap box. Since all three names are mismatched, then just switch the names of the other two boxes to correctly identify the contents of all boxes.

Measuring Mug

Fill the mug about two-thirds full of water. Then tilt it so that water pours off. When the level of water reaches the same height as the up-lifted mug bottom, the vessel is then half full.

Coin Roll

a. The same direction—to the left.

b. Two.

Painting on the Side

Ten ways. 1 = all sides white, 1 = one red face, 1 = two adjacent red faces, 1 = two opposite sides red faces, 1 = three sides red (in line), 1 = three faces red (in right-hand and left-hand L-shape design), 1 = four faces red (in line), 1 = four faces red (two pairs of two in line), 1 = five red faces, 1 = all faces red.

Magic Triangle

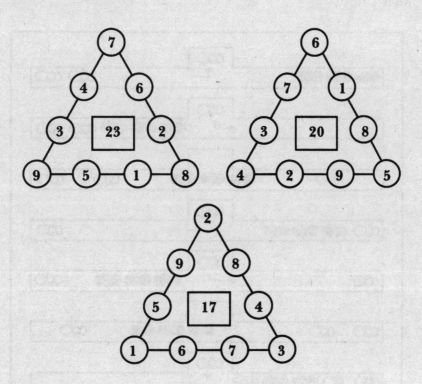

Patterns

Fourteen. Add the upper left number, lower left number, and lower right number together. Then multiply this sum by the number in the upper right corner. The product is in the center of the square.

Frog Jump

Four days. During the first day, the frog jumps up 6 feet and at night slides down 2 feet. The frog begins day two at a height of 4 feet, jumps to 10 feet, but slides back to 8 feet. On day three, the frog jumps to 14 feet, but slides back to 12 feet. On day four, the frog jumps to 18 feet and leaves the well.

Army Ants

Yes. Here's how.

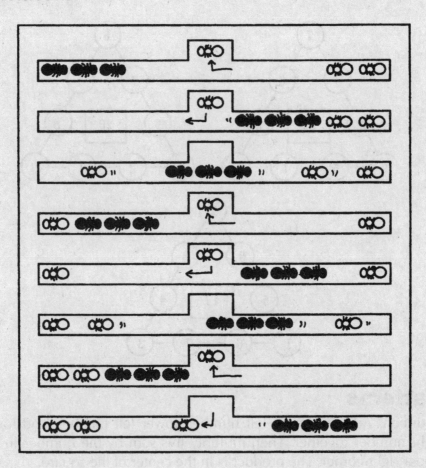

No Sweat

Five girls and two boys. First, subtract the coach's 9 cups from the total amount. Therefore, the boys and the girls together drank 34 cups. The winning combination is five girls (who together drink 20 cups) and two boys (who together drink 14 cups). 20 + 14 = 34 cups.

Go Figure!

Statement 4. The confusing relationship may best be understood by putting the information in a graphic layout. From the drawing, you can see that only statement 4 is true.

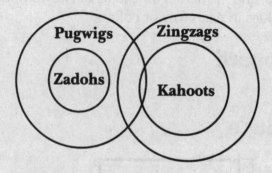

Square Pattern

There are only three distinguishing patterns. All other patterns are obtained by rotating the square.

r	g	b
b	r	g
g	b	r

b	g	r
r	b	g
g	r	b

g	r	b
b	g	r
r	b	g

Bouncing Ball

Approximately 3 meters. The first fall is 1 meter. It rebounds to ½ meter, than falls ½ meter. So now we're at 2 meters. Then the ball goes up and down ¼ meter, then ⅛ meter, then 1/16 meter, and so on. It continues this pattern until it comes to rest (theoretically it would keep going, but in the real world it stops). If we were to add all of these distances up, we'd get: $1 + \frac{1}{2} + \frac{1}{2} + \frac{1}{4} + \frac{1}{4} + \frac{1}{8} + \frac{1}{8} + \frac{1}{16} + \frac{1}{16} + ... = \sim3$ meters.

Complete the Pattern

X = 22; Y = 25. Each circle equals 1, each square equals 5, each triangle equals 10, and the pentagon equals 2. The numbers represent the sums of the values in each row or column.

Checkerboard

Thirty squares.

Cutting Edge

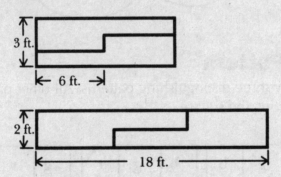

The Die Is Cast

Although all four dice have the same relative orientation of spots, the three spots on the last die tilt from the lower left corner to the upper right corner.

When the other dice are rotated onto this position, their three spots tilt from the upper left to the lower right corner.

Playing with Matches?

Thirty-one matches. If one winner is to be found in thirty-two teams, then thirty-one teams must lose. Since each team can only lose once, the thirty-one losses result from thirty-one matches.

Competing Clicks

Anthony. The actual period is 1 second less than the time given. Emily completes ten clicks in 9 seconds. Buzzy completes twenty clicks in 19 seconds. Anthony completes five clicks in 4 seconds. This gives us the approximate rates: Emily = 1.1 clicks/second, Buzzy = 1.05 clicks/second, Anthony = 1.25 clicks/second.

Another Pattern

Four. The number in the center of each triangle results from dividing the product of the top two sides by the bottom side.

Vive le Flag

Twenty-four combinations. If both of the outside stripes are the same color, you'll have twelve possible combinations (4 x 3 =12).

If all three stripes are a different color, you'll have twenty-four possible combinations (4 x 3 x 2 = 24). However, these twenty-four flags are made up of twelve mirror-image pairs. Just rotate the mirror image one-half turn and you'll produce the other flag. This decreases the stripe combinations to only twelve.

Now let's add the two sets of possible combinations: 12 + 12 = 24 different color patterns.

Pizza Cut

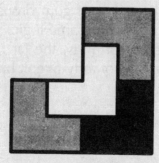

Slip Sliding

You'll get blocked if you don't place the coins in a specific order. Each coin must come to rest on the spot where the previous coin began its journey. Only in this manner can you then place all seven coins.

A, B, See?

10	55	919	545
x10	+55	+191	+455
100	110	1110	1000

Spare Change

$1.19. Jonathan has four pennies, four dimes, one quarter, one half dollar. Added together, they amount to $1.19.

Puzzling Prices

Ten dollars. The trick is not getting fooled into thinking that the book is five dollars.

If the book is "p," then $5 + \frac{1}{2}p = p$.

$5 = \frac{1}{2}p$.

$10 = p$.

Gum Drop

135 gum drops. If forty gum drops are left in the jar, the forty must represent two-thirds of the gum drops that were available when Britt appeared.

Therefore, the total number of gum drops before Britt took her share was sixty. Working with the same logic, you can figure out that before Tanya took her share of thirty, the jar had ninety gum drops. Before Michael took his share of forty-five, it had 135 gum drops.

Go-Cart Crossing

33.3 minutes. To travel 1 mile, go-cart A takes $\frac{1}{6}$ of an hour, go-cart B takes $\frac{1}{12}$ of an hour, and go-cart C takes $\frac{1}{15}$ of an hour. To travel one loop distance ($\frac{1}{3}$ of a mile), it would take each $\frac{1}{18}$, $\frac{1}{36}$, and $\frac{1}{45}$ of an hour, respectively. All three would meet at $\frac{1}{9}$ of an hour intervals. For five meetings to occur, five $\frac{1}{9}$-hour periods must pass. $5 \times \frac{1}{9} = \frac{5}{9}$ of an hour, or about 33.3 minutes.

Table Manners

Two ways. White = female. Black = male.

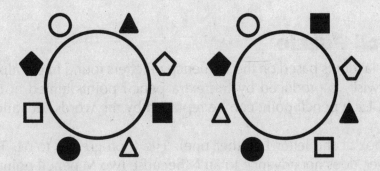

Winning Slip

The contestant picks one of the slips. The slip is placed out of view (possibly eaten). The contestant then asks the MC to read the slip that was not selected. That MC's slip has the word "loser." When the audience hears "loser," they logically conclude that the contestant must have picked the winning slip.

Ancient Man

60 years old. If his whole life is "X years," then:
His boyhood years = $\frac{1}{4}X$
His youth = $\frac{1}{5}X$
His adulthood = $\frac{1}{3}X$
His elder years = 13
$\frac{1}{4}X + \frac{1}{5}X + \frac{1}{3}X + 13 = X$
$X = 60$

Lights Out!

He covers the window as shown here, which meets both conditions.

Pencil Puzzle

V. The layout is based on the sequence of letters found in the alphabet. The "twist" is produced by the extra pencil points aimed at certain letters. Each pencil point can be replaced by the words "advance one step."

Look at the letter L (either one). The L progresses to M. The M, however, does not advance to an N because two M pencil points converge on this next space. The letter then advances one extra step, resulting in an O.

With the same logic, the O leads to an R (advance three steps). The R leads to a V (advance four steps).

Sounds Logical?

Niko. If Sheila picks rock 'n' roll, then according to (1) Ramon must pick jazz and according to (2) Niko must also pick jazz. These selections contradict (3). This rules Sheila out.

If Ramon picks jazz, then according to (1) Sheila must pick rock 'n' roll and the same contradictions surface.

The only person who can select either jazz or rock 'n' roll without any contradictions is Niko.

Triangular Tower

Twenty balls arranged in four levels.

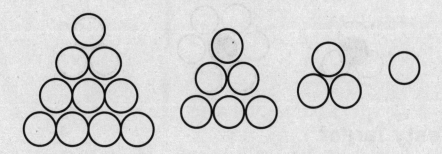

Criss-Crossed

Place one coin on top of the corner coin.

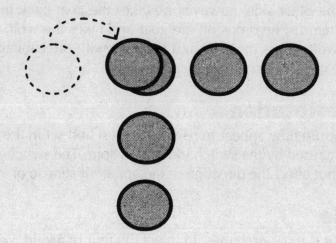

Crystal Building

Twelve tennis balls. Place six in a circle around the middle of the ball. Place three on top and three on the bottom.

Testy Target

Two arrows struck the 8 region (16 points) and seven of them struck the 12 region (84 points). Total: 16 + 84 = 100 points.

Eighth-Century Enigma

On his first trip, the man brings the goat over (leaving the cabbage and wolf behind). On his second trip, he brings over the cabbage. When he lands on the other side, however, he takes the goat back in his boat. When he returns, he drops off the goat and takes the wolf. He transports the wolf across the river and leaves it with the cabbage. He returns once more to ferry over the goat.

Planet Rotation

The sun would now appear to rise in the west and set in the east. This change is caused by the switch in rotation spin. The switch in revolution does not affect the direction of the apparent sunrise or sunset.

Shuffle

The straight is more probable. To select the four of a kind, you need to select "one card out of five cards" four times: $\frac{1}{5}$ x $\frac{1}{5}$ x $\frac{1}{5}$ x $\frac{1}{5}$, or 1 out of 625.

For the straight, the first card can be any card. Then, you'll need to select "one card out of five cards" three times: $\frac{1}{5}$ x $\frac{1}{5}$ x $\frac{1}{5}$, or 1 out of 125—a better probability.

Some Exchange

a. 14 and 9. The sum of all eight numbers is sixty. Each column must have a sum equal to half that, or thirty. To arrive at thirty, you need to lessen one column by five and increase the other by the same amount. This is accomplished by exchanging a 14 for a 9.

b. 2, 1, and 3. As with the previous problem, you can add all nine numbers together, then divide that sum by three.

The result is twenty:	7	2	1
	3	6	2
	<u>10</u>	<u>12</u>	<u>17</u>
	20	20	20

Section 3
CHALLENGING
Critical Thinking
PUZZLES

Introduction

Data, data, and more data. We live in an age when the acquisition and presentation of new knowledge and information is astonishing. From the Internet to CD libraries, new technologies generate the means by which information transfer attains extraordinary dimension.

Since the access and acquisition of new knowledge continues to expand, we must learn to cope with this information overload. We need to develop and nurture thinking skills and strategies that will help us examine, evaluate, and apply new knowledge in a fair-minded manner. That's where critical thinking skills come in.

Although some educators and psychologists use the term "critical thinking" broadly by applying it to a range of thinking abilities, most restrict the use of it to specific strategies that help us better interpret and apply facts.

Educators and psychologists don't agree on the most effective way to develop these skills. Some feel that they should be taught independent of any content, such as real-life situations. This way the strategies are not confused or compromised with the importance of content. As a result, critical thinking skills can be more effectively considered as independent tools that can be applied to a range of circumstances.

Other experts, however, think that content is essential to teaching critical thinking skills. By utilizing real-life situations, students may then appreciate the value of these skills in the analysis of facts. This combination forms an intricate network of connections that produce a deeper understanding of content while offering a thinking platform from which to analyze additional situations.

It is with the latter approach in mind that this book was put together. As in the first two sections, this section uses challenging puzzles as an arena to practice critical thinking skills. So hang on to those brain cells as you tackle this final section.

—Michael

Puzzle Paths

Sam Loyd was one of the most published and brilliant puzzle creators of all time. Born in 1841, Sam was an accomplished chess player by his early teens. He created puzzles based upon the moves of chess pieces. Loyd also produced thousands of other puzzles, many of which still appear today with contemporary twists and slight modifications. The maze below is based upon one of his earliest puzzle ideas. Can you complete the challenge?

The *Amusing Amusement Park* has three rides. It also has three gates with signs that identify the ride to which they lead. The only problem is that the architect forgot the layout of the connecting paths. Can you help? Draw three paths that connect the rides to their gates. The paths can't meet or cross.

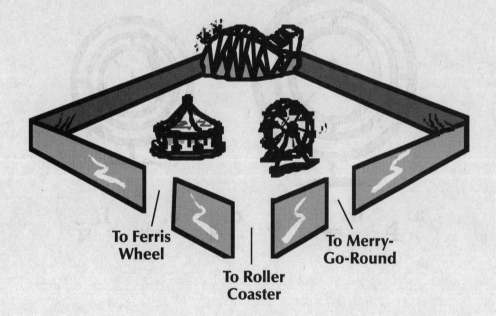

To Ferris Wheel

To Roller Coaster

To Merry-Go-Round

Turn, Turn, Turn

Ever heard of a multiaxial stimulator? Years ago, it appeared as a training device for astronauts and pilots. Nowadays, it's often found at beaches, amusement parks, and fairs. The MAS consists of three loops, each inside of the other. Each loop is free to rotate in only one dimension. The "pilot" is fastened to the middle of the innermost loop. In this position, a person gets to experience all three turning motions at the same time.

   Let's strap the number "4" in this simulator. Suppose each of the loops made one half rotation. How would the "4" appear after it was flipped, turned, and spun halfway in all three dimensions? You can select from the choices below.

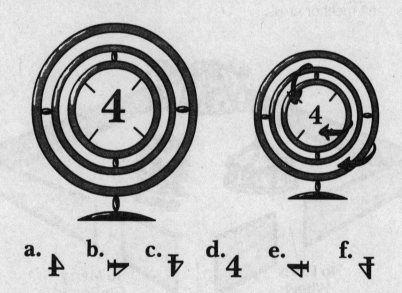

Mind Bend

According to Einstein, in some places the shortest distance between two points is not a straight line! Consider this: In space, the gravitational field of huge objects is strong enough to warp space. In these curved dimensions, the concept represented by a straight line bends to fit the framework of the distorted space. Mind bending, huh?

Here's another type of mind bender. The shape below is made from a single index card. No section of the card has been removed or taped back in place. Can you duplicate its appearance using several snips of a scissors? Have fun!

Whale of a Problem

In spite of their name, killer whales don't hunt and kill people. In fact, these dolphin-like animals prefer to eat smaller marine animals, such as seals and penguins. Biologists believe that rare attacks on humans occur because of misidentification. Obscured by daylight or icebergs, the image of a person may be mistaken for that of a penguin from below.

   Now here's the problem. Acting alone, it takes two killer whales 2 minutes to catch two seals. Based upon this rate, how long will it take a pod of ten killer whales to catch ten seals?

Main Attraction

Like all magnets, a bar magnet has a North and South Pole. At each of these poles, the magnetic force is the strongest. It is powerful enough to attract and repel iron objects. Near the middle of the magnet, however, the force is hardly detectable.

Suppose you have two identical iron bars. Only one of the bars has been magnetized. Suppose you can only pick up and manipulate one bar of these two bars. How can you tell if it is the magnetized or unmagnetized bar?

Runaway Runway

"Good afternoon. This is your captain speaking. We're fourth in line for departure. As soon as these four albatross birds take off, we'll begin our flight. Thank you for your patience."

Strange, but true. Pilots must sometimes compete with birds for runway usage. The same physical principles that lift an aircraft into the sky are at work in our feathered friends. Runways that are constructed to offer better lifting conditions for aircraft inadvertently produce great takeoff locations for birds.

Speaking of runways, here's our puzzle. If an airport has three separate runways, there can be a maximum of three intersections. Suppose there are four runways. What is the maximum number of possible intersections?

Raises and Cuts

Like many modern-day products, paper toweling arose from a factory mistake. A mill-sized roll of paper that should have been cut and packaged into soft bathroom tissue was manufactured thick and wrinkled. Instead of junking the roll, the workers perforated the unattractive paper into towel-sized sheets. And so, the paper towel was born.

Several years ago, Moe and Bo began work at a paper towel factory. At the end of the first week, the owner evaluated both workers. Pleased with Moe, she increased his weekly wage by 10%. Disappointed with Bo, she cut her salary by 10%. The following week, the owner decided to make their salaries more equal. To do so, she cut Moe's new salary by 10%. At the same time, she increased Bo's salary by 10%. Now, which worker earned more?

GEEZ, MOE. YOU SCREW UP YOUR JOB AND THEY MAKE YOU HEAD OF PRODUCT DEVELOPMENT?

PAPER TOWELS

The Race Is On

The material we call rubber is another product of a mishap in the kitchen! Prior to the mid-1800s, rubber was a troublesome material. In the summer heat, it became soft and sticky. In the winter cold, it became hard and brittle. In searching for a way to improve the properties of rubber, Charles Goodyear accidentally spilled a spoonful of a rubber and sulfur mixture onto his stove. When he later examined the solidified spill, he discovered a flexible material that could withstand heat and cold.

Take a look at the two solid rubber wheels below. Both have been modified by retired ice skaters. On the first wheel, 4 pounds of lead are positioned in one central lump. On the second wheel, the same amount of lead is spread out into four 1-pound lumps so that they are positioned closer to the wheel's rim.

Suppose these wheels are released down identical inclines. If we don't consider air resistance, will these wheels accelerate at the same rate?

Screwy Stuff

Take a close look at the two screws below. Suppose they were both turned in a counterclockwise rotation. What will happen to each screw?

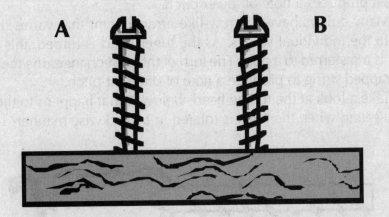

Screws in the Head

The pitch made by a vibrating string is dependent upon several factors, including the tension in the string. The more tightly pulled (greater tension), the higher the pitch. Likewise, if the string is relaxed (less tension), it produces a note of lower pitch.

Many guitars have a screw-like arrangement that varies the tension in the individual strings. As the tuner head is turned, this movement is transferred to a post. The turn of the post changes the tension in its wrapped string to produce a note of different pitch.

Take a look at the tuning heads below. What happens to the pitch of the sound when the head is rotated in a clockwise manner?

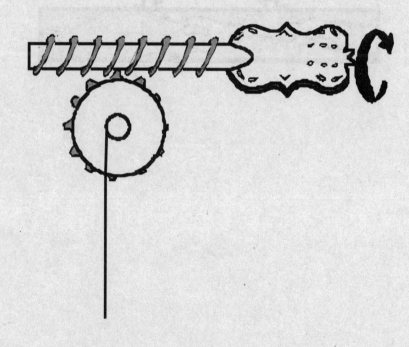

Change of Pace

Here are several puzzles that use a handful of change.

Consider this: I have ten coins in my pocket. The value of these coins is 50 cents. How many coins of each denomination are there?

Okay, so that one wasn't too difficult. How about finding the identity of thirty coins whose value is $1.00?

Spiral²

While exploring the ruins of an ancient city, an archaeologist uncovers an odd structure. The structure is made of stone walls that form a square spiral. The sides of the outside spiral measure 100 feet x 100 feet. The path throughout the entire structure is 2 feet wide.

If the archaeologist walks along the exact center of the path, how far will he travel from the entrance to the end of the spiral?

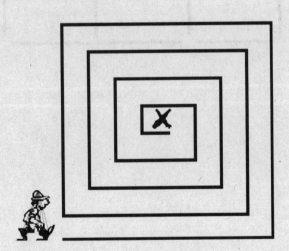

Take 'em Away

This arrangement of toothpicks forms fourteen different squares of various sizes. Can you remove six toothpicks and leave only three squares behind?

Don't Stop Now

Now that you are familiar with the pattern, let's try one more removal problem. Starting with the same twenty-four toothpick grid, remove eight toothpicks and leave exactly three squares behind.

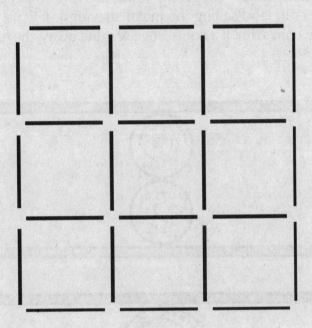

Get Set. Go!

Two cyclists race along a straight course. The faster of the pair maintains an average speed of 30 mph. The slower cyclist averages 25 miles per hour. When the race ends, the judges announce that the faster cyclist crossed the finish line one hour before the slower racer. How many miles long was the racing course?

Coin Roll

Run your fingernail around the rim of a dime or quarter and you'll feel a series of small ridges. These ridges appeared on coins hundreds of years ago. At that time, many coins were made out of silver and other valuable metals. To prevent people from "shaving" the metal from the edge of the coin (and selling the metal shavings), telltale ridges were added to the coin's rim. If a coin's edge was cut away, the telltale ridges would be lost.

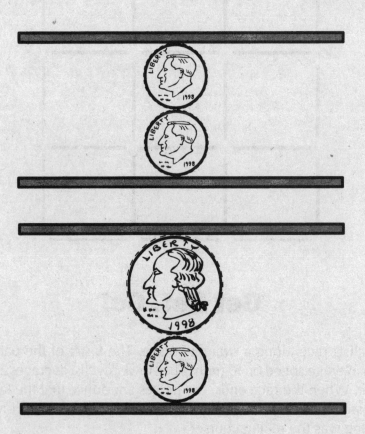

In this problem, we'll use those ridges to prevent the coins from slipping. Consider two dimes within a track formed by parallel chopsticks. Although the coins can move, their snug fit makes both coins move at the same time. Therefore, if we were to rotate one of the dimes,

the other would spin at the same speed but in the opposite direction. This results in both dimes moving along the track and maintaining their relative head-to-head position. Suppose, however, we change our setup and replace one of the dimes with a quarter. If the quarter is rotated along the track, how would its head-to-head position with the smaller dime change?

More Coinage

The four coins are positioned at the corners of a square. The side length of this square (measured from the center of each coin) is 8 inches. Here's the challenge. Can you change the positions of only two coins so that the new square formed by the coin arrangement has a side length slightly more than 5½ inches?

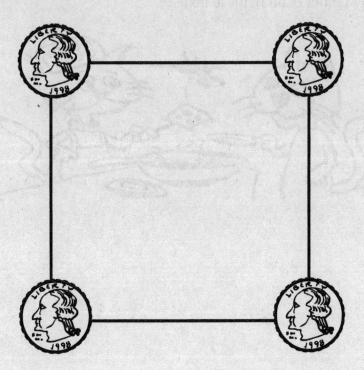

Some Things Never Change

People have written down puzzles for nearly 5000 years. One of the first puzzle collections was recorded about 1650 B.C. on a scroll called the Rhind papyrus. The word *Rhind* comes from the name Henry Rhind, a Scottish archaeologist who explored Egypt. *Papyrus* is a paper-like material that was used as a writing tablet by the ancient Egyptians.

The Rhind papyrus is a scroll that is over 18 feet long and about a foot wide. It was written on, on both sides, by a person named Ahmes. Roughly translated (and somewhat updated), one of the puzzles from the scroll is presented below.

There are seven houses, each containing seven cats. Each cat kills seven mice, and each mouse would have eaten seven ears of corn. Each ear of corn would have produced seven sacks of grain. What is the total number of all of these items?

184

Doing Wheelies

The outer rim of each "double wheel" is twice the diameter of the wheel's inner rim. Suppose the top wheel rotates at ten revolutions per second. At what speed will wheel A and wheel B spin?

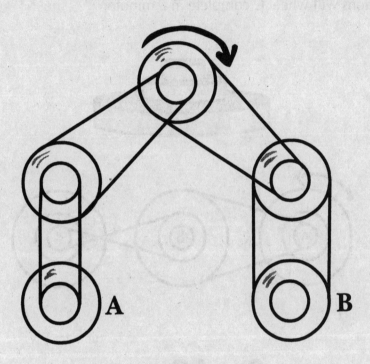

185

More Wheelies

The outermost rim of these wheels is twice the diameter of the middle rim. The middle rim is twice the diameter of the innermost rim. Suppose wheel A rotates at sixteen revolutions per second. How many revolutions will wheel C complete in a minute?

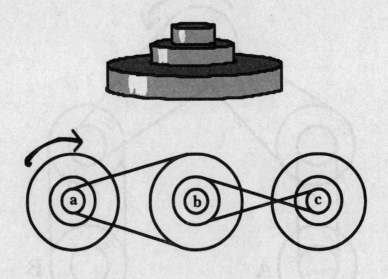

Good Guess

In order to win a free visit to the dentist, students had to guess the exact number of gumballs in a fish bowl. The students guessed 45, 41, 55, 50, and 43, but no one won. The guesses were off by 3, 7, 5, 7, and 2 (in no given order). From this information, determine the number of gumballs in the bowl.

Check It Out

The six sections below are parts of a 5 x 5 checkerboard grid. Can you piece them back together to form the original pattern?

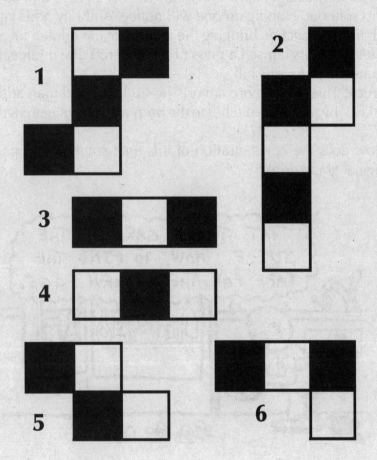

Oops, I Wasn't Concentrating

A pitcher is filled to the brim with grape juice. While raiding the refrigerator, Anthony accidentally knocks the pitcher over so that half of the contents spill out. Hoping no one will notice, Anthony adds tap water to the half-filled pitcher, bringing the volume of the diluted juice to the top. He then pours himself a glass of the watered down juice, leaving the pitcher three-fourths full.

"Yuck! This needs more flavor!" he exclaims and then adds more grape flavor by filling the pitcher to the brim with double-strength grape juice.

How does the concentration of this final solution compare with the original grape drink?

Trying Times

The triangle below is divided into four equal parts. Suppose you can paint one or more of these four smaller parts black. How many different and distinguishable patterns (including the pattern which has no painted triangles) can you form?

Remember, each pattern must be unique and not be duplicated by simply rotating the large figure.

Bridge, Anyone?

Ever heard of Galloping Girdie? If not, perhaps you've seen an old science fiction movie that showed a clip of a large suspension bridge twisting apart and falling into the river below it. That was Galloping Girdie.

It spanned a large river in the state of Washington. Soon after it was constructed, people noticed that winds would cause the bridge to sway and shake. During one incident of heavy winds, the bridge shook so violently that it fell apart into the river below. Bye-bye, Girdie.

Now, it's your turn to design a bridge. To build it, you'll need three ice cream sticks. If you don't have these sticks, you can use three pieces of stiff cardboard. The cardboard sections should be $4\frac{1}{2}$ inches long and $\frac{1}{2}$ inch wide.

Position three cups in a triangular pattern. The cups should be placed so that the edge-to-edge distance between any two of the cups is 5 inches.

Hmm... 5-inch canyons, but only $4\frac{1}{2}$-inch bridges. Your job is to construct a bridge using these three pieces and span the gaps connecting all three cups.

Face Lift

Take a look at the shape below. Although it is made up of four identical cubes, you can only see three of them. The fourth cube is hidden in the bottom backcorner. Imagine picking the shape up and examining it from all angles. How many different cube faces can you count?

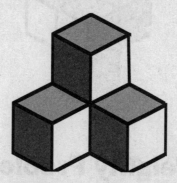

Okay, so it wasn't that hard. Try this one. The "double L" shape is made up of six cubes. The sixth cube is hidden in the back of the middle layer. If you could examine the stack from all angles, how many faces would you see?

Okay, okay, okay. Here's one more. This one consists of only five cubes. Actually it resembles the "double L" shape, except that one of the cubes is removed.

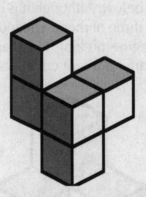

Weighty Problem

Did you know that during periods of weightlessness, astronauts lose bone mass? To prevent any serious loss, people in space must exercise. Stressing and stretching body parts help keep bone material from being reabsorbed into the body.

For a moment, let's imagine our weightless astronaut returning to Earth. She steps onto a scale and weighs herself. When the lab assistant asks her for her weight, she offers an obscure (but challenging) answer.

"According to this scale, I weigh 60 pounds plus half my weight."

Can you figure out how much this puzzling space traveler weighs?

Number Blocks

Take a look at the three stacks of numbered blocks below. Can you rearrange the blocks by exchanging one (and *only* one) from each of the three stacks so that the sum of the numbers in each stack is equal to the sum of numbers in either other stack?

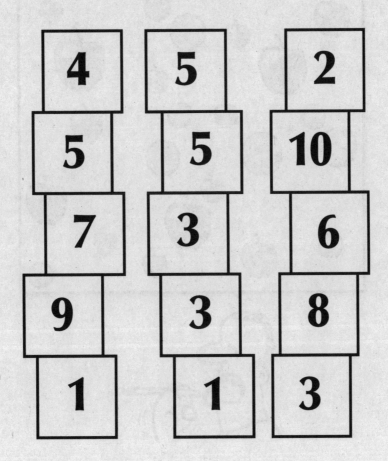

Give Me Five

How many 5's are in the number 5555?

Separation Anxiety

Using three straight lines, separate the apples from the oranges.

Breaking Up Is Hard
to Do... Sometimes

Take a look at the square and triangle below. Both figures are divided into four equal and identical parts so that each part has the same shape of the original figure (only smaller).

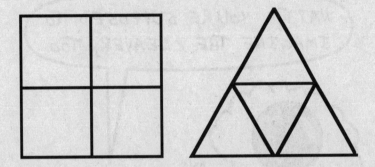

So far, so good. Now try to divide the figure below into four equal and identical parts, each with the same shape as the original figure.

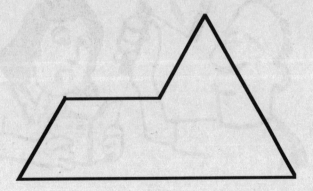

Mind Slice

Close your eyes and imagine a perfect sphere. Now, imagine a cleaver placed at a point anywhere on the surface of the sphere. How does changing the angle of the cleaver slice affect the *shape* of the exposed faces?

Say Cheese

The total surface area of any cube is equal to the sum of the surface areas of each of the six sides. For example, the cheese cube below measures 2 inches on each side. Therefore, the surface area of each side equals 2 inches x 2 inches, or 4 square inches. Since there are six sides, the total surface area of this cube is 24 square inches.

Now, the challenge. Using as many cuts as needed, divide this cube into pieces whose surface area sum is *twice* the surface area of this 2 x 2 cube.

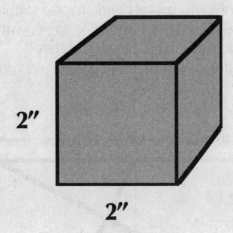

2″

2″

Satellite Surveyor

Satellites that orbit the Earth can see all sorts of things. Spy satellites, for example, have lenses that are powerful enough to "read" license plate numbers on cars. Other types of satellites can "look beneath" the Earth's surface. Some of these images have been used to uncover lost civilizations that have been buried for thousands of years under shifting desert sands.

In this problem, we'll use our satellite to help survey a plot of land.

The basic plot is a square that measures 20 miles on a side. Suppose the midpoint of each side is used as a marker to divide the entire plot into nine plots of various sizes and shapes. Without performing any higher math magic (just stick to plain ol' logic, with a little geometry), what is the area of the shaded central square?

NOTE: Before you bask in premature glory, it is not equal to 100 square miles!

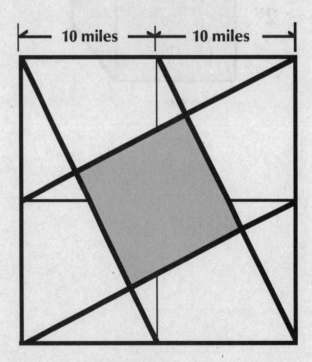

10 miles | 10 miles

Magic Star

For those of you who are tired of magic squares and magic triangles, may we present *The Magic Star?* In this puzzle, you'll have to use the numbers one through twelve. Only one number can be placed in a circle, and all the numbers must be used. When placed correctly, the sum of all rows of four must be the same.

HINT: All of the side sums equal twenty-six.

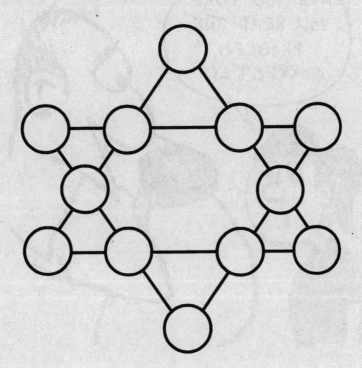

Keep on Tickin'

Divide the face of a watch into three sections. The sum of the numbers included on each section must equal the sum of the numbers on either of the other two sections. Let's not waste any time—the clock is ticking.

Cards, Anyone?

Use a pair of scissors to carefully cut out two unequal corners of an index card as shown below. Can you now use the scissors to cut this modified card into two identical halves?

   NOTE: The identical halves must be formed without flipping either piece over.

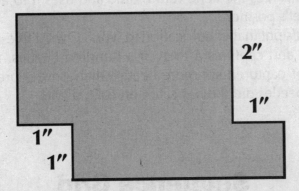

   Let's keep up the cutting challenge. Copy the pattern below onto an index card. Use your scissors to trim off the excess card stock. Now, here's the challenge. Divide this shape into four equal and identical parts that can fit back together to form a perfect square.

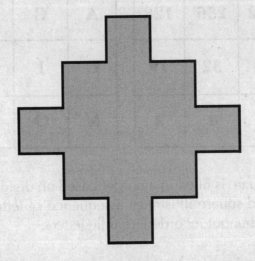

Going Batty

Click, click, click, click. Like submarines, bats have a sonar system called echolocation. They use their echolocation to find objects. The clicking sounds made by bats move outward like the beam of a lighthouse. When the sounds strike an object (such as an insect meal), they are reflected back to the bat's large ears. With incredible speed, the bat's brain analyzes the echo return time and uses it to accurately locate the target's position.

Now, let's put that echolocation to work. Over a five-night period, a bat targets and captures a total of a hundred beetles. During each night, the bat captured six more beetles than on the previous night. How many beetles did the bat catch on each night?

Sequence Grid

A sequence grid is formed by items that are related by their order. Here are two examples. As you can see, the placement of the numbers and letters reflects a sequence.

512	256	128
64	32	16
8	4	2

A	C	E
G	I	K
M	O	Q

The first square is filled in an order based on dividing a number in half. The second square illustrates a sequence of letters that is separated by single (but not recorded) middle letters.

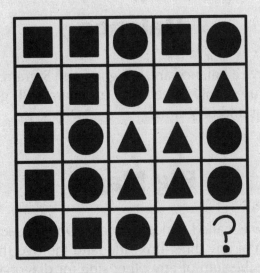

Now that you know what a sequence grid is, here's one to sharpen your puzzling skills on.

Breaking the Rules

A ruler is placed on two pieces of chalk as shown below. As the ruler is pushed, it moves 4 inches ahead. How far did either one of the chalk pieces roll?

Balance

Suppose you have a balance and a 2-gram and 5-gram mass. How can the balance be used only three times to separate 80 grams of fat into piles of 13 grams and 67 grams?

Big Magic

The figure below is called a magic square. Do you see why it's called magic? The sum of any three-box side (and the two three-box diagonals) is equal to the sum of any other side (or diagonal). In this case, they are all equal to fifteen.

8	3	4
1	5	9
6	7	2

The sections belong to a four-by-four magic square. Your job is to assemble these sections into a complete sixteen-box magic square. To do so, you'll *first* have to uncover the sum of the side for this figure.

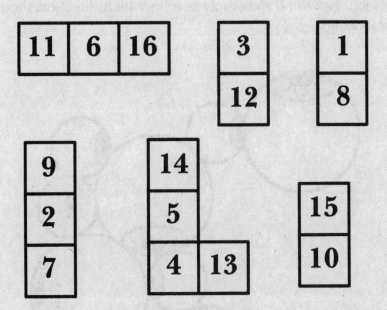

Togetherness

A computer and its monitor weigh a total of 48 pounds. If the monitor weighs twice as much as the computer, how much does each piece of hardware weigh?

Look Over Here

Note the direction in which each eye looks. Can you uncover the pattern? Good. Now find the empty eye. In which direction should this eye be looking?

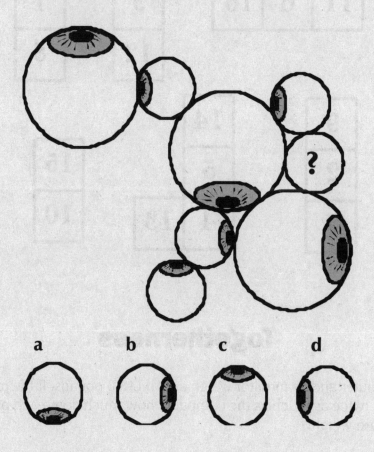

a   b   c   d

Time on Your Hands

Examine the series of three clockfaces shown below. When you uncover the pattern of the hand movement, select from the choice of times the one that will be closest to what the fourth clock should read.

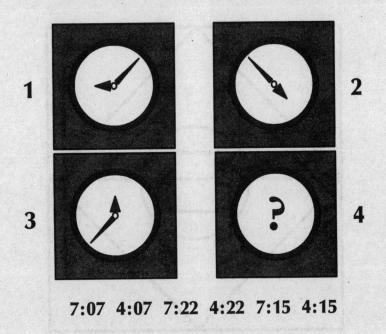

7:07 4:07 7:22 4:22 7:15 4:15

Take Your Pick

Arrange eight toothpicks (on a flat surface) so that they form two squares and four triangles.

One Way Only

Can you trace the following figure using only one continuous line? Place your pencil anywhere on the figure. Then, draw the rest of the figure without lifting your pencil from the page.

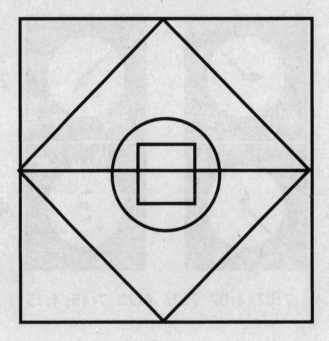

NOTE: This line cannot cross over itself nor retrace any part of its path.

Lasagna Cut

A square pan filled with piping-hot lasagna is set aside to cool. When the hungry chefs return, they discover that a quarter of the lasagna has mysteriously disappeared (as shown below). Frustrated, they decide to divide the remaining piece into four equal portions before any more is eaten. All cuts must be normal—no slicing through the plane of the surface allowed. What is the cutting pattern that will meet the needs of these chefs?

    HINT: The simplest solution requires cutting this meal into eight pieces and supplying each person with two smaller pieces.

Iron Horse Race

Two trains race against each other on parallel tracks. *The Casey Jones Special* is a coal-fed steam engine that travels at a respectable speed. The newer, oil-burning *Metropolitan Diesel* travels 1¹/₂ times the speed of *The Casey Jones Special*. To make the race a closer competition, *The Casey Jones Special* begins the race 1¹/₂ hours before its opponent. How long will it take the *Metropolitan Diesel* to catch up to the slower steam engine?

Thick As a Brick

If the chimney below is complete on all four sides, how many bricks does the whole structure contain?

Here, Art, Art, Art

How quickly can you uncover the perfect five-pointed star hidden in the design below?

Surrounded by Squares

How many squares can you uncover in the pattern below? Don't forget to count the outer border as one of your answers!

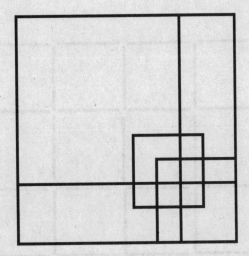

More Cheese

A grocer has a large cube of cheese that she wishes to divide into twenty-seven smaller and equal-sized cubes. To cut out the twenty-seven blocks, she uses two cuts to divide the cube into three slices. She stacks these slices atop of each other and makes two more cuts. Finally, she rotates the cube a quarter-turn and makes the final cut. The result is twenty-seven identical cubes made with six cuts. Is it possible to get the twenty-seven cubes with fewer cuts? If so, how?

Break It Up!

If you look carefully, you'll be able to uncover thirty squares in the toothpick pattern below. Your challenge is to find the fewest number of toothpicks that, when removed, leaves no complete square pattern intact.

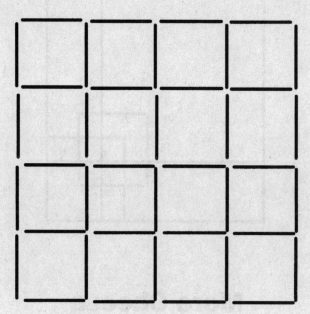

Exactly... Well, Almost

Which of the designs below is unlike the other five?

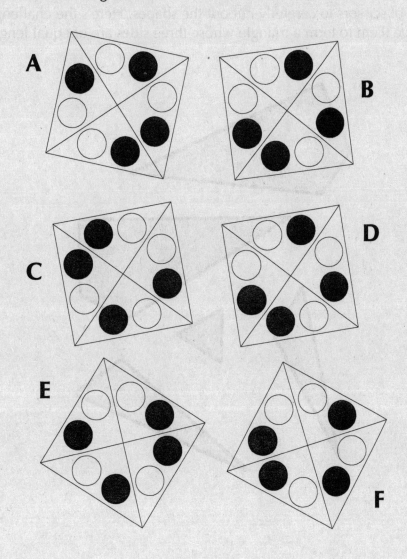

Parts of a Whole

Copy the five shapes shown below onto a separate sheet of paper. Use a pair of scissors to carefully cut out the shapes. Here's the challenge. Arrange them to form a triangle whose three sides are of equal length.

A Game for Losers

The object of this modified game of tic-tac-toe is to lose! In order to win, you must force your opponent to complete three squares in a row. Let's enter a game that has already been started. You are "O" and it is your turn. In which box or boxes should you place your "O" marker to ensure that you win by losing (no matter where your opponent goes)?

217

Roller Coaster, Roll!

Ed and his identical twin brother Ed build roller coaster tracks. They've just completed two hills that are both 40 feet high. As you can see, the slopes of the two hills are somewhat different. Ed (the older twin) rides a car that will travel along on a straight slope. Ed (the younger twin) rides a car that will travel along a curved slope.

If both cars are released at the exact same time, which Ed will arrive at the bottom of this slope first?

Sum Puzzle

Copy the pattern and numbers shown below onto a sheet of paper. Then carefully use a pair of scissors to separate the sheet into nine separate squares. Rebuild the larger square using the following strategy. The sum of any two adjacent numbers must equal ten. Have fun.

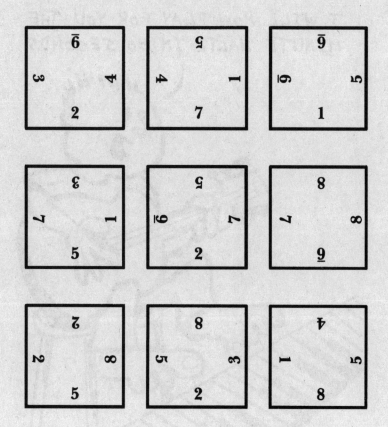

219

A Class Act

There are thirty students in a class. Five of these students do not play any sort of musical instrument. Among the others, eighteen students play guitar. Six of these guitar players also play keyboards. How many of the students in the class play only keyboards?

I WILL NOW PLAY FOR YOU THE MINUTE WALTZ IN 30 SECONDS

Cool Cut

Shut your eyes and try to imagine a perfect ice cube. If you're good at visualizing, you may be able to "see" the edges and faces that are positioned on the far side of the cube. Good. Now, here's the challenge.

With one cut, how can you divide this cube so that a perfect triangular face is exposed? Don't forget, a regular triangle has all three sides of equal length.

Melt Down

Unlike most liquids, water freezes into a solid that is less dense than its former liquid state. Since it is less dense, ice floats in water. At the surface, the ice acts as an insulator to help trap heat within the water below. This layer of frozen insulation actually insulates lakes, rivers, ponds, and oceans from freezing into a complete solid.

Now let's bring this information back to the kitchen. An ice cube floats freely in a glass filled to the brim with water. Will the water level rise or sink as the ice cube melts?

What's the Angle?

An equilateral triangle has three sides that are all of equal length. This familiar shape can be constructed from three identical pieces. Examine the shapes below. Which of these shapes illustrates this building block? Once you've selected the shape, make three copies of it on a separate sheet of paper. Cut out and arrange these pieces so that they form an equilateral triangle.

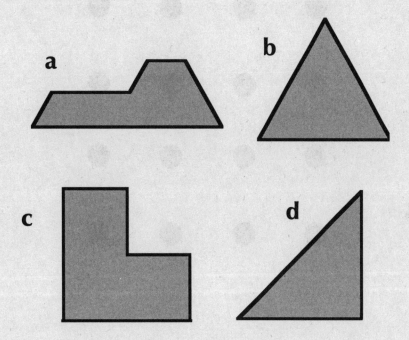

a

b

c

d

Here, Spot, Spot, Spot

Without lifting your pencil from the paper, draw six straight lines that connect all sixteen of the dots below. To make things more of a challenge, the line pattern that you create must begin at the "x".

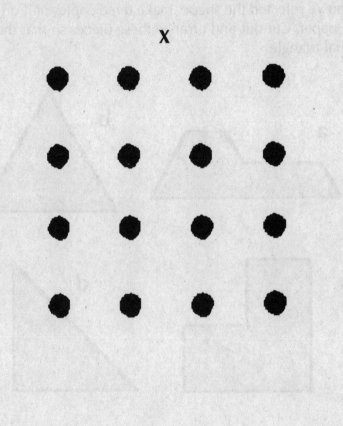

Keeping Time

The strike of a lightning bolt can create a tremendous surge of electricity. If this electric flow reaches the delicate circuits of a computer, it can "burn out" the sensitive components. To prevent against this damage, computers are plugged into surge protectors, which stop the electric flow if a damaging level of electricity is detected.

In this problem, there are no surge protectors. Two electronic clocks are plugged directly into the wall socket. A surge of electricity flows through both clocks and affects their time-keeping circuits. One clock is now 5 minutes per hour fast. The other clock is now 5 minutes per hour slow. In how many hours will the clocks be exactly one hour apart?

Wrap It Up

You will soon engage your intellect in this book's final critical thinking puzzle.

Did you know that fortune cookies didn't originate in China? They were created in the U.S. by the owner of an Asian restaurant who wished to amuse his customers while they waited for their meals to be cooked. Over time, fortune cookies evolved into a treat that is now offered at the end of the meal. That's a wrap. And speaking of wraps...

Take a look at the steps in which the cookie wrapper below was folded. In the final step, two holes were punched through the layers of the folds.

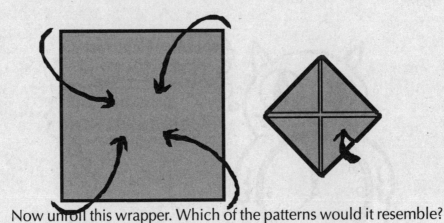

Now unroll this wrapper. Which of the patterns would it resemble?

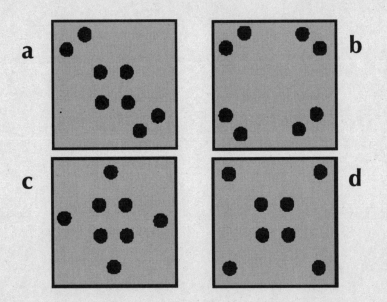

ANSWERS

Balance

First, use the balance to divide the 80 grams into two piles of 40 grams. Then divide one of the 40-gram piles in half. Now balance the 20 grams against the 7 grams produced by the two masses. The 13 grams that are removed from the balance form one pile. The 7 grams added to the 40 grams + 20 grams produces the larger pile of 67 grams.

Big Magic

The sum of the side is thirty-four, and the square looks like this:

1	11	6	16
8	14	3	9
15	5	12	2
10	4	13	7

Break It Up!

Nine toothpicks need to be removed as shown below.

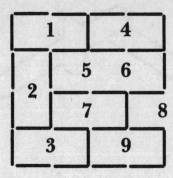

Breaking the Rules

Two inches. Each chalk piece will advance only half the distance covered by the ruler.

Breaking Up Is Hard to Do... Sometimes

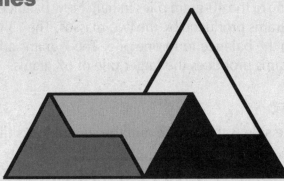

Bridge, Anyone?

The sticks below are arranged so that they support each other in a central triangle formed by overlapping and underlapping supports.

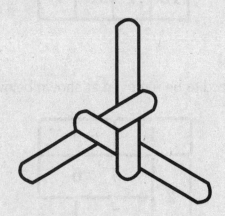

Cards, Anyone?

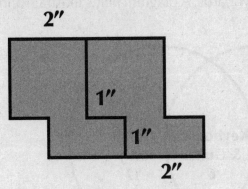

2"

1"

1"

2"

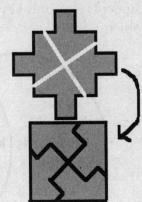

Change of Pace

a. either 5 pennies ($.05) + 4 nickels ($.20) + 1 quarter ($.25) = $.50; or 10 nickels ($.05) = $.50

b. 25 pennies ($.25) + 1 nickel ($.05) + 2 dimes ($.20) + 2 quarters ($.50) = $1.00

Check It Out

A Class Act

Seven students play only keyboards. A diagram helps illustrate and solve this problem.

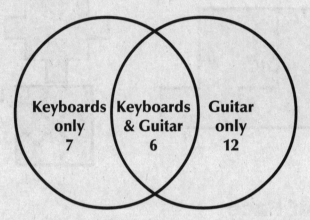

Keyboards only 7 — Keyboards & Guitar 6 — Guitar only 12

Coin Roll

The coins maintain their relative position to each other as they move along the track. What changes is the direction in which the coin images point.

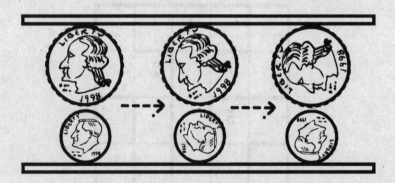

Cool Cut

Make the cut from one corner straight across to the corners as shown below. Each side of this regular triangle that is formed is equal in length to the diagonal of the square.

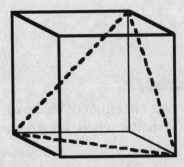

Doing Wheelies

Wheel A would be spinning at five revolutions per minute. Wheel B would be spinning at twenty revolutions per minute. The difference in speed results from the "gearing up" and the "gearing down" from the first wheel set to the second wheel set. The belts between the second and third wheel sets do not affect the spin.

Don't Stop Now

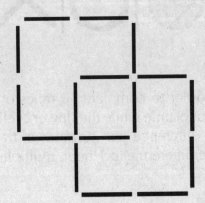

Exactly... Well, Almost

E. It is the mirror image of the other repeating (but rotating) design.

Face Lift

a. Eighteen faces.
b. Twenty-six faces.
c. Twenty-two faces.

A Game for Losers

By placing your "O" marker in either of the boxes indicated below, you are ensured a victory no matter where your opponent places his or her "X"s.

Get Set. Go!

150 miles long. In order to complete 30 miles of distance, the faster cyclist requires 1 hour of time while the slower cyclist needs 1.20 hours. Therefore, the time difference per 30 miles of travel is .20 hours. In order to increase the difference to 1 hour, multiple the 30 miles by 5.

Give Me Five

1111. Easy, unless of course you forget all it takes to solve this problem is to divide 5555 by 5!

Going Batty

The number of beetles captured on each successive night were 8, 14, 20, 26, and 32.

Good Guess

Forty-eight gumballs. Since two guesses were off by seven and no guesses were repeated, these values had to refer to numbers at the opposite extremes of the spread. The two extremes are 41 and 55. If you add 7 to one and take 7 away from the other, you arrive at the middle number of 48.

Here, Art, Art, Art

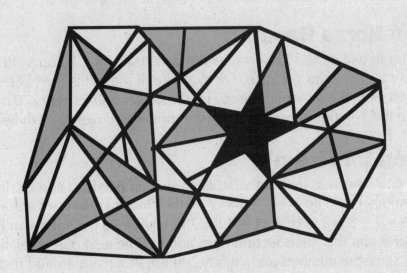

Here, Spot, Spot, Spot

Iron Horse Race

The trains will be tied 3 hours after the faster train (or $4\frac{1}{2}$ hours after the slower train) begins the race. For example, if the trains travel 60 mph and 90 mph, the $4\frac{1}{2}$-hour journey for the slower train covers 270 miles, while the 3-hour journey for the faster train also covers 270 miles.

Keep On Tickin'

First you'll need to find out what each section needs to add to. To get this number, add up every number on the clock's face ($1 + 2 + 3 + 4 + 5 + 6 + 7 + 8 + 9 + 10 + 11 + 12 = 78$). Divide 78 by 3 and you'll get 26—the sum that each section must add to. The next part is relatively easy, since the numbers are already laid out in a ready-to-add pattern.

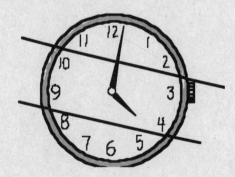

Keeping Time

Six hours. In 6 hours, the slow clock will be exactly 30 minutes behind while the fast clock will be exactly 30 minutes ahead of time.

Lasagna Cut

Each person gets one large and one small triangular piece.

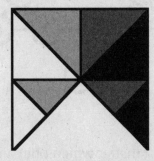

Here's a slightly different pattern that produces four similarly shaped slices (if we assume the connecting points between the triangle pairs remain uncut).

Look Over Here

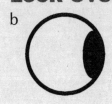

b   The direction of the look is based upon the number of neighboring eyes that are in contact with the eye's circumference. Eyes that "touch" three other circles (such as the circle in question) have a pupil that points to the right.

Magic Star

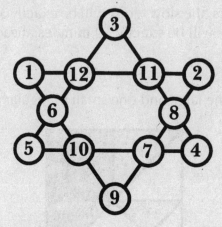

Main Attraction

Take either bar (it doesn't matter which one) and touch one end of the bar to the middle of the other bar. If the bar you are holding is a magnet, then its pole will cause the nonmagnetized bar to move. If, however, you've picked up the nonmagnetized bar, no attraction will occur. That's because neither of the poles is being touched.

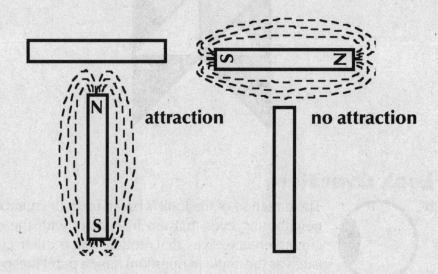

attraction   no attraction

Melt Down

The level of water will not change. Although the top of the cube floats above the surface of the water, the amount of water in the entire ice cube can fill a space equal to the dimensions occupied by the part of the cube that is under the water's surface. In other words, as the ice cube turns to water, it produces the same amount of water as the space occupied by the submerged part of the cube.

Mind Bend

Place three parallel cuts in the card. Two of the cuts should be positioned on one side, while a single central cut should be made on the opposite side (as shown below). Then place a twist in the card so that half of the upper surface is formed by the "bottom-side" of the card. For extra fun, you might want to tape the folded card by all of its edges to the desk (making it more difficult to uncover the baffling "twist").

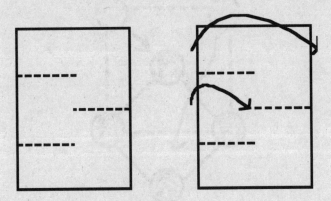

More Cheese

No. Six cuts are the fewest number of cuts needed to produce the twenty-seven smaller cubes. Stacking doesn't result in fewer cuts. Think of it this way: that innermost cube of the twenty-seven must be formed by a cut on each of its six sides.

Mind Slice

The angle of the cut will not affect the shape at all. All cuts will produce faces that are perfect circles. The feature that does change with the cutting angle is the circle size.

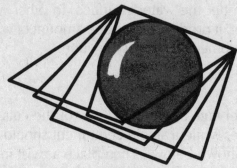

More Coinage

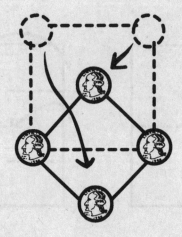

More Wheelies

480 revolutions. Since wheel B's rim is four times longer than wheel A's rim, it spins at one-fourth the speed (4 rps). Likewise, wheel B's rim is twice as long as wheel C's rim. Therefore, wheel C's rim spins twice as fast (8 rps). In 1 minute, C wheel will complete 60 x 8 revolutions, or 480 revolutions.

Number Blocks

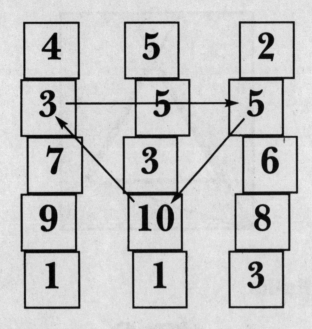

One Way Only

Start here →

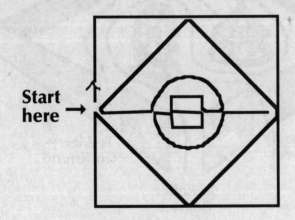

Parts of a Whole

Puzzle Paths

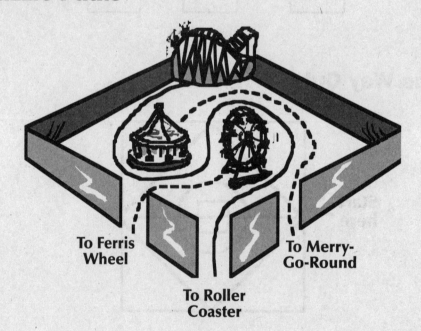

To Ferris
Wheel

To Roller
Coaster

To Merry-
Go-Round

Oops, I Wasn't Concentrating

It is weaker than the original solution. In order to have the original concentration, Anthony would have to add grape juice that is $2\frac{1}{2}$ times the regular strength.

Raises and Cuts

They are now both earning the exact same amount. To prove this, let's take a sample first-week salary of $100 for both Moe and Bo. After the first adjustment, Moe earned $110 while Bo earned $90. During the second adjustment, Moe was cut by $11 to $99. At the same time, Bo was increased by $9 to $99.

Runaway Runway

Six intersections as shown below.

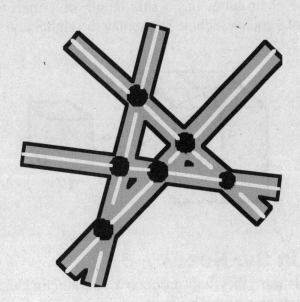

Roller Coaster, Roll!

Young Ed. The car that travels along the curved slope accelerates faster. This extra speed results from the quick drop in the path that allows the car to quickly pick up speed as the car moving down the straight slope accelerates at a slower and more uniform rate.

Satellite Surveyor

80 square miles. If you examine the dissected grid, you'll uncover that the composite shapes include side-by-side pairs that can be joined to form four squares. The total area is 20 x 20, or 400 square miles. Each of the five identical squares contains one-fifth, or 80 square miles.

Say Cheese

Make three cuts that divide the cube into eight smaller but equal cubes. Each of these eight cubes has a side length of 1 inch to produce a surface area of 6 square inches. The sum of the eight cube surface areas is 48 square inches.

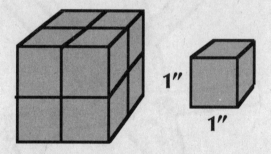

Screws in the Head

As the threads turn, they will produce a counterclockwise motion in the gear of the tuning post. This motion will decrease the tension in the string to produce a note of lower pitch.

Screwy Stuff

The threads of screw A form a spiral that would "go into" the wood block. In contrast, the opposite spiral of screw B would result in this screw moving out of the wooden block.

Separation Anxiety

Sequence Grid

Triangle. The grid is filled by a series of number sequences. The first sequence consists of only one member—a square. The second and adjoining sequence includes a square + circle. The third sequence expands to include a square + circle + triangle. The complete sequence from which the "?" can be determined is square + circle + triangle + triangle + circle + circle.

Some Things Never Change

$7 + 49 + 343 + 2401 + 16,807 = 19,607$.

Spiral²

The complete path from entrance to center is 5000 feet. To obtain this distance, determine the total area of the structure (10,000 square feet). Now mentally unroll the spiral. Divide the 10,000-square-foot area by the area associated with one foot of forward travel. Since the corridor is 2 feet wide, the area for a single foot of forward motion is 2 square feet. Dividing 10,000 by 2, we arrive at the total distance of 5000 feet.

The Race Is On

The wheel with the centrally placed lead will accelerate fastest. This behavior reflects a property of physics that ice skaters execute during their moves. As a skater spins, the speed of the spin can be adjusted by altering his or her distribution of weight. As the arms extend, the spinning skater slows. As the arms draw in, the spin accelerates.

Sum Puzzle

Surrounded by Squares

Thirteen squares.

Take 'em Away

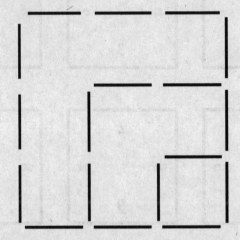

Take Your Pick

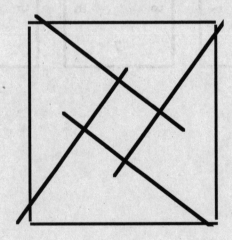

Thick As a Brick

Sixty bricks. You don't have to count all of the bricks. Just count the bricks in the uppermost layer (twelve) and multiply by the number of layers (five) so that you arrive at a total number of sixty bricks.

Time on Your Hands

7:22. For each given time, the minute hand advances a quarter of a complete counterclockwise rotation, while the hour hand advances three-eighths of a complete counterclockwise rotation. The final arrangement looks like this:

Togetherness

The computer weighs 16 pounds and its monitor weighs 32 pounds.

Trying Times

Eight unique triangles as shown below.

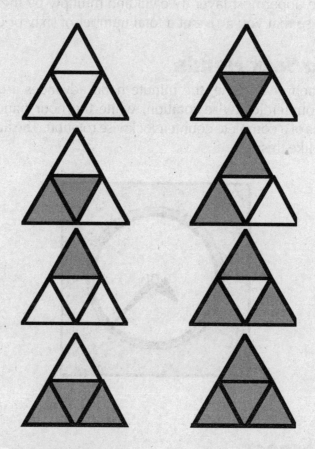

Turn, Turn, Turn

F.

Weighty Problem

120 pounds. If she needs to add "half of her weight" to get her full weight, then the weight that she does tell (60 pounds) must be half of her total. Therefore, 60 pounds is half of her weight. 60 + 60 = 120 pounds. If this doesn't seem right, just work it backwards starting with the 120 pounds.

What's the Angle?

a. Three copies of this shape are positioned as shown here.

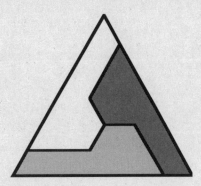

Whale of a Problem

Two minutes. The amount of time needed to catch the seals doesn't change. Since two whales can catch two seals in 2 minutes, it is logical to assume that a single whale can catch one seal in that same period of time. Likewise, three whales can catch three seals in 2 minutes. As long as the number of whales is equal to the number of seals, the time doesn't change. Therefore, ten killer whales will also take 2 minutes to catch ten seals.

Wrap It Up

d. Here's what you see as you unwrap the folds.

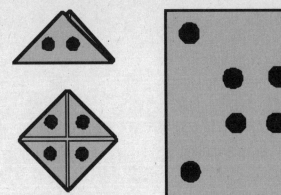

INDEX  Answers appear on pages in *italics*.

GIANT BOOK OF MENSA MIND CHALLENGE

J.J. Mendoza Fernández
Jaime & Lea Poniachik
Tim Sole & Rod Marshall

The Main Street Press

10 9 8 7 6 5 4 3 2

Published In 1999 by Sterling Publishing Company, Inc.
387 Park Avenue South, New York, N.Y. 10016

Material in this collection was adapted from
Quick-to-Solve Brainteasers
© J. J. Mendoza Fernández
Hard-to-Solve Brainteasers
© Jaime & Lea Poniachik
and
Nearly Impossible Brain Bafflers
© Tim Sole & Rod Marshall

Distributed in Canada by Sterling Publishing
c/o Canadian Manda Group
One Atlantic Avenue, Suite 105
Toronto, Ontario, Canada M6K 3E7

Distributed in Great Britain and Europe by Cassell PLC
Wellington House, 125 Strand
London WC2R 0BB, United Kingdom

Distibuted in Australia by Capricorn Link (Australia) Pty Ltd.
P.O. Box 6651, Baulkham Hills, Business Centre,
NSW 2153, Australia

Manufactured in the United States of America.

CONTENTS

SECTION ONE
Quick-to-Solve BRAIN TEASERS

SECTION TWO
Hard-to-Solve BRAIN TEASERS

SECTION THREE
Nearly Impossible BRAIN BAFFLERS

QUICK-TO-SOLVE
BRAIN
TEASERS

This section contains many different types of puzzles: numerical puzzles, logic puzzles, word games, lateral thinking puzzles, riddles, etc. Most of them are extremely short and can be solved mentally in just a minute or two. When writing is required, a small slip of paper should be more than adequate.

The purpose of these puzzles is to entertain. The correct answer is not always obvious. The reader will notice that the puzzles are often misleading or involve humor in the answer. Therefore, use your imagination, be alert, and have an open mind when trying the puzzles.

The **answers** for this section can be found on **pages 59** through **83**.

NUMBERS

1234567890

1

How many times can you subtract 6 from 30?

2

What number can you subtract half from to obtain a result that is zero?

3

How can half of 12 be 7?

4

Find two positive numbers that have a one-digit answer when multiplied and a two-digit answer when added.

5

Find two whole, positive numbers that have the same answer when multiplied together as when one is divided by the other.

6

Find two positive numbers that have the same answer when multiplied together as when added together.

7

Find a two-digit number that equals two times the result of multiplying its digits.

8

Find three whole, positive numbers that have the same answer when multiplied together as when added together.

9

What two two-digit numbers are each equal to their right-most digit squared?

10

Find the highest number that can be written with three digits.

COMPARING NUMBERS

11

The ages of a father and a son add up to 55. The father's age is the son's age reversed. How old are they?

12

How much do 10 pieces of candy cost if one thousand pieces cost $10?

13

An outlet and a light bulb cost $1.20. We know that the outlet costs $1 more than the light bulb. How much does each cost?

PERCENTAGES

14

If 75% of all women are tall, 75% are brunette, and 75% are pretty, what is the minimum percentage of tall, brunette, pretty women?

15

Thirty-two students took a nationwide exam and all the students from New York passed it. If the students from New York made up exactly 5% of the total number of the students that passed the test, how many students passed it and how many students were from New York?

16

Of the 960 people in a theater, 17% tipped 5 cents to the usher, 50% of the remaining 83% tipped 10 cents, and the rest tipped nothing. How much did the usher get?

OTHER NUMBERS

17

What must you do to make the equation below true?
81 x 9 = 801.

18

There are 100 buildings along a street. A sign maker is ordered to number the buildings from 1 to 100. How many "9's" will he need?

19

How many tickets with different points of origination and destination can be sold on a bus line that travels a loop of 25 stops?

20

We know that humans have up to 100,000 hairs. In a city with more than 200,000 people, would it be possible to find two or more people with the same number of hairs?

COUNTING

21

All my ties are red except two. All my ties are blue except two. All my ties are brown except two. How many ties do I have?

22

A street that's 30 yards long has a chestnut tree every 6 yards on both sides. How many chestnut trees are on the entire street?

23

A pet shop owner is in the countryside. If he says, "one bird per olive tree," there is one bird too many. However, if he says, "two birds per olive tree", there are no birds left over. How many birds and olive trees are there?

24

In a singles tennis tournament, 111 players participated. They used a new ball for each match. When a player lost one match, he was eliminated from the tournament. How many balls did they need?

25

Peter and John had a picnic. Peter had already eaten half of the muffins when John ate half of the remaining muffins plus three more. There were no muffins left. How many muffins did they take to the picnic?

26

A shepherd says to another, "If I give you one sheep, you will have twice the number of sheep that I have, but if you give me one, we will both have the same number of sheep." How many sheep did each shepherd have?

27

If I put in one canary per cage, I have one bird too many. However, if I put in two canaries per cage, I have one cage too many. How many cages and birds do I have?

28

If $1\frac{1}{2}$ sardines cost $1\frac{1}{2}$ dollars, how much would $7\frac{1}{2}$ sardines cost?

29

If a brick weights 3 pounds plus $\frac{1}{2}$ a brick, what's the weight of $1\frac{1}{2}$ bricks?

30

If $1\frac{1}{2}$ dozen sardines costs $9\frac{1}{2}$ dollars, how much do 18 sardines cost?

31

If $1\frac{1}{2}$ men can eat $1\frac{1}{2}$ pies in $1\frac{1}{2}$ minutes, how many pies can 3 men eat in half an hour?

32

Yesterday afternoon, I went to visit my friend Albert, who is a painter. While I was watching him paint, I told him, "No wonder it takes you so long to finish a painting. Since I arrived, you have entered the studio twelve times." How many times did he leave the studio?

33

If two ducks are swimming in front of another duck, two ducks are swimming behind another duck, and one duck is swimming between two other ducks, what is the minimum number of ducks?

34

Two people are flipping coins. Each time, they bet $1 apiece. At the end, one person won $3 and the other one won three times. How many games did they play?

MEASURING TIME, VOLUME, LENGTH, ETC.

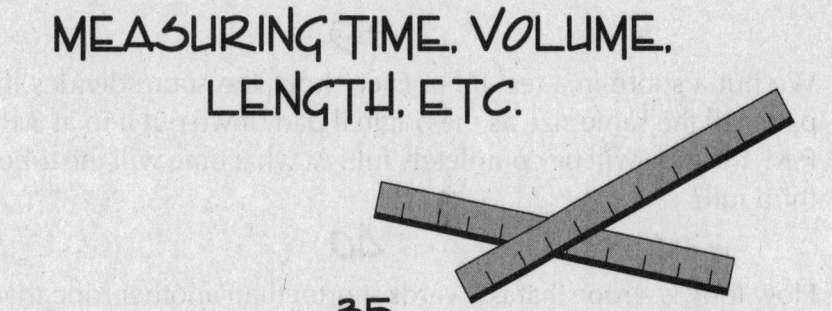

35

A bottle with a cylindrical shape at the bottom and with an irregular shape at the top is filled halfway to the top with liquid. The cylindrical part contains approximately three-fourths of the capacity of the bottle and we wish to determine the exact percentage of liquid that the bottle contains. We cannot open it and we can only use a ruler. What must we do?

36

If one nickel is worth five cents, how much is half of one half of a nickel worth?

37

Two soldiers have been ordered to do the following chores:
   1. Peel potatoes.
   2. Do the dishes.
   3. Mow the lawn.
Each of these chores, when done by one person, takes one hour. If they start at 8 A.M., what could they do to take as little time as possible if they have only one knife, one lawn mower, and one sink with room for one person?

38

A spider spins its web in a window frame. Each day, it spins an area equal to that of the amount already completed. It takes 30 days to cover the entire window frame. How long would two spiders take? (In the case of the two spiders, each of them spins an amount equal to the area of the existing part of the web made by that particular spider.)

39

We put a spore in a test tube. Every hour the spore divides into three parts, all the same size as the original part. If we put it in at 3 P.M., at 9 P.M. the tube will be completely full. At what time will the tube be one-third full?

40

How long is a rope that is 2 yards shorter than another rope that is three times the length of the first rope?

41

If a post is 6 yards longer than half of its own length, how long is the post?

42

How much mud (measured in liters) is there in a rectangular hole 2 meters wide, 3 meters long, and 3 meters deep?

43

One mother gave 25 books to her daughter and another mother gave her daughter 8 books. However, between both daughters they only increased their collection by 25 books. How can this be?

COMPARING TIME, VOLUME, LENGTH, ETC.

44

Emily is taller than Ann and shorter than Dolores. Who is the tallest of the three?

45

Rose is now as old as Joan was six years ago. Who is older?

46

If Emily speaks in a softer voice than Ann, and Dolores in a louder voice than Ann, does Emily speak louder or softer than Dolores?

47

James is sitting between John and Peter. Philip is sitting on Peter's right. Between whom is Peter sitting?

48

What has more value, one pound of $10 gold coins or half a pound of $20 gold coins?

49

A man went into a store and bought an umbrella for $10. He gave the salesperson a $50 bill. The salesperson went to the bank to get change. Two hours later, the bank teller went to the store claiming that the $50 bill was counterfeit, so the salesperson had to exchange it for a real one with the bank teller. Between the customer and the bank, how much did the store lose?

50

We have two pitchers, one with one quart of water and the other with one quart of wine. We take a tablespoon of the wine and mix it in the pitcher of water. Then we take a tablespoon from this pitcher and mix it into the pitcher with the wine. Is there more wine in the water pitcher or more water in the wine pitcher? What would have happened if after pouring a spoonful of wine into the water, we had not mixed it well?

51

A sultan wanted to offer his daughter in marriage to the candidate whose horse would win the race. However, the rules of the race stated that the winner would be the one in last place. He didn't want the race to last forever, so he thought of a way to solve this. What was it?

WEIGHTS

52

On one side of a scale we have a partially filled fish bowl. When we put a fish in the bowl, the total weight of the bowl increases by exactly the same as the weight of the fish. However, if we hold the fish by the tail and partially introduce it into the water, will the total weight be greater than before introducing the fish?

53

We have a scale and a set of weights in a field. The scale is not very accurate, but it is consistent in its inaccuracies. How can we know the exact weight of four apples?

54

A little bird weighing 5 ounces is sleeping in a cage. We put the cage on a scale and it weighs one pound. The bird then wakes up and starts flying all over the cage. What will the scale indicate while the bird is in the air?

55

We have 10 sacks full of balls. All sacks contain balls weighing 10 ounces each, except one of the sacks, which contains balls weighing 9 ounces each. By weighing the balls, what would be the minimum number of weighings required (on a scale that gives weight readouts) to identify the sack containing the defective balls?

56

Now we have 10 sacks that contain either 10-ounce balls or 9-ounce balls. Each sack has at least 1,000 balls, and all the balls in one sack are the same weight. However, we do not know how many sacks contain the 9-ounce balls or which ones they are. How can we identify these sacks by weighing the balls (on a scale that gives weight readouts) in the fewest number of tries?

CHAINS

57

I have six pieces of a chain, each piece made up of 4 links, and I want to make a single straight chain out of them. The blacksmith charges 10 cents for cutting each link and 50 cents for welding a link. How much will the chain cost?

58

A lady arrives at a hotel where rooms are $10 per night. When she checks in, she does not have enough money, but she offers to pay with a clasped gold bracelet. The bracelet has seven links, each valued at $10. What would be the fewest number of cuts necessary to let her stay for one week if she wants to pay one day at a time?

59

"And then I took out my sword and cut the thick chain that was linked to two posts into two pieces," said the samurai.

"That is not true," said the monk.

How did the monk know the samurai's story was untrue?

MIXING

60

We have 10 glasses sitting in a row. The first five are filled with water and the other five are empty. What would be the minimum number of glasses needed to move so that the full and the empty glasses alternate?

61

In five plastic cups there are five marbles, each of different colors: white, black, red, green, and blue. We mark each cup randomly with the initial of one of the colors. If the white, green, red, and blue marbles are in their respective cups, how likely is it that the black marble is in its cup?

62

We have 8 pairs of white socks and 10 pairs of black socks in a box. What would be the minimum number of socks that we need to take out of the box to ensure that we get one pair of the same color? (Imagine that you cannot see the color when you are picking them from the box.)

63

We have 8 pairs of white socks, 9 pairs of black socks and 11 pairs of blue socks in a box. What would be the minimum number of socks that we need to take out of the box to ensure that we get one pair of the same color? (Imagine that you cannot see the color when you are picking them from the box.)

64

We have 6 pairs of white gloves and 6 pairs of black gloves in a box. What would be the minimum number of gloves that we need to take out of the box to ensure that we get one pair? (Imagine that you cannot see the color when you are picking them from the box.)

65

We have six white marbles, four black marbles, and one red marble in a box. What would be the least number of marbles that we need to take out of the box to ensure that we get three of the same color?

66

Distribute ten marbles in three plastic cups so that every cup contains an odd number of marbles. You must use all ten.

67

Distribute nine marbles in four boxes so that each box contains an odd number of marbles, different from the three other boxes. You must use all nine.

68

We have three boxes. One contains two black marbles, the second box contains two white marbles, and the third box contains one black and one white marble. The boxes are marked BB, WW, BW. However, no code corresponds with the marbles in its box. What would be the least number of marbles that must be randomly picked, from one or several boxes, to identify their contents?

CLOCKS

69

A schoolteacher uses a five-hour hourglass to keep track of class time. One day, he sets the hourglass at 9 A.M. and while he is teaching his class, a student inadvertently inverts the hourglass. Another student, who notices this, sets the hourglass to its initial position at 11:30 A.M. In this way, the class ends at 3 P.M. At what time did the first student invert the hourglass?

70

A clock gains half a minute every day. Another clock doesn't work. Which one will show the correct time more often?

71

What time is it when a clock strikes 13 times?

72

In a conventional clock, how many times does the minute hand pass the hour hand between noon and midnight?

73

If a clock takes two seconds to strike 2, how long will it take to strike 3?

74

When I gave Albert a ride home, I noticed that the clock in his living room took 7 seconds to strike 8. I immediately asked him, "How long do I have to wait to hear it strike 12?"

75

A clock takes five seconds when striking 6. How long will it take when striking 12?

CALENDAR

76

A Roman was born the first day of the 30th year before Christ and died the first day of the 30th year after Christ. How many years did he live?

77

On March 15, a friend was telling me, "Every day I have a cup of coffee. I drank 31 cups in January, 28 in February and 15 in March. So far, I drank 74 cups of coffee. Do you know how many cups of coffee I would have drunk thus far if it had been a leap year?"

78

If yesterday had been Wednesday's tomorrow and tomorrow is Sunday's yesterday, what day would today be?

79

Mrs. Smith left on a trip the day after the day before yesterday and she will be back the eve of the day after tomorrow. How many days is she away?

80

A man was telling me on a particular occasion, "The day before yesterday I was 35 years old and next year I will turn 38." How can this be?

81

A famous composer blew out 18 candles on his birthday cake and then died less than 9 months later. He was 76 at the time of his death and had composed *The Barber of Seville*. How could this happen?

WORDS

82

Find a commonly used word that ends in T, contains the letters VEN, and starts with IN.

83

If you can speak properly, you will be able to answer the following question. Which is correct, "The yolk of an egg is white" or "The yolk of an egg are white"?

84

What is the opposite of "I AM NOT LEAVING"?

85

What 11-letter word is pronounced incorrectly by more than 99% of Ivy League graduates?

86

What 7-letter word becomes longer when the third letter is removed?

87

Five times four twenty, plus two, equals twenty-three. Is this true?

88

Paris starts with a "p" and ends with an "e." Is this true?

89

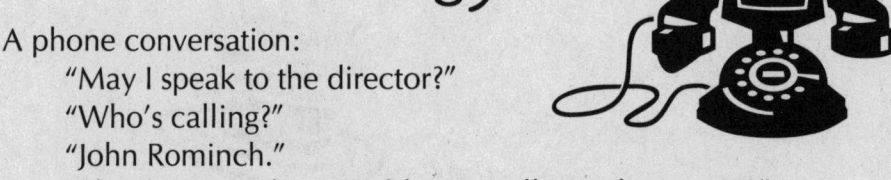

A phone conversation:
  "May I speak to the director?"
  "Who's calling?"
  "John Rominch."
  "I beg your pardon. Could you spell your last name?"
  "R as in Rome, O as in Oslo, M as in Madrid, I as in
      Innsbruck..."

"I as in what?"
"Innsbruck."
"Thanks. Please go ahead."
"N as in Nome..."
This does not make sense. Why?

90

What can you always find in the middle of a taxicab?

91

Is the sentence "This statement is false" true or false?

92

What occurs once in June and twice in August, but never occurs in October?

93

"I must admit that I was not serious when I was telling you that I was not kidding about rethinking my decision of not changing my mind," my friend was telling me. So, is he really going to change his mind or not?

94

A criminal is sentenced to death. Before his execution, he is allowed to make a statement. If his statement is false, he will be hanged, and if his statement is true, he will be drowned. What should he say to confuse the jury and thus save his life?

COUNTING RELATIVES

95

A woman has five children and half of them are male. Is this possible?

96

A friend was telling me, "I have eight sons and each has one sister." In total, how many children does my friend have?

97

Ann's brother has one more brother than sisters. How many more brothers than sisters does Ann have?

98

"I have as many brothers as sisters, but my brothers have twice the number of sisters as brothers. How many of us are there?

FAMILY TIES

99

A doctor has a brother who is an attorney in Alabama, but the attorney in Alabama does not have a brother who is a doctor. How can this be?

100

John wonders, "If Raymond's son is my son's father, how am I related to Raymond?"

101

If your uncle's sister is related to you, but is not your aunt, what is the relation?

102

A group of paleontologists found a prehistoric cave and one of them is congratulated by a younger son, who writes a telegram to his dad explaining the discovery. Who discovered the cave?

103

The other day, I heard the following conversation:
"Charles is related to you the same way I am to your son."
"And you are related to me in the same way Charles is to you."
How are Charles and the second man related?

104

Can someone marry his brother's wife's
mother-in-law?

105

Ann is looking at the portrait of a gentleman. "He is not my father, but his mother was my mother's mother-in-law," she says. Who is this gentleman?

106

Do you know if the Catholic Church allows a man to marry his widow's sister?

107

A friend of mine was looking at a photo when she said, "Brothers and sisters? I have one. And this man's father is my father's son." Who was in the photo?

108

A friend of mine was looking at a photo when he said,"Brothers and sisters? I have none. But this man's son is my father's son." Who was in the photo?

109

Two women are talking on the street. When they see two men coming, they say, "There are our fathers, our mother's husbands, our children's fathers, and our own husbands." How can you explain this?

QUICK LOGIC

110

What was the biggest ocean in the world before Balboa discovered the Pacific Ocean?

111

How many cookies could you eat on an empty stomach?

112

Three mature and hefty women were walking in San Francisco under one regular-size umbrella. Why didn't they get wet?

113

What can a pitcher be filled with so it is lighter than when it is full of air?

114

A dog is tied to a 15-foot long leash. How can the dog reach a bone that is 20 feet away?

115

I went into a store and found out that it cost $3 for 400, which meant that each part cost $1. What did I want to buy?

116

Last week, my uncle Peter was able to turn his bedroom light off and get into bed before the room was dark. The light switch and the bed are ten feet apart. How did he accomplish this?

117

How can you make 30 cents with only two coins if one of the coins is not a nickel?

118

The only barber in my town likes foreigners to go into his shop. Last week, he was telling me, "The truth is that I'd rather give two foreigners haircuts than to give a haircut to one person in town." What was the logic behind this?

119

My brother Mark says he is able to place a bottle in the middle of a room and by crawling on the floor, he can slide into it. How can this be?

120

Last Friday I flew to San Diego. It was a scary flight. About an hour after getting onto the plane, I saw a very thick fog and then the engines stopped due to lack of fuel. Why didn't we die?

121

While eating out, my brother-in-law Paul found a fly in his coffee. After taking the cup away, the waiter came back with a different cup of coffee. My brother-in-law got upset and returned it, saying that the coffee in the second cup was the same as in the first one. How did he know?

122

You find shelter in a mountain lodge on a windy night. When you go in, you only find a match, a candle, a sheet of newspaper, and a torch. You need to light the fireplace. What would you light first?

123

A mother has six children and five potatoes. How can she feed each an equal amount of pototoes? (Do not use fractions.)

124

The giraffe and its offspring are walking in a field. The little giraffe tells a friend, "I am the daughter of this giraffe, although this giraffe is not my mother." How can you explain this?

125

A farmer has twenty sheep, ten pigs, and ten cows. If we call the pigs cows, how many cows will he have?

126

Where must a referee be to blow the whistle?

127

In the event of an emergency, can a Muslim baptize a Catholic?

128

It occurs once in a minute, twice in a week, and once in a year. What is it?

129

One night, when my uncle Emil was reading a book in the living room, his wife turned off the light and the living room became completely dark. However, my uncle continued reading. How is this possible?

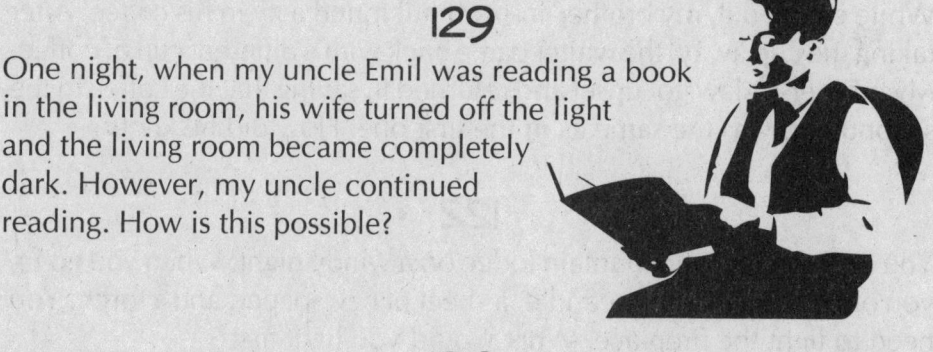

130

A man says, "I am going to drink water because I don't have water. If I had it, I would drink wine." What does he do for a living?

131

Imagine you are a taxi driver and you are driving a 1978 yellow cab. Your passengers are an older couple, and they want to travel 6 miles. You are driving at 40 miles per hour with the tank one-third full, when, 2 miles into the trip, the tank is down to one-quarter full. Ten minutes later, the trip is over. What is the name and age of the cab driver?

132

A railway line has a double track, except in a tunnel where there was no room for a double track. A train goes into the tunnel in one direction, and another one enters in the opposite direction. Both trains are traveling fast. However, they do not crash. Why?

133

My son was telling me yesterday, "Four days ago, my school's soccer team won a game 4 to 1, although none of the boys on my school's team scored any goals. Also, the other team didn't score against itself accidently." How can this be?

134

Last Thursday, my aunt Martha forgot her driver's license at home. She was traveling down a one way street in the wrong direction and did not stop at an intersection to let pedestrians go. A policeman was watching her, but did not give her a ticket. Why?

135

Three friends went out for drinks. The waiter brought them a check for $30, so each one of them paid $10. When the waiter took the cash, he realized he had made a mistake, and the check was for $25 instead. When he gave their change back, each friend got a dollar and they left the remaining two dollars as a tip. Therefore, each customer paid $9; multiplied by 3 this equals $27; plus $2 for the tip equal $29. Where is the remaining dollar?

136

A 16-year-old boy was driving a moped down a one-way street in the wrong direction. A policeman stopped him and gave him a ticket. The policeman paid the ticket himself. Can you find a logical explanation for this?

137

The butcher, his daughter, the fisherman, and his wife won the lottery and divided the prize into three. How can this be?

138

My friend Albert the butcher wears a size 13 shoe, is six feet tall, and wears a 42-long suit. What does he weigh?

139

There are five apples in one basket and five people in a room. How can you distribute the apples so that each person receives one and there is one apple left in the basket?

140

A man is doing his work. He knows that if his suit tears, he will die. Can you guess his job?

141

We have just invented two words: to sint and to sant. You cannot sint or sant in the street or in the office. You can do both things in the bathroom, the swimming pool, and the beach, but in the swimming pool and the beach you cannot sint completely. You cannot sint without clothes on and you need little or no clothing to sant. Can you guess what the words mean?

142

My cousin Henry can guess the score of a soccer game before the game begins. How can that be?

143

Before my husband left on a trip, he left me $150 in cash and a $500 check. However, when I went to a bank to cash the check, I found out that the account only had $450. How could I cash the check?

144

A bus stops three times during the ride. The ticket costs 12 cents to the first stop, 21 to the second stop, and 25 to the third stop. A man gets on at the start of the route and gives the driver 25 cents. Without talking to the passenger, the driver gives him a ticket to the last stop. How did the driver know?

145

You've probably heard the expression "two's company and three's a crowd." But what's the simplest way to describe four and five?

146

Mary, riding her white horse, decies to go into the forest. How far can she go?

147

What animal eats with its tail?

148

How can you light a match under water?

149

What three shapes can a saber have for it to fit in a sheath?

150

"This parrot can repeat anything it hears," the owner of the pet shop told Janice last week. So my sister bought it. Yesterday she went to return it, claiming that the parrot had not even said one word. However, the pet shop owner had not lied to her. Can you explain this?

151

A man and his son were in a car accident. The boy had a fracture and injuries to one leg and was taken to a nearby hospital in an ambulance. When he was in the operating room, the surgeon said, "I cannot operate on him! He is my son!" Explain this.

152

Who do black sheep eat less grass than white sheep?

LOGIC

153

My cousin Mary dropped an earring in her coffee, but the earring did not get wet. How could this be?

154

I have a book where the foreword comes after the epilogue, the end is in the first half of the book and the index comes before the introduction. What book is it?

155

How can you explain that one lady works alone as a bartender, yet there is a COUPLE that works behind the counter?

156

My uncle Raphael bought a coin in the flea market for 10 dollars. The coin has the head of Emperor Augustus and is dated 27 B.C. The other side is illegible. It is a fake, however. What proves that it is not a true ancient Roman coin?

157

An Air France plane crashes along the border of Portugal and Spain. Rescue teams from both countries are called to the site of the crash to help the victims. In which country do you think the survivors will be buried?

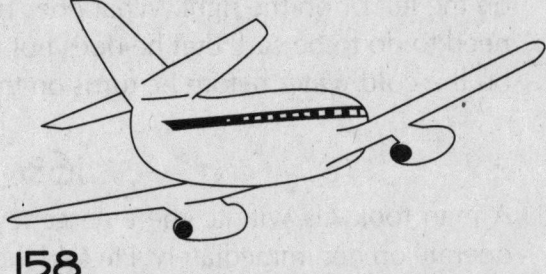

158

The director of a large company asks the security guard working the night shift to call him a cab, because he needs to take a red-eye flight to New York. The guard tells him not to board the plane, because he had just had a dream that the director would have an accident. To be safe, the director decides to wait until the next morning. During the trip, he reads in the paper that the red-eye flight had crashed. When he returns from his trip, he thanks the guard and gives him a bonus. Then he fires him. Why did he fire him?

159

My cousin Edward got soaked while he was walking on the street yesterday. He did not have an umbrella or a hat, so when he got home, his clothes were completely wet. However, not a hair on his head got wet. Why?

160

My sister Sophie lives on the 28th floor of a 32-story building. When my aunt Emily visits her, she takes the elevator to the 25th floor and then walks up the stairs. On her way down, she takes the elevator at the 28th floor all the way down to the ground floor. Why does she do this?

161

A man was sleeping in a hotel. In the middle of the night, he woke up and could not go back to sleep. He picked up the phone and called someone. As soon as he hung up, he fell sound asleep. He did not know the person he was calling. Why did he call that person?

162

When he goes to the bathroom, a man does not know if the hot water faucet is the one on the left or on the right. What does he need to do to be sure that he does not turn on the cold water before he turns on the hot water?

163

A man took his wife to the emergency room. The doctor decided to operate on her immediately. He told the husband that whether the wife died during the operation or survived, he would charge $1,000. The woman did not survive the operation. The husband did not pay anything. Why not?

164

The brothers Albert, Ben, Carl, and Don wear shirt sizes 37, 38, 39, and 40, respectively. Their mother bought one blue shirt for each one of them and embroidered their first initials on the left side. She placed three initials correctly. How many different ways can this happen?

165

If the date of the last Saturday of last month and the first Sunday of this month do not add up to 33, what month are we in?

166

The priest in my hometown announced last year that on a particular day he would walk on water for half an hour. The river was not dry and we could all see that the priest was actually able to walk on water. How did he manage?

167

Two miners go home after work. One of them has his face covered with soot and the other has a clean face. The one with a clean face wipes it with a handkerchief and the one with the dirty face does not do anything. Why?

168

What is there in the middle of a cigar?

169

A remote town has two hair salons. The first one has a dirty mirror, a floor covered with hair, and the hairdresser has an awful haircut. In the second one, the mirror and floor are very clean and the hairdresser has a great haircut. Where would you go and why?

170

A man ordered a glass of white wine and a glass of red wine at a bar. He took the glass of white wine in his right hand and the one with red in his left hand and drank both. He paid and left. The next day, he did the same. When he was leaving, the waiter asked him:

"I did not know that firemen drank that way."

The man smiled and left. How did the waiter know that he was a fireman?

171

Three meteorologists left a meeting in the middle of the night, during a heavy rain.

"The weather will remain like this until the next full moon," said one of them.

"I agree. And 96 hours from now, the sun will not shine," said the second one.

"I agee more with you than with the first forecast," said the third one.

Why was the third meteorologist so sure?

172

A criminal took his wife to the movies to watch a western. During a gunshot scene he killed his wife with a bullet to her heart. When he left the movies with his wife's dead body, nobody tried to stop him. How did he manage this?

173

In the 5th century A.D. a king was taking his daily bath when he received a huge crown that he had ordered made from one of his bars of gold. He knew that the crown and the gold weighed the same, although he suspected that part of the gold had been replaced with lighter materials, such as copper or silver. How did he find out quickly?

174

If I take two apples out of a basket containing six apples, how many apples do I have?

175

How much will a 38° angle measure when observed under a microscope that magnifies ten times?

176

John Peterson was born in Albany in 1938, on a date not divisible by 2, 3, or 5, and in a month that does not contain the letters "e" or "i". When does he become one year older?

177

A passenger traveling by bus between Springfield and Capital City noticed that due to the heavy traffic, it took him 80 minutes to reach his destination at an average speed of 40 mph. On his return trip, he took the bus and it took him 1 hour and 20 minutes at the same average speed and with less traffic. Do you know why?

178

A man traveling in a taxi is talking to the driver. After a while, the driver tells him, "You must excuse me, but I am deaf and cannot hear a word of what you are saying." The passenger stops talking. After he gets out of the cab, the passenger realizes that the driver had lied to him. How?

179

A friend told me the following story: "I was drinking a Coke in a bar when a man wearing a mustache came in and ordered a glass of water. As the waiter came back with his water, he pointed a gun at the customer. The customer got startled, but then calmed down and thanked the waiter." How can you explain what happened?

180

A 30-year-old man married a 25-year-old woman. She died at the age of 50 and her husband was so devastated that he cried for years. Ten years after he stopped crying, he died. However, he lived to be 80.
How many years was he a widower?

181

Two rich men, now bankrupt, came across each other one day. After exchanging greetings and catching up with what had happened in their lives, they compared how much money each had. The first one had 80 dollars and the second one had only 42 dollars. However, two hours later, between both of them they had more than 84 million dollars in cash. None of them had inherited anything, won the lottery, or received payment for a debt or loan. How could this be?

182

I am sitting at a table. Ten flies are on the table.
With one swat, I kill three flies.
How many flies are left on the table?

INTELLIGENCE AND SKILLS

183

How can you drop a matchbook match from five feet above the ground so that it comes to rest with one of its thin edges touching the ground?

184

How can you drop an egg a distance of three feet without breaking it?

185

How can you divide a round pie in eight equal pieces by cutting only three straight lines?

186

Two thin ropes hang from the high ceiling of an empty room, just too far apart from each other to be grabbed with both hands at the same time. How can you tie a knot with both rope ends using only a pair of sharp scissors?

187

A sparrow has fallen into a hole in a rock. The hole measures three inches in diameter and is three feet deep. Due to the depth of the hole, the sparrow cannot be reached by hand. We cannot use sticks or canes, because we could hurt the bird. How can you get the bird out?

188

A homeless man runs out of cigarettes. He looks for cigarette butts since he knows that he can make one new cigarette out of every three butts. He picks up nine butts. If he smokes one cigarette per hour, how many hours can he smoke for?

189

How can you make a hole in a paper napkin and then fit your body through it without tearing the napkin?

190

How can you form four equilateral triangles with six toothpicks of equal length?

191

You go on a picnic with your friends. Each one of them wants a different amount of oil and vinegar in his salad. However, you've already mixed the oil and vinegar in one bottle. How can you please everyone at the picnic?

192

The maximum length of a postal package is 30 inches. How can you mail an iron bar that measures 40 inches in length without bending it?

193

How can you tie a knot with a napkin by holding one end in each hand without letting go of it?

194

If you cut a circle the size of a nickel in a piece of paper, can you pass a silver dollar through it?

195

A six-foot-long rope is tied to a hook fixed to the ceiling of a room. We tie a mug by the handle to the loose end of the rope. If you cut the rope in half, how can you prevent the mug from falling? (There is nothing between the floor and the mug. Nobody is holding on to the mug.)

196

Two thick ropes hang from a high ceiling attached to hooks three feet apart. The ends touch the ground. Without using anything else, and considering that you will die if you fall from one-quarter of the height of the room, how can you cut the largest amount possible of each rope with a knife?

197

You are playing table tennis on the beach when your only ball falls into a hole in the sand that someone else had used for their beach umbrella. The hole is only slightly larger in diameter than the ball. How can you take the ball out without digging?

198

A truck is about to go under a bridge, although its load is two inches higher than the clearance of the bridge. It is a very heavy load, so it cannot be unloaded. How can it pass under the bridge in a quick and simple way?

199

How could you throw a tennis ball so that after traveling a short distance, it stops and returns following the same path? The ball cannot hit or be tied to anything.

200

A brick measuring 5 centimeters high, 20 centimeters long, and 10 centimeters wide falls off a dike causing a leak that must be stopped immediately. How can you stop the leak with a saw and a wooden cylinder measuring 5 centimeters in diameter?

201

With your pants on, can you put your right hand in your left pocket and your left hand in your right pocket?

202

I bet that you alone cannot take off your left shoe using only your right hand. I will not touch you or interfere with your movements. How can I prevent this?

203

How can you pour wine out of a corked bottle that is half full without breaking or damaging the bottle or the cork, and without taking out the cork?

204

You keep some of your diamonds in a jewelry case with a sliding cover. To keep thieves away, you put a scorpion inside the case. One day you need to take some of the diamonds. How can you do it without taking the scorpion out, while protecting your hands from its bites, only taking a few seconds, and leaving the case in the same way you originally had it?

205

I am going to make you a bet: "On this folded piece of paper I have written down the prediction of something that might or might not happen in the next five minutes. Put it in your pocket. On this blank piece of paper, write "YES" if you think that it will happen and "NO" if you think it will not happen. I'll bet you a cup of coffee that you cannot guess right." What have I written on the paper? (It is something that can be proven.)

206

Your rich relative gathers the family together to tell them, "I will leave my inheritance to the one who can collect the exact number of pennies equaling half the number of days that I have left to live." What would you do to inherit the fortune?

207

How can two people step on one page of newspaper so that they can't touch each other without stepping off the newspaper?

208

A friend told me, "I can do something that you are not able to, no matter how hard you try." What could it be?

209

A bottle is standing on a rug (or upside down on a dollar bill). Can you take out the rug or the bill without turning or touching the bottle and without help from anybody else?

210

Set an imaginary finish line somewhere (for example, a point on the wall 10 feet away from you). Find a method of advancing so that even though you always move ahead, you never reach the finish line.

211

Yesterday, someone dared me to jump over a ballpoint pen on the floor. I could not, even though I'm a good jumper. How come I wasn't able to?

INVESTIGATIONS AND TRIALS

212

A plane was hijacked. The hijacker demanded two parachutes and ten million dollars. Once he got both, he jumped off the plane during the night and while in flight. Why did he need two parachutes?

213

One rainy day, my cousin Ernest found a dead body lying next to a strange package. He could not see any footprints in the area. Because of the temperature of the body, Ernest knew that the man had been dead for less than one hour. What was in the package? How did the man get there?

214

A man walking along a rural road was being sought by the police. When he saw a patrol car approaching him, he thought of running toward the forest. Instead, he ran 20 yards toward the approaching car. Why?

215

Stella was telling my cousin Ernest that her husband once fell asleep in the opera and started dreaming of being on a plane that was hijacked. The hijacker demanded to fly to an African country. People complained, screamed, and fainted. The hijacker was pointing a gun to Stella's husband's head. At this point, the husband started to move and make noise. Stella tapped her husband on the shoulder and he got so startled that he fell on the floor and died from the impact. Ernest immediately said, "This story is impossible." How did he know?

216

My cousin Ernest solved this case. A man was hanged, his feet half a meter above the ground, in the middle of a very hot room, hanging by

a rope tied to a hook from the ceiling. The room was completely empty and had some moisture on the floor. On the other side of the door there was a ladder, which must have been used by the victim. However, the investigation proved that the victim had no place to lean the ladder against to reach the rope. That is how Ernest realized that this was not a murder, but a suicide. How could it have happened?

217

Last winter, my cousin Ernest went on a ski vacation. At the airport, he read in the papers that a famous couple had been skiing and the wife had died in an accident. Her well-known husband was the only eyewitness. After talking to a travel agent, my cousin was able to deduce that it had not been an accident. What did he find out from the travel agent?

218

A medieval count organized a court trial in which he gave the defendant a chance to save his life if he could pick a white marble out of a bag containing, in the count's words, one white marble and one black marble. The accused knew that this was a trick, because he had seen the count place two black marbles in the bag. However, he went ahead and took out a marble. What did he do to save his life?

219

During the war, my cousin Ernest was captured and put into a prison cell. It was in the basement, with a dirt floor, armored walls, and a water tank 10 feet from the ground. There was no furniture and no object to reach the water tank with. How did Ernest manage to drink?

220

My cousin Ernest, amateur private investigator, was able to figure out the weapon used in a suicide case. The man had been stabbed, but the weapon was nowhere in the room. The room was locked from the inside. The deceased had the only key. During the investigation, they found out that the weapon had been thicker than typical knives. What was the weapon? Where was it?

221

When Ernest went to visit his friend Albert, he found him dead on his desk with a bullet through the head. He saw a cassette player and decided to listen to the tape. He hit "play" and heard, "This is Albert. I just got a call saying that someone is on his way here to kill me and that he will be here in less than three minutes. I hear steps. Someone is opening the door." At that point, my cousin knew that it was not Albert's voice on the tape, but the killer's. How did he know that?

222

A man has been killed in a room locked from the inside with a vertical deadbolt. The killer was able to lock it from the outside. How did he do this?

223

A businessman was working in his home office when he realized he had left a five-dollar bill in the book he had been reading. He called his butler to bring him the book from the library. When he got the book, the bill was no longer there. He then questioned the maid and the butler. The maid remembered seeing the bill between pages 99 and 100 in a book to the left of a business book. The butler did not recall seeing the bill, but was sure the book was to the right of the business book, because to the left of it there was a statistics book.

Who is lying?

224

On the 29th of last month, there was a double murder on the express train from Paris to Berlin. The engineer and the conductor were killed at the same time, even though they were at opposite ends of the train. This was confirmed by a police detective, who was at the exact center of the train and heard both gunshots at the same time.

When my cousin was told this story, he realized that both victims did not die at the same time.

How did he figure it out?

225

Two people were accused of murder. In a court trial, one had been acquitted and the other had been found guilty. When the judge had to sentence the guilty man, he said, "This is the strangest case that I have ever presided over. Even though you have been found guilty, the law obliges me to set you free." Can you explain this?

226

My cousin Ernest was once kidnapped. He knew they would either take him to New York City or to Sydney, Australia. When they took his blindfold off, he could see he had been locked in a room without windows. There was only a table, a bed, a chair, and a sink. However, Ernest was able to figure out which city he was in. How did he do it?

227

These are the clues to a robbery and murder in a ground floor office:

A. The killer had to be one of these three people: the muscled engineer, the obese director, or the perky secretary.

B. The stolen goods were taken out from the open window. There were light footprints under it in the snow.

C. The footprints matched the director's shoes, which were found next to the crime weapon.

D. Only one bullet was found, although there were two wounds to the body, one to the chest and the other to the right hand.

Who was the killer? Why were there two wounds?

RIDDLES

228

I climbed up a cherry tree, where I found cherries. I did not pick cherries, nor did I leave cherries. How can you explain this?

229

What animal walks on all fours in the morning, on two legs at noon, and on three legs at dusk?

230

What is so fragile that when you say its name you break it?

231

Among my siblings I am the thinnest. I am in Paris, but I am not in France. Who am I?

232

I can only live when there is light, although I die if the light shines on me. What am I?

ELEMENTS IN MOVEMENT

233

A ship is anchored offshore. In order for the crew to reach the rafts, they must descend a 22-step ladder. Each step is 10 inches high. The tide rises at a ratio of 5 inches per hour. How many steps will the tide have covered after 10 hours?

234

A 100-meter-long train moving 100 meters per minute must pass through a tunnel of 100 meters in length. How long will it take?

235

A train headed for Barcelona leaves Madrid at midnight, at a constant speed of 60 kilometers per hour. Another train leaves Barcelona at the same time, heading for Madrid at a constant speed of 40 kilometers per hour. The distance between both cities is 600 kilometers. The train that left from Madrid stops for half an hour when both trains cross. Which train was closer to Madrid when they crossed?

236

My uncle Lou takes the subway to the movies or the theater every evening. He always takes the first subway that stops at the station close to his home, no matter which direction it is heading. If the subway is heading north, he will go to the theater. If it is heading south, he will go to the movies. Both trains run every 10 minutes. However, nine time out of every ten, my uncle ends up at the movies. How can you explain this?

237

A cyclist takes 2 minutes and 13 seconds for every full lap of a circuit. Answer in 10 seconds:
How long will he take to do 60 laps?

238

My bird can fly faster than any supersonic plane. How can this be?

239

Albert, who was just back from his trip around the world in a sailboat, asked me, "What part of my boat has traveled the longest distance?" Do you know the answer to that?

240

If we tie a light oxygen tank to a bird so that it can breathe on the moon, would the bird fly faster, slower or the same speed as it does on earth? (Remember that there is less gravity on the moon.)

241

What can a train passenger do to be in a tunnel the least time possible while the train is going through a 100-meter long tunnel?

242

Two trains travel on parallel tracks in opposite directions, at 70 and 50 miles per hour. When the trains are 60 miles apart, a bird flying at 80 miles per hour leaves the first train and flies off to the second. It keeps on flying back and forth until both trains cross. How many miles does the bird fly?

243

We drag a large stone over three logs measuring 50 inches in circumference each. What distance does the stone cover each time the logs make one rotation?

244

Two trains are moving on the same track in opposite directions. One goes 80 meters per minute and the other 120 meters per minute. After 12 hours, they are 1700 meters apart. How far apart will they be one minute before they collide?

245

A snail is climbing up a one-meter-high wall. It advances three centimeters per minute and then stops for one minute to rest, during which it slides back down two centimeters. How long will the snail take to reach the top of the wall?

246

A young man gets on the end car of a train. Just as the train passes by Cat City, he leaves his suitcases and walks at a steady pace to find a seat. After five minutes, he reaches the front car. Not finding a seat, he returns at the same pace to where his luggage is. At that point, the train passes by Dog City, which is five miles from Cat City. How fast is the train going?

247

A journey by ship between New York and London takes seven days. Ships leave from both ports at the same time every day. During the trip, how many other ships will a ship come across?

248

A regular LP record measures 30 centimeters in diameter. The outer blank (non-recorded) area is 5 millimeters in width. The non-playable center area measures 10 centimeters in diameter. The grooves are ¼ millimeter apart. What is the distance traveled by the needle during the time that the record is playing?

249

A man is walking at night at a steady pace. As he passes by a street lamp, he notices that his shadow becomes longer. Does the top of the shadow move faster, slower, or the same when the shadow is longer as when it is shorter?

250

A kid who is in the back seat of a car is holding the string of a helium balloon. The balloon is floating without touching the roof of the car, and the windows are closed. When the car accelerates, where does the balloon go? And when the car turns, where does it go?

251

A train goes from north to south, although at all times there are certain areas of the train that are moving in a south-to-north direction. What are these areas?

252

A railway track measures 5 kilometers in length and its ties are one meter apart. A child ties a can to a dog's tail. As the dog starts running along the tracks, it increases its speed by one meter per second every time it hears the noise of the can hitting a tie. If the dog starts to run at a speed of 1 meter/second and the can hits all of the railway ties, what is the dog's speed at the end of the track?

253

Two athletes ran in a 100-meter race. When the runner with the number "1" on his jersey reached the finish line, the runner with number "2 had only run 95 meters. In a second race, the number "1" runner had to start 5 meters behind the start line. If both ran at the same speed as in the first race, who won this time?

254

A driver always leaves the office at the same time, gets to the director's house at the same time, picks him up, and takes him to the office. One morning, the director decides to leave one hour earlier and he starts walking to the office along his usual route. When he sees the car, he gets in and continues his trip. He reaches the office 20 minutes earlier than usual. How long was he walking for?

255

In a river without a current, a ship leaves from a certain point, goes three miles up the river, turns around and goes back to the point of departure in 20 minutes. If the river has a current of two miles per hour and the ship did the same trip at the same speed (with respect to the water), would the trip last more or less than 20 minutes?

256

A mountaineer starts rapidly climbing up a mountain trail at 6 A.M. He makes frequent and irregular stops to rest or eat. He reaches the summit at 6 P.M. At 6 A.M. the next day, he starts his way back following the same route, stopping only once to eat. He reaches the starting point at 6 P.M. Is there a point on the way where he passes at exactly the same time on both days?

OUTDOORS

257

Which is warmer, a two-inch-thick blanket or two blankets one-inch-thick each?

258

Three ice cubes are melting in a glass of water. Once they have completely melted, has the water level of the glass changed?

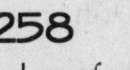

259

A super-accurate bomb, one that always hits the bull's-eye and destroys it, hits an indestructible fort. What will happen?

260

A man gets up 180 times every night and sleeps for at least 7 hours at a stretch. Where does he live?

261

I had just made myself a cup of coffee when I realized I had to run upstairs for a moment. I did not want the coffee to get cold, and I had to add milk at room temperature. Should I add the milk before I go up or after I get back?

262

A raft loaded with rocks is floating in a swimming pool. We mark the level of water in the swimming pool and on the raft. If we drop the rocks into the pool, what will happen to the water level in the pool and to the flotation line of the raft? Will they go up or down?

263

A boat is floating in a pool. We mark the flotation line. If we drop rocks into the pool and make the water level rise five inches, will the water rise more or less than five inches compared to the mark we made on the boat?

264

Two ivy branches sprout out of a tree trunk from the same point at ground level. One wraps around four times to the right, the other wraps around five times to the left, and their ends meet. Without counting the ends, how many times do both branches of ivy intersect?

265

An African trader is visiting different tribes in a raft loaded with sacks of salt, which he trades according to their weight in gold. When he is about to trade them, he realizes that the scale is broken. How can he trade the same weight of salt for gold?

A LITTLE BIT OF EVERYTHING

266

We have a bottle of wine approximately three-fourths full. We want to leave an amount of wine in the bottle equal to exactly half of the total capacity of the bottle. How can we do it without using anything to help us?

267

We have three glass pitchers. One is a three-quart pitcher and is empty. The twelve-quart one is also empty. The third one is clear in color and irregular in shape. It contains acid. It has two marks, a two-quart mark and a five-quart mark. The level of acid is a little less than five quarts.

We want to take out exactly three quarts of acid, but when we try it, the three-quart pitcher breaks. What can we do to take out the desired amount by pouring it into the twelve-quart pitcher, which is the only one left?

268

A man was used to walking at a regular pace. He never wore a watch, although he had a very accurate clock at home. One day, he forgot to wind it and the clock stopped. He went to a friend's house two miles from his home to ask the time. He spent the afternoon with him and when he came back home, he set the clock to the exact time. How did he know the exact time?

269

We have two similar coins and we make one spin on the edge of the other. How many times does the spinning coin turn on itself each time it takes an entire lap around the stationary one?

270

Mr. Brown, Mr. White, and Mr. Red are in a meeting. The three are wearing ties that are the three colors of their last names, although no man's tie matches his name. Mr. Brown asks the man with the white tie if he likes red, but cannot hear the answer. What is the color of each man's tie?

271

We mark three random points on a sphere. How likely are the three points to be in the same hemisphere?

272

Can you draw a square with two straight lines?

LAUGHS

273

My cousin Henry can predict the future when he pets his black poodle. Is that possible?

274

An older woman and her young daughter, a young man, and an older man are traveling in the same compartment of a train. When the train passes through a tunnel, they hear a kiss and a slap. As the lights come back on, they can see the older man with a black eye. This is what each of the passengers thought:

The older woman: "He deserved it. I am glad my daughter can defend herself."

The daughter: "I cannot believe he preferred to kiss my mother or that young man over kissing me."

The older man: "What is going on here? I didn't do anything! Maybe the young man tried to kiss the girl, and she mistakenly slapped me."

The young man: "I know what really happened."

Do you know what happened?

275

An electric train runs at 60 mph heading south toward a wind blowing at 30 mph. What is the direction of the smoke from the train?

276

If Albert's peacock jumps over the fence onto Edward's property and lays an egg there, whose egg is it?

277

What can you have in an empty pocket? (Apart from air, of course.)

278

What did the twelve apostles make?

279

My cousin Herbert told me yesterday, "I can easily bite my eye." How can this be?

280

It sings and has ten feet. What is it?

281

Mary married John two years ago. She did not bring any money into the marriage and did not work during these two years, but she made her husband a millionaire. How did she do it?

282

My cousin Herbert told me this morning, "I can easily bite my good eye." How can he do this?

283

What can elephants make that no other animal can?

284

Last Thursday I walked back home from work (2 miles), and noticed a strange man following me the entire way. Once I got home, the man was still there walking around my building (a 100-by-100-yard-square building). Later on, I saw he had fallen asleep next to the street lamp at the entrance of my building. During which lap did he fall asleep?

285

How can you get into your home if there is a dangerous dog inside that doesn't know you and belongs to your wife's friend?

286

A turtle, a gopher, and a hare are walking one behind the other in a straight line.
"I am first," said the turtle.
"I am second," said the gopher.
"I am first", said the hare.
How can you explain these statements?

287

What activity can only be done at night?

288

My cousin Robert was pushed into a well measuring six feet in diameter and 10 feet deep, with smooth walls and its bottom covered with water. How did he emerge from the well?

289

Every day, a cyclist crosses the border between Spain and France carrying a bag. No matter how much customs officials investigate him, they do not know what he is smuggling. Do you?

ANSWERS

1. Only once, because the second time you will be subtracting from 24 instead of 30.

2. The number 8. (It is made up of two zeroes, one on top of the other.)

3. By using Roman numerals. The upper half of XII is VII.

4. 1 and 9.

5. Any number and 1.

6. 2 and 2.

7. It is easy to eliminate possibilities. For example, it has to be an even number; none of the digits can be zero (or else the product would be zero); and the product of the digits must be less than or equal to 48 (otherwise two times the product would have three digits). If you think of the remaining possibilities, you will find the answer, $36 = 2 \times 3 \times 6$.

8. 1, 2, and 3, because $1 \times 2 \times 3 = 1 + 2 + 3 = 6$.

9. $25 = 5^2$ and $36 = 6^2$.

10. $9^{9^9} = 9^{387420489}$, which is a number with more than 369 million digits.

11. The father is 41 and the son is 14.

12. 10 cents.

13. $1.10 for the outlet and $0.10 for the light bulb.

14. $3 \times 75 = 225$ qualities distributed among 100 persons, so at least 25% of them have all three.

15. The number of passing grades is a whole number less than 32, and 5% of it is also a whole number. It can only be 20. If 20 is the number of passing grades, the number of students from New York that took the test is one.

16. If half of the 83% tip the usher 10 cents and the other half doesn't, it is the same as if all 83% had tipped him 5 cents, which is the same amount as what the remaining 17% tipped. The usher received 4,800 cents, or more simply, 48 dollars.

17. Turn the page upside-down. It will read 108 = 6 x 18.

18. He will need twenty "9's," one for the numbers 9, 19, 29, 39, 49, 59, 69, 79, 89, 90, 91, 92, 93, 94, 95, 96, 97, and 98, and two for 99.

19. At each stop, passengers can buy a ticket for any of the 24 remaining stops. Therefore, the number of tickets will be 25 x 24 = 600.

20. Let's imagine that the inhabitants are as different as possible (one will be bald, another will have only one hair, another two, another three, and so on, until we get to someone having 100,000 hairs). Inhabitant number 100,002 will have the same number of hairs as someone among the first 100,001 inhabitants. The total population is more than 200,000 people, which means that there will be more than 100,000 inhabitants with the same number of hairs as other people in town.

21. Three: one red, one blue and one brown.

22. There are 6 chestnut trees per side, making a total of 12.

23. Two birds and one olive tree.

24. There is only one winner, so the remaining 110 players were defeated in 110 matches. Therefore, they used 110 balls.

25. Twelve muffins. When John ate half the remaining muffins plus three more to leave none, he must have eaten six muffins. So Peter ate half the muffins and left six, meaning that there were 12 to start.

26. The shepherd that is talking had 5 sheep and the other one had 7.

27. Three cages and four canaries.

28. Each sardine costs 1 dollar. Therefore, 7½ sardines would cost 7½ dollars.

29. Since $\frac{1}{2}$ brick weighs 3 pounds, $1\frac{1}{2}$ bricks weigh 9 pounds.

30. Since 18 sardines is the same as $1\frac{1}{2}$ dozen, they cost $9\frac{1}{2}$ dollars.

31. Since 1 man eats 1 pie in $1\frac{1}{2}$ minutes, 1 man eats 20 pies in 30 minutes, which means 3 men eat 60 pies in 30 minutes.

32. 11 times (one fewer than the number of times he went in).

33. Three ducks.

34. The person who won three games must have also lost six games, since his opponent won $3. In total, they played 9 games.

35. We measure the inside diameter and the height of the liquid, obtaining the volume of the liquid. Then, we turn the bottle upside-down and measure the volume of the empty part. If we add both, we obtain the total capacity of the bottle and can calculate the percentage of the liquid. An easier way is to measure only both heights, because both have the same size base.

36. $0.0125

37. By leaving a task half done (for example, peeling potatoes) so that the next soldier can finish it, they can do all the tasks in 1 hour and 30 minutes.

38. 29 days. One spider would have covered half of the space on the 29th day, and on the 30th day would repeat what had been done, covering the space completely. Two spiders would each have covered half of the space in 29 days, therefore covering the entire area.

39. At 8 P.M. Each hour the volume triples, so it is one-third full one hour before it is full.

40. If the length of the rope + 2 yards = 3 times the length of the rope, then the rope is 1 yard long.

41. If the length is 6 yards + half the length, then half the length is 6 yards. Therefore, it is 12 yards long.

42. No mud at all, because a hole can only contain air.

43. There are only three people, a daughter, her mother, and her grandmother. The mother received 25 books from the grandmother and then gave 8 to her daughter.

44. Dolores is taller than Emily, who is taller than Ann.

45. Joan is 6 years older than Rose.

46. Emily speaks in a softer voice than Dolores (Emily < Ann < Dolores).

47. Peter is sitting between Philip (on his right) and James (on his left).

48. A pound of $10 gold coins has twice the amount of gold than half a pound of $20 coins. Therefore, it is worth more.

49. The store lost $40 given as change plus the value of the umbrella, $10. The transaction was only between the sales person and the customer. The bank teller did not take part in the transaction.

50. The pitcher with water contains exactly the same amount of wine as water in the pitcher of wine. Both pitchers have the same volume of liquid before and after mixing water and wine, so mixing them makes no difference.

51. He made each candidate ride another candidate's horse. Each one would, of course, try to come in first, because in that way the owner of the horse that a particular candidate was riding would lose the race.

52. The weight of the fish bowl increases by the same amount as the weight of the liquid displaced by the fish.

53. If it is a traditional scale with two dishes, you can place the apples in one dish and dirt in the other until they balance. Then, replace the apples with weights and you will know the weight of the apples. If it is a spring scale, you weigh the apples first, then write down the mark on the scale and replace the apples with weights until you reach the previous mark. The weights will show the real weight of the apples.

54. The reaction of the air that the little bird is pushing down in order to fly will partially affect both the dish of the scale and the floor of

the room. The scale will show one pound minus some portion of the 5 ounces that the bird weighs.

If the cage were sealed, the air would affect only the dish of the scale and the scale would continue to read one pound.

55. One weighing. Take one ball from the first sack, two from the second, three from the third, and so on until you reach the last sack, from which you take ten balls. Since $1 + 2 + 3 + ... + 9 + 10 = 55$, if all of the balls weighed 10 ounces each, the total weight would be 550 ounces. In this case the weight will be $550 - N$, where N is the number of the sack containing nine-ounce balls.

56. We identify each sack by the number of balls taken from it. We must find a way to obtain different results from all possible sums of the digits that identify the sacks. The easiest way would be powers of 2: 1, 2, 4, 8, 16, ... (2^0, 2^1, 2^2, 2^3, 2^4, ...). Therefore, we will take one ball from one sack, two from another, four from another. etc.

The resulting weight will be $1023 - N$, where N can only be obtained by adding certain sack numbers. If N is 27 ounces, the sacks containing 9-ounce balls will be those from which we took 1, 2, 8, and 16 balls, because, using just the powers of 2, 27 can only be obtained by adding $1 + 2 + 8 + 16$.

Let's call "1" the sack from which we took 1 ball, "2" the one from which we took 2 balls, "3" the one from which we took 4 balls, etc. The number 27, in binary, is 11011. The position of the 1's in this binary sequence reveals the solution. The 1's are in first, second, fourth, and fifth position, which means that the sacks containing the 9-ounce balls are 1, 2, 4, and 5.

57. The best solution is to open four links from one of the pieces and use them to join the remaining five parts in one chain. The total cost will be $4 \times 60 = 240$ cents, or $2.40.

58. By cutting the third link, we obtain three pieces of one, two, and four links each. The first day, she pays with the one-link part. The second day, she pays with the two-link part and gets the one-link part back as change. The third day, she pays with the loose link. The fourth day, she pays with the four-link part and receives back the three links, and so on.

59. The minimum number of parts that could have been left is 3 (the link that is cut and the two disconnected parts of the chain). The maximum number will be 6, as shown in the figure below.

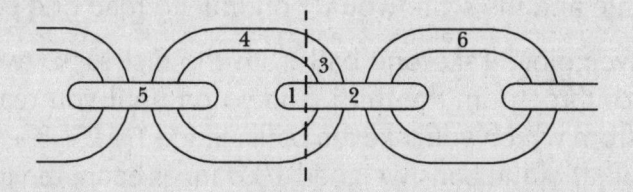

60. Two glasses. Pick up the second glass, pour its contents into the ninth glass, and put it back. Then pick up the fourth glass, pour its contents into the seventh glass, and put it back. Note that the seventh and ninth glasses are not moved.

61. 100% probability, because if four marbles are in their corresponding cups, the fifth one must be in its corresponding cup, too.

62. Three. The first two can be of different colors, white and black, but the third sock will be one of these two colors, and thus complete one pair.

63. Four. There are three different colors, so the first three socks may not match, but the fourth one will match one of the previous three socks.

64. 13. The first 12 gloves can be six white left gloves and six black left gloves. Therefore, the 13th glove will make a pair with one of the previous 12 gloves. No matter what the first 12 gloves are, if no two have made a pair yet, the 13th will.

65. 6. The worst case is to take two white, two black, and the red marble. The sixth marble has to be either white or black.

66. Put five marbles in one cup, four in another and one in another. Put the cup with one marble inside the one containing four. There are other solutions, all based on the same trick. Another solution, for example, involves putting three marbles in one cup, three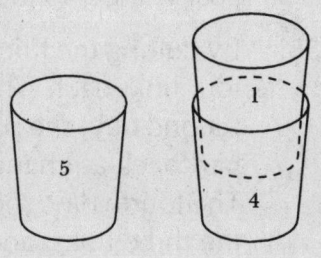

marbles in the second cup, and four marbles in the third cup, and then putting the second cup inside the third one. This leaves three marbles in the first cup, three marbles in the second cup, and seven marbles in the third cup.

67. Put one marble in one box, three in another box and five in a third one. Then place the three boxes inside the fourth box.

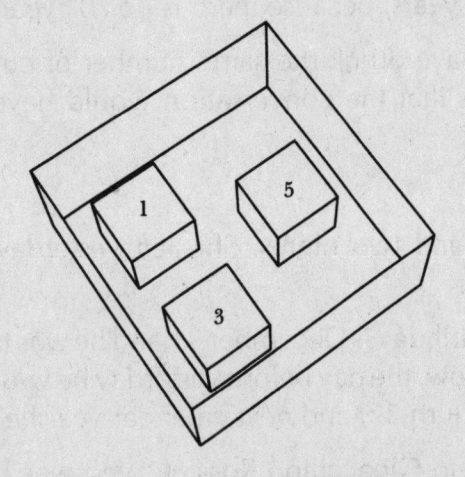

68. Take one marble from the box marked BW. If it is white, the other marble must also be white. This means that the box marked BB must have black and white marbles and the box marked WW must have only black marbles. You can apply the same principle if the first marble you take is black.

69. After being inverted twice, the hourglass continued working in its initial position. Therefore, the extra hour that it measured was a consequence of these two inversions, half an hour each time. If it was inverted for the second time at 11:30, the firt time had to be a half-hour earlier, at 11:00.

70. The clock that doesn't work will show the precise time twice a day, but the fast one will take 2 x 60 x 12 = 1440 days to show the precise time. Therefore, the broken clock shows the correct time more often.

71. Time to have the clock fixed.

72. Ten times (you can verify it yourself).

73. Four seconds (it takes two seconds between 2 consecutive strikes).

74. Four hours, the time between 8 and 12.

75. There is 1 second between 2 strikes. Therefore, it will take 11 seconds for the clock to strike 12 times.

76. He lived 59 years, because there is no "0" year.

77. He would have drunk the same number of cups of coffee. The difference is that the conversation would have taken place on March 14.

78. Friday.

79. Three days and two nights. She left yesterday and will return tomorrow.

80. The man's birthday is December 31 and he was talking on January 1. He is 36 now, the day before yesterday he was 35, this calendar year he will turn 37, and next calendar year he will turn 38.

81. It happened to Gioacchino Rossini, who was born on February 29, 1792, and who died on November 13, 1868. Remember that 1800 was not a lear year. All years that are divisible by four are leap years, except those that end in "00." They are only leap years if they are divisible by 400.

82. INVENT.

83. Neither. The yolk of an egg is yellow.

84. It is not "I am going in" or "I am not going in." The opposite is "I am leaving."

85. The word "incorrectly."

86. Lounger.

87. It's a matter of language. Consider "four twenty" as $4.20. Then it is true.

88. Yes. "Paris" starts with a "p," and "ends" starts with an "e."

89. The phone operator was trying to get the spelling of the man's last

name. Therefore, it makes no sense to ask, "I as in what?" The operator had already understood it was an "I."

90. The letter "i."

91. Let's suppose it is false. By saying "This statement is false," it becomes true and vice versa. Therefore, to be false it has to be true and vice versa. It is a paradox.

92. The letter "u."

93. He will not change his mind.

94. His statement must be "I will be hanged." If they want to hang him, the sentence is true, and therefore, they will not be able to hang him. For the same reason, he cannot be drowned because his statement would be false and they could not drown him if his statement is false. (Based on *Don Quixote,* by Cervantes.)

95. Yes, as long as the other half are male, too. She has five sons.

96. Nine children.

97. Three more brothers than sisters. Ann's brother has one more brother than sister. Ann is one of the sisters, so Ann will have one fewer sister than her brother has and one more brother than her brother has.

98. Seven. The only possible solution is that the person talking is a woman and there are four women and three men.

99. The doctor is a woman.

100. John is Raymond's son.

101. Your mother.

102. The son's mother.

103. The second man is Charles's grandson.

104. No, because it would be his mother.

105. The man is Ann's uncle.

106. If the man left a widow, then he is dead. Therefore, he cannot get married.

107. She was looking at a photo of her nephew.

108. He was looking at a photo of his father.

109. Two widowers have one daughter each and decide to marry each other's daughters. This conversation takes place once they are married and with children. Their wives are the ones talking.

110. The Pacific Ocean. Even though it had not been discovered or named by Balboa, it was still the biggest ocean.

111. One cookie, because after eating one you would no longer have an empty stomach.

112. Because it wasn't raining.

113. Holes.

114. By walking and dragging the rope with it. The puzzle does not say that the leash is tied to something.

115. The number 400 to hang on a house. This number is formed by three digits, at $1 each.

116. It was daytime, so the room was light.

117. With one quarter and one nickel. The puzzle says that one of the coins is not a nickel, and it is true since a quarter is not a nickel.

118. Because he earns double by giving a haircut to two foreigners instead of to only one person in town.

119. He goes to the next room and by crawling toward the bottle, he slides into the room.

120. The plane had not yet taken off.

121. He had already put sugar in his coffee.

122. The match.

123. By serving mashed potatoes.

124. It is a male giraffe, so it is the father and not the mother of the offspring.

125. Ten cows. We can call the pigs cows, but it doesn't make them cows.

126. He must always be behind the whistle.

127. There is no reason to baptize him. If he is Catholic, he is already baptized.

128. The letter "e."

129. My uncle Emil is blind, and he was reading in Braille.

130. He is a farmer. He needs plenty of water, so if he lacks water he has no income and he won't be able to buy or even make wine.

131. At the beginning of the puzzle, it says that you are the cab driver. Therefore, the answer is your name and age.

132. One of the trains went into the tunnel hours after the other.

133. It was a girls' team.

134. My aunt Martha was a pedestrian, too.

135. The customers paid $27, $25 to cover their bill and $2 as a tip for the waiter.

136. The driver of the moped was the policeman's son.

137. The butcher's daughter is the fisherman's wife.

138. Since he's a butcher, he weighs meat.

139. The first four people pick one apple each, and the fifth one takes the basket with the apple in it.

140. Either a deep-sea diver or an astronaut.

141. "To sint" means to take off your clothes, and "to sant" is to go into the water to bathe.

142. Because before the game begins, the score is always 0-0.

143. I deposited $50 in my bank account to have enough funds to cash the check.

144. The passenger gave the driver 25 cents in the form of four nickels and five pennies.

145. Nine.

146. As far as half of the forest, because if she went any further, she would be leaving the forest, instead of going into it.

147. All the animals that have one, because as far as we know, no animal takes it off to eat.

148. You just have to light a match under a container with water.

149. Straight, arced, or spiral.

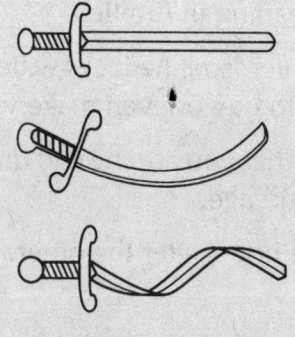

150. The parrot was deaf.

151. The surgeon was the boy's mother.

152. Because there are fewer black sheep than white sheep.

153. She dropped her earring into her coffee beans.

154. The dictionary. The work "foreword" comes before "epilogue," "end" is in the first half of the dictionary, and "index" comes before "introduction."

155. The girl's name is Anne COUPLE.

156. If it were an authentic coin, it could not have "B.C." (This system was created after Jesus died, not before he was born.)

157. Neither country, because they are survivors.

158. What the director actually needed was a real night shift guard that did not sleep at work, even if he could predict the future in his dreams.

159. My cousin Edward is bald. Therefore, his hair cannot get wet.

160. My aunt is really short and the button for the 25th floor is at the highest point she can reach.

161. The neighbor was snoring. That is why he couldn't sleep. When he made the call, the person woke up and stopped making the noise.

162. He must turn on both faucets at the same time.

163. The woman died before the operation.

164. If three of the letters are correct, the fourth one must be too. Therefore, there is only one way.

165. The same month you are reading this.

166. The river was frozen.

167. When he sees his coworker, the miner with the clean face assumes that his face is also dirty and wipes it. The miner with a dirty face sees his coworker with a clean face and assumes that his is also clean.

168. The letter "g."

169. Hairdressers don't cut their own hair. Therefore, the clean hairdresser gave the bad haircut and the dirty hairdresser gave the perfect haircut. Thus, it is better to go to the dirty salon.

170. The customer was in his firefighter uniform.

171. Because in 96 hours it would again be night.

172. It was a drive-in theater. He killed her in the car. On his way out, nobody noticed that the woman was dead in the car.

173. First he immersed the crown in a container of water and measured the level of the water. Then he removed the crown and immersed the gold bar, measuring the water level. If the levels were not the same, the gold had been mixed with another metal.

174. Two apples.

175. It will still be 38°.

176. On his birthday.

177. He took the same time in both cases, because 1 hour and 20 minutes equals 80 minutes.

178. If the cab driver had been deaf, he would not have heard the address the passenger had given him. He only mentioned he was deaf when the passenger didn't stop talking.

179. The waiter scared his customer who had the hiccups. That is why the customer thanked the waiter.

180. If he became a widower when he was 55 and died when he was 80, he was a widower for 25 years.

181. One was standing at the main door of a bank and his friend was standing at the back door. There was 84 million dollars in the safe of the bank. Therefore, "between both of them" they had that amount of money.

182. I killed three flies. They remain. The rest would have flown away immediately.

183. By bending the match and then dropping it.

184. Drop it and catch it before it hits the ground.

185. Cutting it either of these ways.

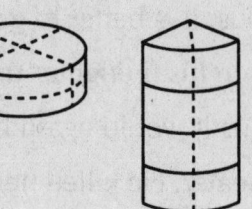

186. Tie the scissors to one of the ropes and make it move like a pendulum. Then take the other end of the rope and grab the scissors as they come toward you. Then tie the knot.

187. By gradually pouring sand into the hole. The bird will keep moving so that it is not buried in the sand, forcing it higher until it comes out.

188. He makes three cigarettes out of the nine cigarette butts. Every time he smokes one cigarette, he has one new cigarette butt. In total, he smokes four cigarettes and, therefore, smokes for four hours.

189. Cut it either of these ways:

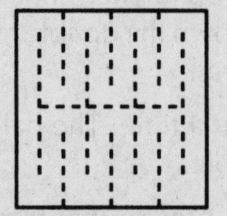 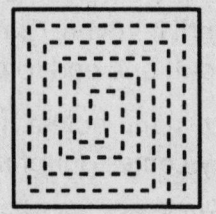

190. In two dimensions there is no solution, but it is possible in three dimensions, where you can form a tetrahedron.

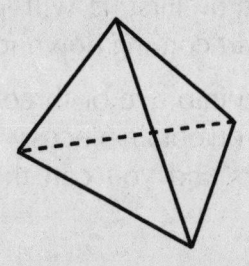

191. Oil floats in vinegar. All you have to do is to tilt the bottle. To pour vinegar, you have to turn the bottle upside down and by pulling off the cork a little, you can let the desired amount of vinegar out.

192. By placing it diagonally in a 30-by-30-inch package.

193. Cross your arms and hold a tip of the napkin in each hand. When you uncross your arms, the knot will be formed.

194. Yes, very easily, by folding the paper and then wrinkling it as shown below.

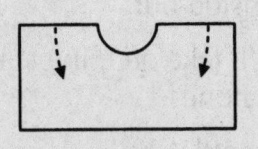 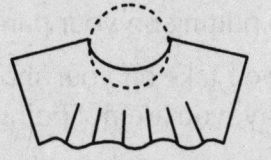

195. Make a knot with a loop at the base of the rope, and then cut the loop. The knot will be still holding the ends of the rope.

196. First, tie the lower ends. Then climb up the first rope and cut the second one, close to the ceiling, leaving an end long enough to form a loop. (You can instead cut it off entirely if you can slide the

rope through the hook.) Hanging from the loop, cut the first rope at the hook. Be careful not to drop it. Then slide the rope through the loop until it's even. Climb down the double rope and, once on the floor, pull one end to get it all.

197. Pour water in the hole a little at a time. The ball will rise until it completely comes out of the hole.

198. By releasing some air from the tires so that they lower the total height of the truck more than two inches. The truck can then easily go under the bridge.

199. By tossing it upward. First it will go up, then it will stop momentarily and start coming down following the same path.

200. By cutting the wood into two or three pieces, 20 centimeters in length. In this way, you obtain pieces with a rectangular surface of 5 by 20 centimeters and you can then put them in the hole, stopping the leak.

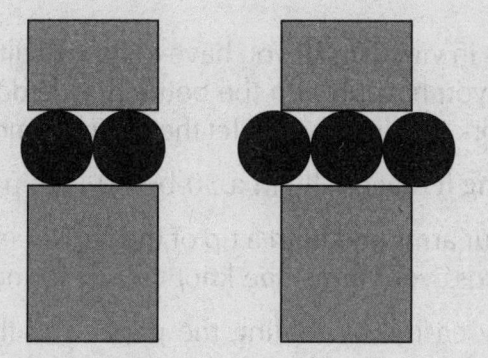

201. Yes, by putting on your pants inside-out.

202. When you take off your shoe, I'll take off mine at the same time. That way, you are not doing it alone.

203. By pushing the cork inside the bottle.

204. By turning the box upside down and sliding the lid enough to make some diamonds fall. The close it, turn it back to its original position, and put it back in its place.

205. The paper reads, "You will write the word 'NO' on the paper." If you write "NO," you are indicating that it will not happen,

although it has really happened. If you write "YES," you are indicating that it will happen, although it actually has not happened. No matter what you write, you will not get it right.

206. Save one penny every other day. When he dies, you will have the exact amount.

207. Place the newspaper page under a closed door. Each person steps on one end of the page so that they cannot touch each other without opening the door. To open the door, they would have to step off of the paper.

208. Something that specifically involves you. For example, crawling under your legs. Your friend can crawl under your legs, but you cannot crawl under you own legs.

209. Roll up the rug (or the bill) starting on one end until it reaches the bottle. Then, continue rolling it slowly so that the bottle moves until it is entirely off the rug. During this process, only the rug is touching the bottle.

210. Always advance half the distance remaining to the wall. In this way, there will always be some distance between you and the wall. The distance left approaches zero, but it never actually reaches zero.

   If we consider d as the initial distance to the wall, the distance traveled is $d \times (\frac{1}{2} + \frac{1}{4} + \frac{1}{8} + \frac{1}{16} + \ldots + \frac{1}{2^n})$.

211. Because they placed the ballpoint pen on the ground leaning against a high wall.

212. To make the authorities think that he was going to jump with a hostage. If they thought that, they would not give him a defective parachute.

213. There were no footprints. Therefore, the man and package fell from the sky. The package was the parachute that had not opened up. That is why the man was dead.

214. He was on a long bridge, so he had to run 20 yards toward where the police car was approaching from in order to get off the bridge. Then he ran toward the forest.

215. The husband died before he woke up. Therefore, nobody could have known what he had been dreaming about.

216. The man used the ladder to tie the rope to the hook. Then, he took it out of the room and brought in a big block of ice. He stood on the block of ice to hang himself. The moisture on the floor came from the ice melting down.

217. He talked to the travel agency where the couple had bought their tickets and found out that the husband had ordered a one-way ticket for his wife and a round-trip ticket for himself.

218. He took out one marble and swallowed it before someone else could see its color. This forced the count to take out the other marble. It was black, of course, so they all assumed that the previous one had been white.

219. He dug up the dirt with his hands to form a little mound. He then stepped on the mound to reach the water.

220. The man stabbed himself with an icicle. The ice melted. This explains why there was no weapon.

221. If Albert had stopped the cassette player when the killer came in, the tape would not have been rewound. This means that the killer had listened to the tape to make sure that the imitation was perfect.

222. The killer blocked the deadbolt with a chunk of ice. When the ice melted down, the door locked itself.

223. The maid, because pages 99 and 100 are two sides of the same sheet of paper.

224. If the police detective heard the shots at the same time, it means that the men could not have died at the same time. If both sounds had occurred at the same time at opposite ends of the train, he would have first heard the one from the front car, because the speed of the train was added to the speed of sound. For the sound from the back of the train, the speed of the train was subtracted from the speed of sound. For the detective to hear both shots at once means the man at the back of the train was killed first.

225. The guilty man was one Siamese twin, and his twin was innocent.

226. New York City is in the Northern Hemisphere and Australia is in the Southern Hemisphere. Due to the earth's movement, water and air masses turn in different directions in both hemispheres. In the Southern Hemisphere, they turn clockwise, while in the Northern Hemisphere, they turn counterclockwise. When he saw the direction of the water draining from the sink, he knew where he was.

227. The footprints were not very deep, which means that they could not belong to a very heavy person. Therefore, they had to belong to the secretary, who had changed shoes to hide her crime.

> Both wounds must have occurred when the victim placed a hand on his chest before the gunshot and the bullet crossed his hand before going into his chest.

228. I climbed up a cherry tree that had two cherries and picked only one. I left the other one on the tree. I did not "pick cherries," because I "picked a cherry."

229. Humans. When we are little, we crawl on all fours. When we are adults, we stand on two feet. When we are old, we use a cane.

230. Silence.

231. The letter "i."

232. A shadow.

233. None. The ship floats and it always weighs the same in the water. It will rise with the tide, so its flotation line will always be the same. So the ladder will still be 22 steps.

234. Two minutes. During the first minute, the front of the train will pass through the tunnel and during the second minute, the rest of the train will pass through the tunnel.

100 m   100 m

235. When they crossed, they were both in the same place. Therefore, they were both equidistant from Madrid.

236. The trains going to the movies arrive one minute earlier than the other ones. So if my uncle arrives at a random time, nine time out of ten the movie train will come first.

237. Two hours and thirteen minutes. (If you multiply by 60, the minutes become hours and the seconds become minutes.)

238. If you put my bird inside any supersonic plane and make it fly in the same direction as the plane, it will be going faster than the plane.

239. The top of the highest mast in the boat traveled a distance 2 d feet longer than the lowest point of the boat, which is d feet lower.

240. A bird cannot fly on the moon because there is no air to suspend it.

241. The passenger should sit at the end of the train and when the train enters the tunnel, he should run toward the front of the train. The time he spends in the tunnel will be shorter than if he had remained seated.

242. The combined speed of the trains is 50 + 70 = 120 miles per hour. It will take them half an hour to travel the 60 miles between them. During this time, the bird will travel 40 miles.

243. 100 inches. The stone moves relative to the log and the log to the terrain.

244. The combined speed of the trains is 80 + 120 = 200 meters per minute. One minute before crashing, they will be 200 meters apart.

245. You might think that the snail would take 200 minutes in traveling 100 centimeters, but you have to realize that at the end of the 194th minute it will be 3 centimeters away from the end. This means that in the 195th minute, the snail will reach it and will not slide down again. The answer is 195 minutes.

246. The young man took ten minutes to go to the other end of the train and back. During this time, the man's suitcases have traveled five miles. The train travels five miles every ten minutes, which makes the speed 30 miles per hour.

247. Fifteen, counting the times that they meet at a port while one ship is leaving and the other arriving. Thirteen, if we do not count these crossings. When the ship leaves, there are already seven ships on the way that it will come across at some point during the journey. It will also cross with the one ship that leaves when it leaves and the seven other ships that will depart during the ship's journey. The figure below represents this situation. The arrow indicates a ship that leaves New York destined for London. The dotted lines indicate the ships it passes.

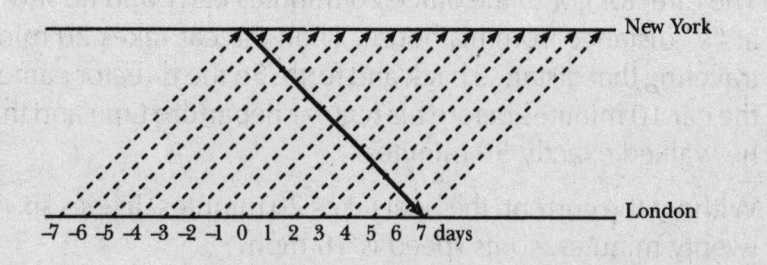

248. The needle will travel approximately 9.5 centimeters (the radius of the record minus the non-playable areas, 15 - 5 - 0.5 = 9.5 centimeters.) Actually, the speed of the record and the number of grooves do not affect the result. The needle moves in an arc of a circle whose radius is the length of the tonearm.

249. This point maintains a constant speed, independent of the length of the shadow.

250. When the card speeds up, the inertia pushes the air back inside the car, compressing the air behind the balloon and thus pushing the balloon forward. When the car turns, the balloon will move toward the inside of the turn.

251. The lower ends of the rim of the wheels. Their trajectory is shown below:

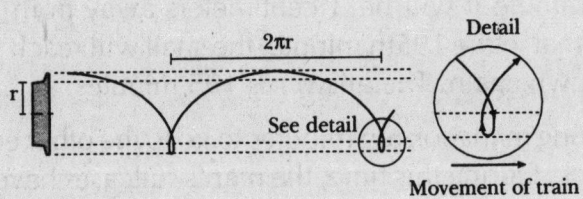

When the train goes in one direction, those points move in the opposite direction.

252. If the dog went faster than 330 meters per second (the speed of sound), it could not hear the noise of the can. So that is the fastest the dog can run.

253. Because the speed ratio was the same, runner number "1" won. We can verify this mathematically:

$$V_1/V_2 = {}^{100}/_{95} = {}^{105}/_{X_2} \qquad x_2 = 99.75 \text{ meters}$$

254. The director got to the office 20 minutes early and he saw the car at "x" distance from his house. Then the car takes 20 minutes in traveling that distance back and forth. So the director came across the car 10 minutes before his regular departure time and therefore he walked exactly 50 minutes.

255. Without the current, the boat takes 20 minutes. It goes six miles in twenty minutes, so its speed is 18 mph.

   With a current, the first trip would be $V_1 = 18 - 2 = 16$ mph, taking $T_1 = {}^{D_1}/V_1 = {}^{3}/_{16} = 11$ minutes and 15 seconds. The return trip would be $V_2 = 18 + 2 = 20$ mph, taking $T_2 = {}^{3}/_{20} = 9$ minutes.

   The total trip, in this case, would take 20 minutes and 15 seconds, which is more than the trip without the current.

256. There is such a spot. Let's imagine that on the same day that one person was climbing down, the other was climbing up. They must have met at a certain point of the trip. This is the spot we are looking for.

257. Two blankets one-inch-thick each, because the air between them also acts as insulation.

258. No. It hasn't because the total weight of the ice is equal to the volume of water moved.

259. This can never happen. These are two contradictory concepts. If one of them exists, the other cannot possibly exist as well.

260. At the North or South Pole.

261. I must pour it before going upstairs, because the coffee will lose more heat before adding the milk rather than after. (Matter loses heat proportionally to the difference in temperature with the surrounding environment.)

262. The flotation line will be lower, because the raft will be lighter. The water level of the pool will also be lower, because the volume of water that the rocks move when they are in the raft is larger than the volume of water the rocks move when they are at the bottom of the pool. When the rocks are on the raft, they move a volume of water equal to the weight of the rocks. When the rocks are at the bottom of the pool, the volume of the water moved is qual to the actual volume of the rocks. Since rocks are denser than water, this is the smaller of the two volumes.

263. The flotation line will be the same, because the weight of the boat does not change.

264. Eight times, as shown below.

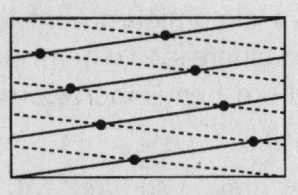

265. While the raft is loaded with the salt, he must mark the flotation line. Then, he must unload the salt and load the raft with gold until the water level reaches the flotation line. This means that the weight of the salt and the gold will be equal.

266. Place the bottle horizontally and let the wine gradually pour out until the horizontal surface of the wine is at the middle of the bottle, as shown in the illustration.

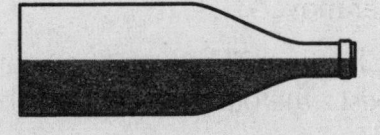

267. Put pieces of glass of the broken pitcher in the pitcher containing acid until the level reaches the five-quart mark. Then pour the acid until it reaches the two-quart mark.

268. Before leaving home, he wound the clock and set it for 12:00. When he got back home, he knew exactly how long he had been out because of his own clock.

At his friend's house, he checked the time. Once he was back home, he subtracted the time he was at his friend's house from the total time indicated by the clock. The remainder was used in walking to and from his friend's house. He divided this number into two and added the result to the time that he saw on his friend's clock when he was leaving his friend's house.

269. Two turns on itself. (You can actually try this yourself.)

270. Mr. Brown does not wear a brown or white tie. Therefore, it has to be red. Mr. White's tie can't be white, so it must be brown. That leaves Mr. Red with the white tie.

271. The maximum distance for the first two points is when they are on opposite ends of a circumference of that sphere. The circumference divides the sphere in two hemispheres. The third point has to be in one of these hemispheres. Therefore, it will certainly happen.

272. The puzzle says to draw a square "with two straight lines." The easiest solution is the one shown in the illustration following,

which shows a square with two straight lines.

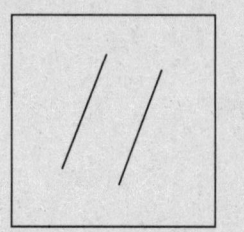

273. It is possible to predict it. That doesn't mean that he is right in his predictions.

274. This puzzle is based on an old joke. What really happened was that the young man kissed his own hand and then slapped the older man in the face.

275. There is no smoke coming out of an electric train.

276. Peacocks don't lay eggs. Peahens do.

277. A hole, for example.

278. One dozen.

279. He has a glass eye.

280. A quintet.

281. When he got married, he was a billionaire. Because of his wife's spending habits, he became a millionaire.

282. He can take out his dentures and bite his good eye with them.

283. Baby elephants.

284. During his last lap.

285. You can go in through the door.

286. The hare was lying. (The first paragraph of the puzzle gives the order.)

287. Staying up at night.

288. Wet.

289. Bicycles.

HARD-TO-SOLVE
BRAIN
TEASERS

The brainteasers in this section have two purposes: to let you have fun and to train your mind.

You don't need any special knowledge to solve them. It's a matter of thinking a little about the questions and applying common sense.

The puzzles are organized by order of difficulty. If you cannot find the answer to a problem and feel like giving up, refer to the **"Hints"** (**pages 139** through **143**) for some clues to finding the answer.

Solving these brainteasers can be a good activity for a solo player or a group, and can be turned into a game of competition.

The **answers** for this section can be found on **pages 145** through **168**.

1. TWINS

Peter and Paul are twin brothers. One of them (we don't know which) always lies. The other one always tells the truth. I ask one of them:
"Is Paul the one that lies?"
"Yes," he answers.
Did I speak to Peter or Paul?

2. TWIN STATISTICS

Suppose that 3% of births give rise to twins. What percentage of the population is a twin: 3%, less than 3%, or more than 3%?

3. PLACE YOUR CARDS

You have three cards: an ace, a queen, and a six. One is a diamond, one is a heart, and one is a spade, although not necessarily in that order.
The diamond sits between the queen and the heart.
The six is immediately to the right of the spade.
Write in the picture below where each card is located.

4. THE PROFESSOR AND HIS FRIEND

Professor Zizoloziz puts 40 matches on the table and explains a game to his friend Kathy.

Each player in turn takes 1, 3, or 5 matches. The winner is the one who takes the last match. Kathy chooses to go first and takes 3 matches.

Who do you think will win this game, Kathy or the professor?

5. IRREGULAR CIRCUIT

Two cars start from point A at the same time and drive around a circuit more than one mile in length. While they are driving laps around the circuit, each car must maintain a steady speed. Since one car is faster than the other, one car will pass the other at certain points. The first pass occurs 150 yards from point A.

At what distance from A will one car pass the other again?

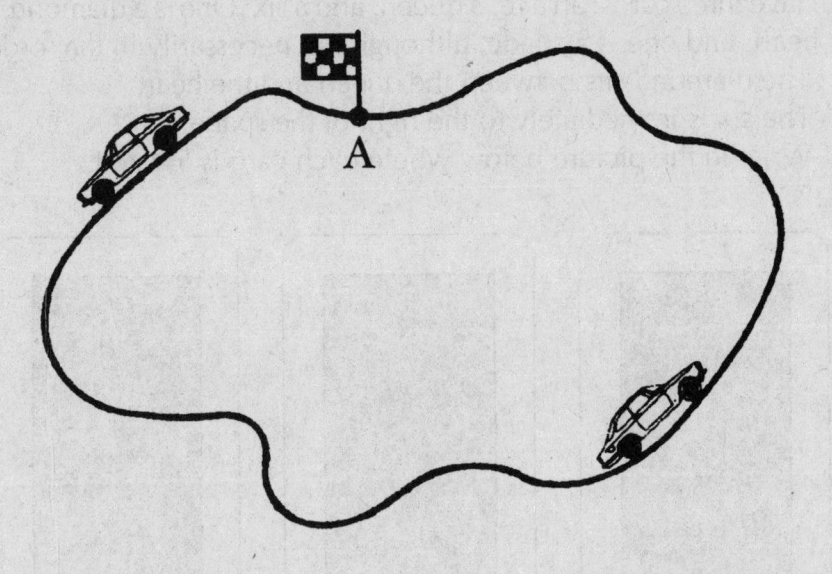

6. ECONOMICAL PROGRESSION

Below are four terms in an arithmetic progression (a series in which the difference between terms is constant, in this case 50):

5, 55, 105, 155

Notice how the four terms use only three different digits: 0, 1, and 5.
Can you find six terms in an arithmetic progression that use only three different digits?

7. SKIN AND SHOES

A white man is wearing a pair of white shoes, a black man is wearing a pair of black shoes, and a red-skinned man is wearing a pair of red shoes. In a gesture of friendship, they decide to exchange shoes. When they are done, each man has on one shoe from each of the other two men.

How many shoes will you have to look at to know which color of shoe each man is wearing on each foot; that is, which color shoe each man wears on his right foot and which color each man wears on his left foot? Note that when you look at a shoe, you can see that man's skin color.

8. UP AND DOWN

This morning I had to take the stairs because the elevator was out of service. I had already gone down seven steps when I saw Professor Zizoloziz on the ground floor coming up. I continued descending at my usual pace, greeted the professor when we passed, and was surprised to see that when I still had four more steps to go, the professor had gone up the whole flight. "When I go down one step, he goes up two," I thought.

How many steps does the staircase have?

9. WHAT MONTH—I

A month begins on a Friday and ends on a Friday, too. What month is it?

10. WHAT MONTH—II

The result of adding the date of the last Monday of last month and the date of the first Thursday of next month is 38. If both dates are of the same year, what is the current month?

11. EVE'S ENIGMA

After heaven, the earth, the grass, and all the animals were created, the snake, who was very smart, decided to make its own contribution.

It decided to lie every Tuesday, Thursday and Saturday. For the other days of the week, it told the truth.

"Eve, dear Eve, why don't you try and apple?" the snake suggested.

"But I am not allowed to!" said Eve.

"Oh, no!" said the snake. "You can eat it today since it is Saturday and God is resting."

"No, not today," said Eve, "Maybe tomorrow."

"Tomorrow is Wednesday and it will be too late," insisted the snake.

This is how the snake tricked Eve.

What day of the week did this conversation take place?

12. BROKEN M

We have formed six triangles by drawing three straight lines on the M. That's not enough. Starting with a new M, form nine triangles by drawing three straight lines.

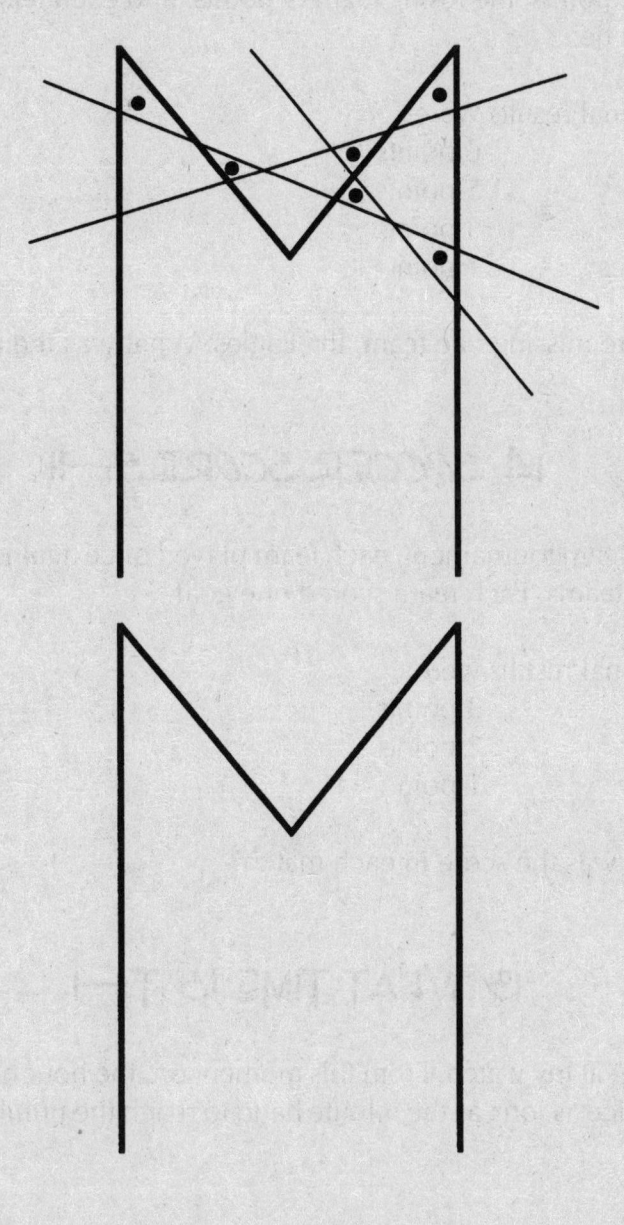

13. SOCCER SCORES—I

A soccer tournament has just ended. Five teams participated and each one played once against each of the other teams. The winner of a match received 2 points, the losing team O points, and each team received 1 point for a tie.

The final results were:

Lions	6 points
Tigers	5 points
Bears	3 points
Orioles	1 point

We are missing one team, the Eagles. What was their point total?

14. SOCCER SCORES—II

In a three-team tournament, each team played once against each of the two other teams. Each team scored one goal.

The final results were:

Lions	3 points
Tigers	2 points
Bears	1 point

What was the score in each match?

15. WHAT TIME IS IT—I

I'm looking at my watch. From this moment on, the hour hand will take exactly twice as long as the minute hand to reach the number six. What time is it?

16. WHAT TIME IS IT—II

I'm looking at my watch. From this moment on, the hour hand will take exactly three times longer than the minute hand to reach the number six. What time is it?

17. WHAT TIME IS IT—III

I'm looking at my watch. The hour hand is on one mark and the minute hand is on the next one. (By marks, we mean minute marks.) What time is it?

18. WHAT TIME IS IT—IV

I'm looking at my watch. The hour hand is on one mark and the minute hand is on the previous one. (By marks, we mean minute marks.) What time is it?

19. PROHIBITED CONNECTION

Using numbers 1, 2, 3, 4, 5, and 6, put each of them in a circle. There is only one condition. The circles connected by a line cannot have consecutive numbers. For example, 4 cannot be connected with 3 or 5.

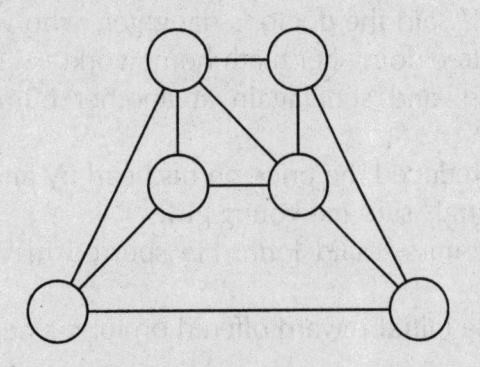

20. CONCENTRIC

The big square has an area of 60 square inches. Is there a fast way to figure out what the area of the small square is?

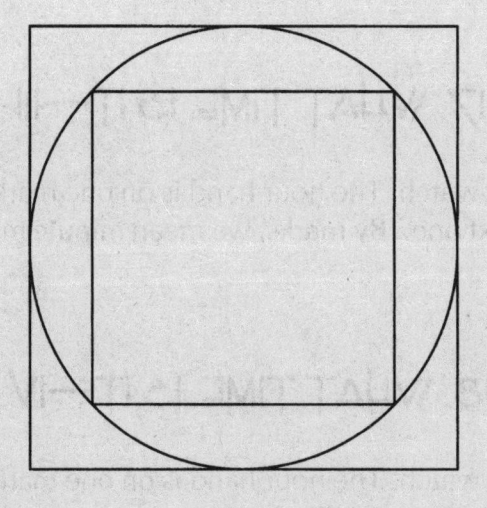

21. JOHN CASH

John Cash saw his face on a poster nailed to a tree. As he approached, he saw "WANTED, DEAD OR ALIVE." Under his picture, it read "REWARD:____DOLLARS."

There was a three-digit figure on the poster. John drew his Colt and shot at the first number (in the hundreds column).

He had just reduced the price on his head by five times.

"Good Lord!" said the doctor's daughter, who was sitting on the other side of the tree doing her math homework.

John blushed, and shot again at another number (in the tens column).

He had just reduced the price on his head by another five times.

"Nice shooting!" said the young girl.

"Thank you, miss," said John. He spurred his horse and never returned.

What was the initial reward offered on John's head?

22. RUSSIAN ROULETTE

Russian roulette was created by Count Ugo Lombardo Fiumiccino, who successfully died during his first presentation of it.

He placed six jars on a shelf, as in the drawing below. After staring at them, he closed his eyes and told his friend to fill them up with the ingredients, making sure that each jar contained an ingredient other than the one shown on its label.

When she was finished, the count asked:

"Dear Petrushka, would you be so kind as to tell me where the salt is?"

"Under the jar containing snuff," answered Petrushka.

"My dear friend, would you tell me where the sugar is?" he asked.

"Immediately to the right of the jar containing coffee," she answered.

Ugo Lombardo Fiumiccino, confirming his desire to commit suicide, reached immediately for the jar containing arsenic.

Where is the arsenic?

23. NEW RACE

Two cars start traveling from two different points and in opposite directions in a circuit race at a constant speed. The cars cross for the first time at point A. The second time is at point B. The third time is at point C, and the fourth one is again at point A.

How much faster is one car going than the other?

24. THE CALCULATOR KEYS

Several times Professor Zizoloziz mentioned that he feels uncomfortable looking at his pocket calculator. Yesterday, he was elated because he had found the reason why. The layout of the keys from 1 to 9 and the "minus" and "equal" signs look like they are doing subtraction. It's an incorrect one, however, because 789 minus 456 does not equal 123. Zizoloziz thought of changing the numbers to achieve a correct equation. He changed 7 with 3, then 3 with 4, and 9 with 6, resulting in 486 - 359 = 127. He made only three changes to achieve this.

Using the keyboard below as a reference, can you obtain a correctly subtracted number with only two changes?

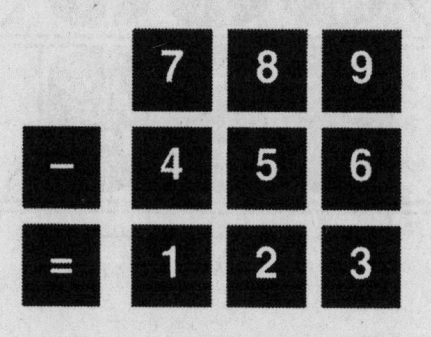

25. NICE DISCOUNTS

A bookstore has a nice discount policy. If you buy a $20 book today, you get a 2% discount on your next purchase. If you buy a $15 book, you get a 1.5% discount on your next purchase. If you have to buy three books that cost $10, $20, and $30, you could buy the $30 book today, the $10 book tomorrow (on which you'll get a 3% discount), and the $20 book the following day (on which you'll get a 1% discount). Or you could buy the $30 book and the $20 book today, and the $10 book tomorrow (with a 5% discount).

What is the cheapest way to buy five books priced at $10, $20, $30, $40, and $50?

26. ENIGMATIC FARES

Professor Zizoloziz always adds the five digits on a bus transfer. Yesterday, he rode route 62 with a friend. As soon as he got the tickets, which were consecutively numbered, he added the numbers on them and then told his friend that the sum of all ten digits was exactly 62. His logical friend asked him if the sum of the numbers on either of the tickets was by any chance 35. Professor Zizoloziz answered and his friend then knew the numbers on the bus tickets.

What were the numbers on the two bus tickets?

27. HOROSCOPE

An indiscreet young man asks his beautiful mathematics teacher her age. She responds, "Today's date is my age, although before this week is over there will be another day with a date one fifth of the new age that I will be."

What is the teacher's sign of the zodiac?

28. STRANGERS IN THE NIGHT

The midnight train is coming down the Strujen-Bajen mountains. Art Farnanski seems to be dozing off in his seat.

Someone knows that this is not true.

At the station, all the passengers get off the train, except one. The conductor comes and taps him on the shoulder to let him know they have arrived. Art Farnanski does not answer. He is dead.

"His heart?" asks Commander Abrojos, looking at the dead body.

"Strychnine," answers the forensic doctor.

Hours later, the four people that had shared the train compartment with the dead man are at the police station.

The man in the dark suit:
"I'm innocent. The blonde woman was talking to Farnanski."

The blonde woman:
"I'm innocent. I did not speak to Farnanski."

The man in the light suit:
"I'm innocent. The brunette woman killed him."

The brunette woman:
"I'm innocent. One of the men killed him."

That same morning, while he is serving him coffee, the waiter at the Petit Piccolo asks commander Abrojos:

"This is an easy case for you, isn't it?"

"Yes," answers the commander. "Four true statements and four false ones. Easy as pie."

Who killed Farnanski? (Only one person is guilty.)

29. MONTE CARLO

The famous playboy Hystrix Tardigradus explained to a beautiful woman his system for playing roulette:

"In each round, I always bet half of the money I have at the time on red. Yesterday, I counted and I had won as many rounds as I had lost."

Over the course of the night, did Hystrix win, lose, or break even?

30. THE FOREIGNERS AND THE MENU

A particular inn always offers the same nine dishes on its dinner menu: A, B, C, D, E, F, G, H, and I.

Five foreigners arrive. Nobody tells them which dish corresponds to which letter and so they each select one letter without knowing what they will eat.

The innkeeper arrives with the five dishes ordered and puts them in the center of the table so that they can decide who eats what.

This goes on for two more nights.

The foreigners, who are professors of logic, were able to deduce by the dishes they ordered which letter represents which dish.

What could have been the dishes ordered each of the three nights?

31. FORT KNOX JUMPING FROGS—1

The first puzzle of this series is very well known. We included it here, though, because it is good practice for the following puzzles, since they all use the same method of moving coins.

Make a line of eight coins. In four moves, make four piles of two coins each.

A move consists of taking one coin, skipping over two others, and piling it on top of the next one.

The answers list one of several possible solutions for all of the puzzles in this series.

32. FORT KNOX JUMPING FROGS—II

Place 14 coins in the shape of a cross, as shown in the illustration. In seven moves as described in Puzzle 31, make seven piles of two coins each. Note: Only move the coins in a straight line; do not change directions.

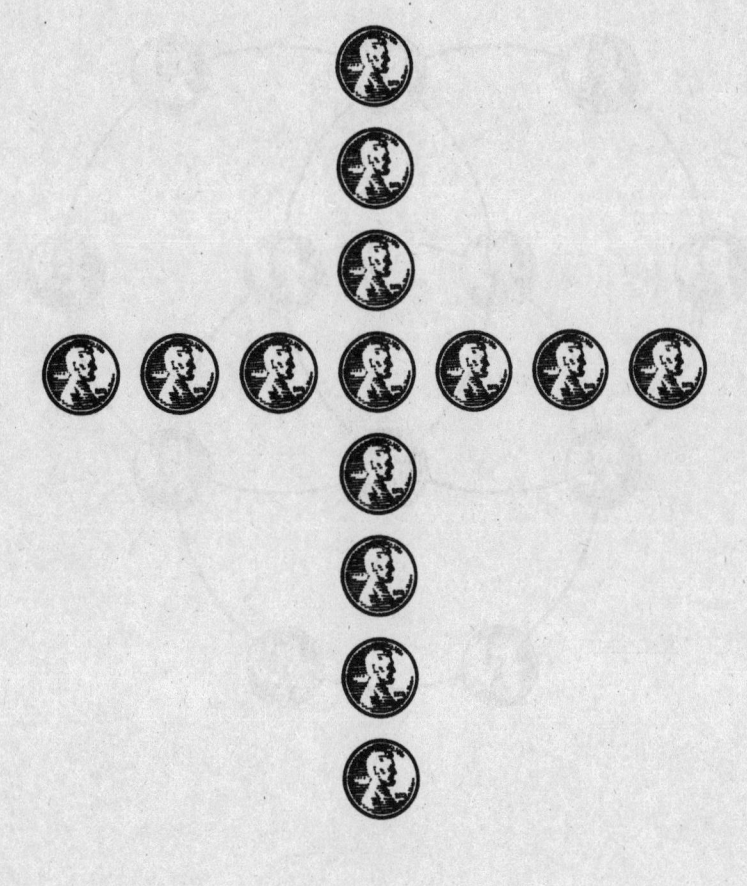

33. FORT KNOX JUMPING FROGS—III

Place 12 coins on the three rings as shown in the illustration below. In six moves as described in Puzzle 31, make six piles of two coins each. Note: Only move the coins around their own rings and always go clockwise in direction.

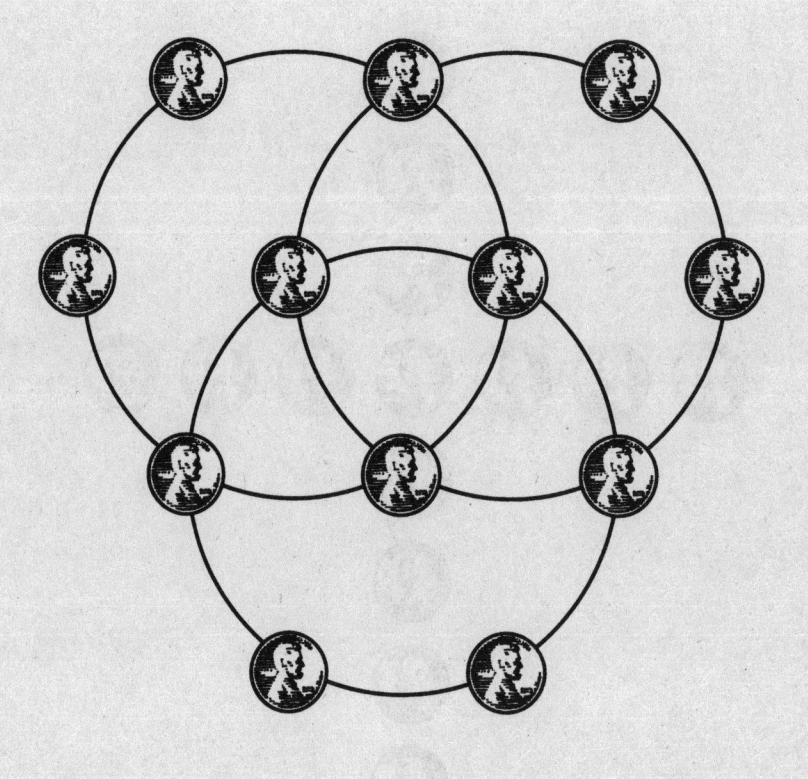

34. FORT KNOX JUMPING FROGS—IV

Place 20 coins in the shape of a star as shown in the illustration below. In ten moves as described in Puzzle 31, make ten piles of two coins each. Note: Only move the coins along the straight lines and do not turn corners.

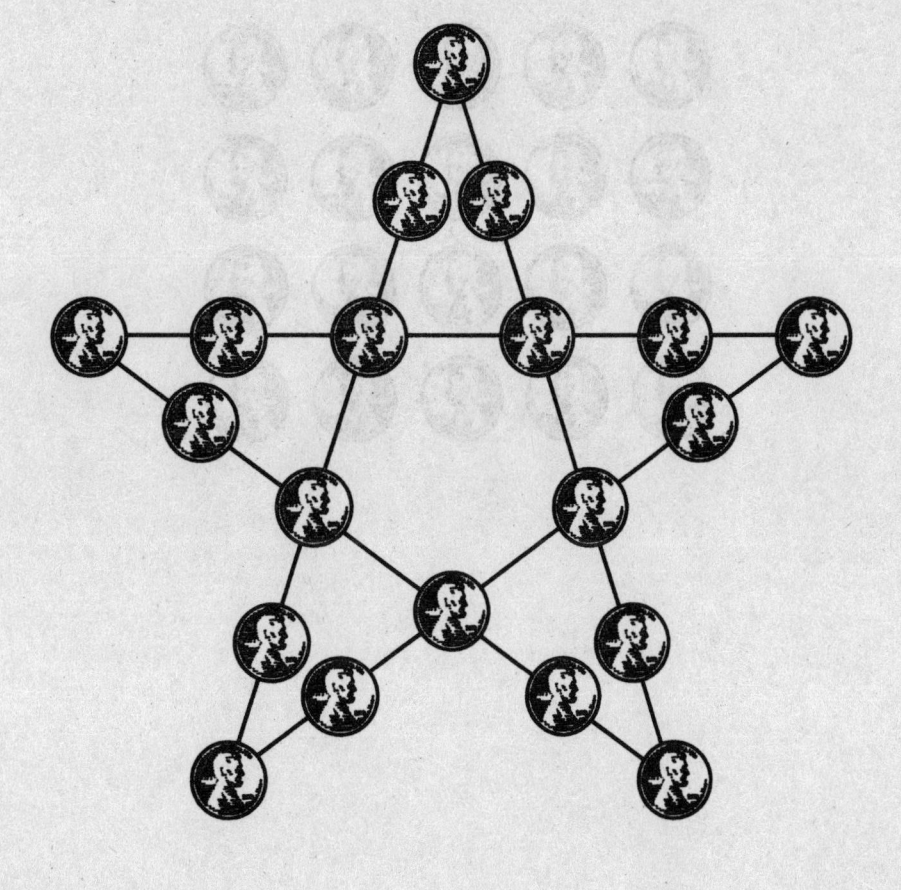

35. FORT KNOX JUMPING FROGS—V

Place 20 coins in a four-by-five rectangle as shown below. In ten moves as described in Puzzle 31, make ten piles of two coins each. Note: Coins can move only in a straight line and cannot move diagonally.

36. THE HAREM

The story goes that the harem of the Great Tamerlan was protected by a door with many locks. The vizier and four slaves were in charge of guarding this door.

Knowledgeable of the weaknesses of men, the Great Tamerlan had distributed the keys in such a way that the vizier could only open the door if he was with any one of the slaves, and the slaves could only open it if three of them worked together.

How may locks did the door have?

37. THE DIVIDING END

My ID number is quite remarkable. It's a nine-digit number with each of the digits from 1 to 9 appearing once. The whole number is divisible by 9. If you remove the rightmost digit, the remaining eight-digit number is divisible by 8. Removing the next rightmost digit leaves a seven-digit number that is divisible by 7. This property continues all the way down to one digit. What is my ID number?

38. THE ISLAND AND THE ENGLISHMEN

On a deserted island (except for a small group of Englishmen) there are four clubs.

The membership lists reveal that:

a) Each Englishman is a member of two clubs.

b) Every set of two clubs has only one member in common.

How many Englishmen are there on the island?

39. LOGIC APPLES

Four perfect logicians, who all knew each other from being members of the Perfect Logicians' Club, sat around a table that had a dish with 11 apples in it. The chat was intense, and they ended up eating all the apples. Everybody had at least one apple, and everyone knew that fact, and each logician knew the number of apples that he ate. They didn't know how many apples each of the others ate, though. They agreed to ask only questions that they didn't know the answers to:

Alonso: Did you eat more apples than I did, Bertrand?

Bertrand: I don't know. Did you, George, eat more apples than I did?

George: I don't know.

Kurt: Aha!

Kurt figured out how many apples each person ate. Can you do the same?

40. ADDED CORNERS

Using the numbers from 1 to 8, place one in each shape with one condition: The number in each square has to be the sum of its two neighboring circles.

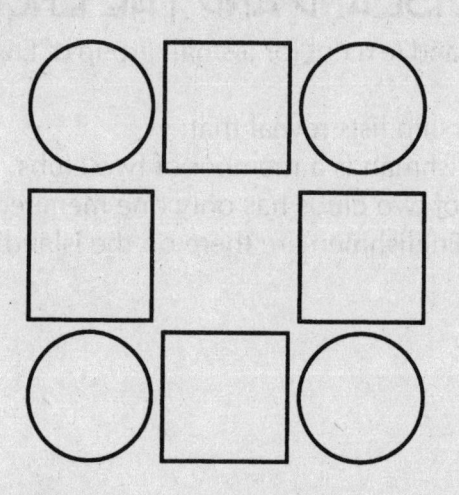

106

41. RECTANGLES

The vertical rectangle (solid line) has an area of 40 square inches.
Find out in a quick way the area of the inclined rectangle (dotted line).

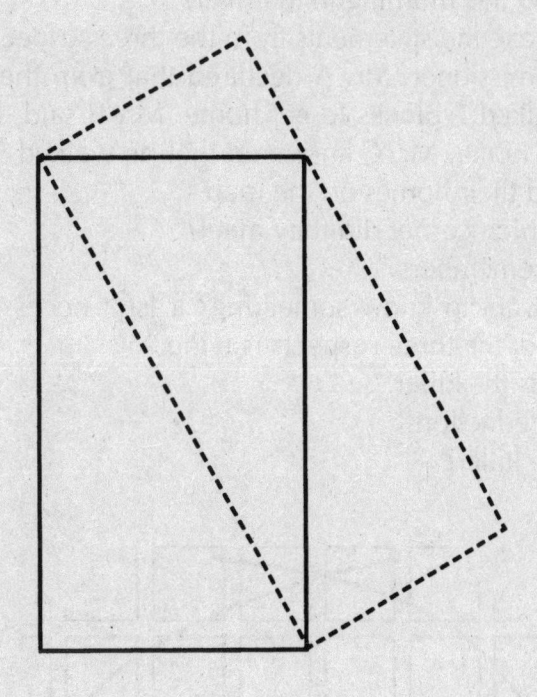

42. A WARM FAREWELL

At a train station, the Porter family is saying good-bye to the Robinson family. We don't know who is leaving and who is staying.

Each of the members of the Porter family say farewell to each of the members of the Robinson family. To say good-bye, two men shake hands, and both a man and a woman and two women kiss once on the cheek.

An eyewitness to the event counted 21 handshakes and 34 kisses.
How many men and how many women were saying good-bye?

43. FOUR MINUS ONE IS A CRIME

Messrs. A, B, C, and D met last night in a corner in the circled area. After the meeting, each of them went home, except for one, Mr. D, who was discovered dead this morning in the river.

"Did you take the statements from the three suspects?"

"Yes, commissioner. Mr. A declared that from the corner of the meeting he walked 7 blocks to get home. Mr. B said that he walked 6 blocks to get home. Mr. C answered that he walked 5 blocks to get home. I marked their homes on the map."

"And in which corner did they meet?"

"Nobody remembers."

"Do you want to know something? It isn't necessary, because I know that one of the three suspects is lying."

"And that is the killer!"

"Brilliant deduction!"

Who is the killer?

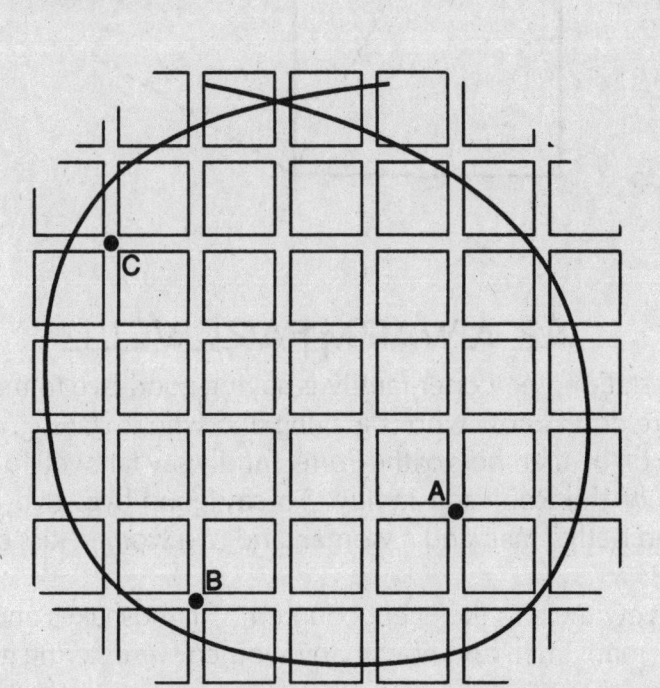

44. ON THE ROUTE OF MARCO POLO

On his way east, Marco Polo passed five little villages along a straight road. At each village a road sign points to one of the other four villages. Below are the five signs, in no particular order. Can you add the corresponding arrows to the four signs that have lost them? (The five signs are all on the same side of the road.)

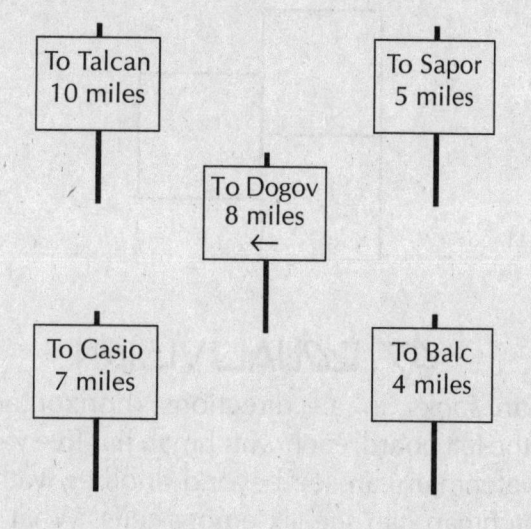

45. ON THE ROAD

On my way to Philadelphia, I pass five mileposts that indicate their respective distances to Philadelphia. The mileposts are at fixed intervals. What's curious is that each milepost has a two-digit number, and together the five mileposts use all the digits from 0 to 9 once. What is the smallest distance that the closest milepost can be from Philadelphia? (As usual, mileposts don't begin with 0.)

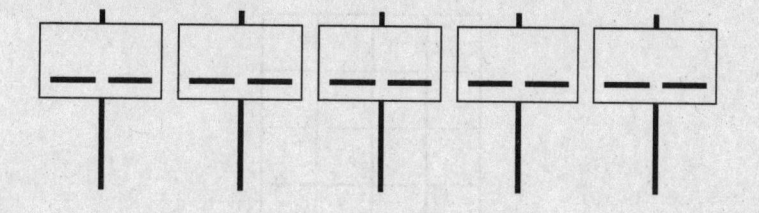

46. TOUCHING SQUARES

Shown here are three squares on a table with each one touching the other two squares. If you want to place squares so that each square touches exactly three other squares (not counting corner-to-corner or corner-to-side contact), how may squares do you need? All squares must lie on the table surface.

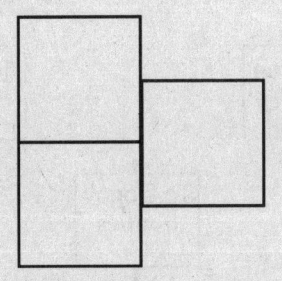

47. EQUAL VISION

Each watchman looks in all directions (horizontal, vertical, and diagonal). On the left board, each watchman has five vacant cells under his gaze. (A watchman can see beyond another watchman.) On the right, each watchman can see six empty cells. What's the maximum number of watchmen that can be placed so that each sees seven empty cells?

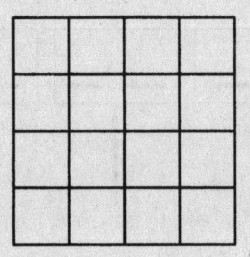

110

48. BLOOD AND SAND

"You are the killer!" declared Commissioner Abrojos. His assistant, Inspector Begonias, slanted his eyes and looked around. They were alone in the room.

"I don't understand," he said.

"You are the killer!" the commissioner repeated.

Here is the story:

Yesterday, responding to a phone call, Inspector Begonias visited the mansion of millionaire Lincoln Dustin at around 7 P.M. The millionaire was dead in his office. There were blood stains on the carpet around the desk. Begonias inspected the place. He questioned the butler, who told him that Lincoln Dustin always led a perfectly ordered life. Every day, at noon, Mr. Dustin started the hourglass, the one that was now next to his dead body. At exactly midnight, the hourglass finished and Lincoln Dustin would go to sleep.

Begonias thought this was all very interesting, but not so useful for his investigation. That same night, the butler's call woke him up.

"Inspector!" cried the butler, "The hourglass did not finish at midnight, but at 3 A.M.!"

Begonias told all of this to Commissioner Abrojos.

"Let's suppose," said the commissioner, "that Mr. Dustin was able to turn the hourglass to leave us a clue as to the time of the crime."

Begonias nodded.

"In that case," continued the commissioner, "you told me that you had gone to the mansion around 7 P.M., which makes me think that you are the killer."

This is how they reached the conversation at the beginning of our puzzle.

Begonias could not believe it.

"I never thought," he said sadly, "that you would do this to me."

"Come on, Begonias, aren't you going to try to find an excuse?"

The inspector thought for a moment, going over the events of the previous day.

"The hourglass!" he cried. "I remember now. When I inspected the room I saw that the hourglass was on a handwritten note."

"Do you mean that the victim wrote the name of the killer? I don't believe that."

"Not at all!" said Begonias. "I wanted to read the note, so I lifted the hourglass and then I must have turned it upside down by mistake."

"What time was it then?"

"7 P.M."

"My dear friend, this clears you as a suspect!" said the commissioner.

Suppose that Mr. Dustin was able to invert the hourglass before dying. At what time did he die? Why did the commissioner consider Begonias as a suspect?

49. INTERNATIONAL SUMMIT

At a recent international summit, five delegates (A, B, C, D, and E) participated. This is what we observed:

1. B and C spoke English, although when D joined them, they all changed to Spanish, the only common language among the three of them.

2. The only common language among A, B, and E was French.

3. The only common language between C and E was Italian.

4. Three delegates could speak Portuguese.

5. The Most common language was Spanish.

6. One of the delegates spoke all five languages, another one spoke four, one spoke three, one spoke two, and the other only spoke one language.

What languages did each delegate speak?

50. MISTER DIGIT FACE

Place each of the digits 1 to 9, one digit per blank, so that the product of the two eyes equals the number above the head, and the product of each eye and mouth equals the number on the respective side of the face.

51. DIGIT TREE

Using each digit from 1 to 9 once, make seven numbers so that each number is equal to the sum of the numbers in the circles that are connected to it from below. (The numbers can be more than one digit.) There are two slightly different answers.

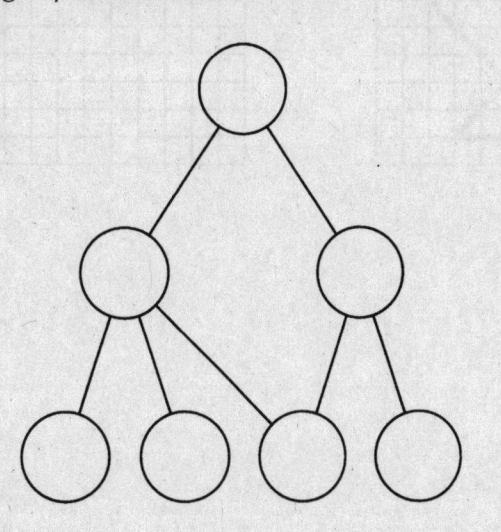

52. FIGURES TO CUT IN TWO

Each one of the following figures can be divided into two equal parts (that may be mirror images of each other). The dividing lines can follow the grid or not. The grid is only to provide proportion to the figures.

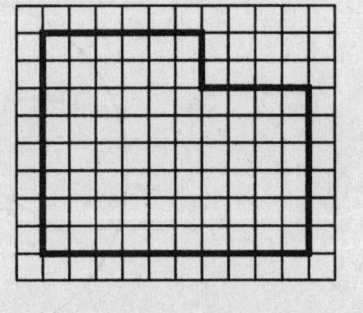

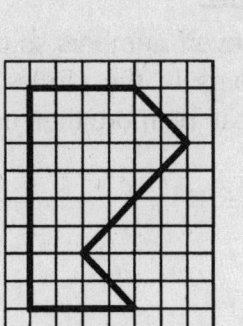

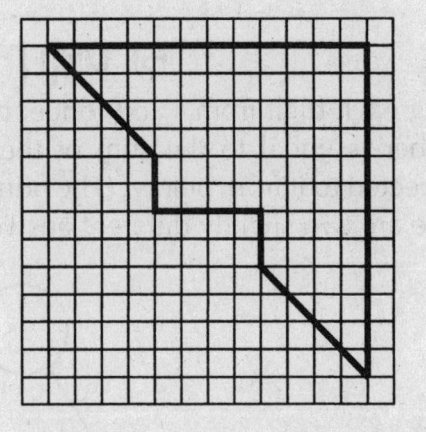

53. SEGMENTS

Place the digits 1 to 9 (using each digit once, one digit per box) so that:

• the boxes containing the 1 and 2 and all the ones between them add up to 12,

• the boxes containing the 2 and 3 and all the ones between them add up to 23,

• the boxes containing the 3 and 4 and all the ones between them add up to 34,

• the boxes containing the 4 and 5 and all the ones between them add up to 45.

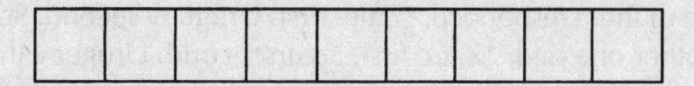

54. MULTIPLE TOWERS

As the elevator rises along the eight-floor tower, it forms a series of three-digit numbers by combining the 72 in the elevator with the digit on the floor. What's more, these three-digit numbers are multiples of 2, 3, 4, etc., up to 9. (That is, on the lowest floor, 726 is evenly divisible by 2, on the next floor, 723 is evenly divisible by 3, and so on.) Can you find another arrangement for the digits 0 to 9 (using each digit once, one digit per box) so that the elevator isn't 72 and the combinations of the elevator with the level form an appropriate multiple?

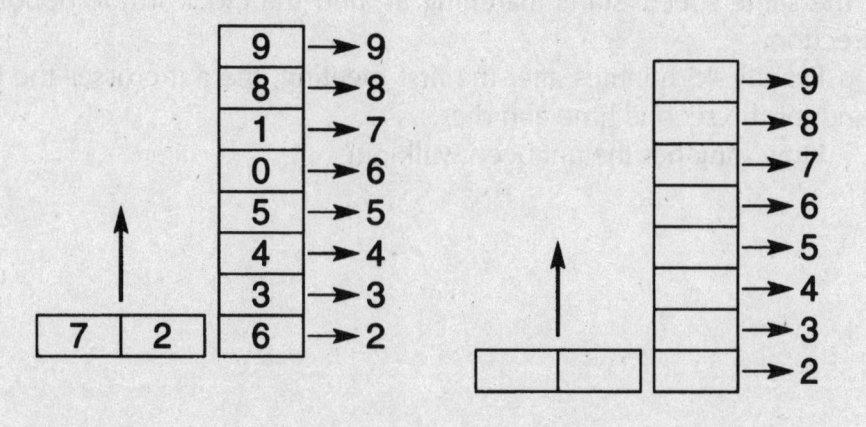

115

55. EARTHLINGS

August 2002.

The spaceship landed.

"Earth!" they shouted.

They knew that earthlings are divided into three groups: those who always tell the truth, those who always lie, and those who do both, alternating between true and false statements, starting with either.

"Let's go!" said the captain.

The aliens approached three earthlings, who each were from a different group, and asked, "Who won the last World Cup? Who came in second? Who came in third?

One of them responded, "Zaire first. Uruguay second. Spain third.

Another one said, "Zaire first. Spain second. Uruguay third."

The third one said, "Uruguay first. Spain second. Zaire third."

The aliens returned to their space ship and flew back to where they came from.

Do you know which response was the true ranking in the World Cup?

56. THE ANT AND THE CLOCK

Precisely when the big hand of the clock passes 12, an ant begins crawling counterclockwise around the clock from the 6 mark at a consistent speed.

When reaching the big hand of the clock, the ant turns around and, at the same speed, starts marching around the clock in the opposite direction.

Exactly 45 minutes after the first meeting, the ant crosses the big hand for the second time and dies.

How long has the ant been walking?

57. HIDDEN WORD—I

A four-letter word belongs in the rectangle below. You are given several clues to help guess what it is.

    In the column markd "2," you have words that share exactly two letters in the same position as the hidden word. For example, if the hidden word were REDO, in column 2 we could put DEMO, BEDS, DODO, etc. Column 1 contains words that share exactly one letter in the same position as the hidden word. In the example above, REDO being the hidden word, column 1 could have NODS, ROAD, etc.

    Column 0 has words that do not share any letter in the same position as the hidden word. For our example, column 0 could have GAME, HARD, etc.

    Now find the hidden word.

0	1	2
CULT	SOME	VEST
	HINT	HOSE

58. HIDDEN WORD—II

A three-letter word belongs in the rectangle below. Given the words below, figure out what it is.

0	1	2
HAS	CON	SON
	CAB	

59. HIDDEN WORD—III

A five-letter word belongs in the rectangle below. Given the words below, figure out what it is.

0	1	2
BALKS	MILES	MUSHY
GUSTO	GAUDY	PATES

SECRET NUMBER

In the first field of the first row of every illustration we have written (in invisible ink) a number formed by four different digits between 0 and 9.

The following rows indicate attempts to find out the secret number. Each try has, in the column to the right, its grade with letters R (right) and B (bingo). Each R indicates that this number has one digit in common with the secret number, but in a different position. Each B indicates that the number has one digit in common with the secret number in the same position.

Find out the secret number in the following tables.

60. SECRET NUMBER—I

				B	B	B	B
8	9	5	1	R	R		
2	1	6	9	R	B		
3	6	9	4	R	B		
4	7	2	1	R	B		
1	2	3	7	R	R	R	

118

61. SECRET NUMBER—II

6	2	5	3	R			
				B	B	B	B
8	1	4	7	R	R		
2	5	7	1	B			
3	6	0	9	R	R		
9	6	8	7	B	B		

62. SECRET NUMBER—III

				B	B	B	B
1	0	2	9	R			
3	4	6	2	R	R		
5	8	4	9	R	R		
8	5	2	1	R	R		
4	2	8	5	R	R	R	

63. SECRET NUMBER—IV

				B	B	B	B
3	9	2	0	R	R	R	
8	7	4	5	B			
9	0	7	5	R	R		
8	3	9	7	R	R	R	

64. SECRET NUMBER—V

				B	B	B	B
1	2	5	9	R			
1	3	8	9	R	B		
1	3	5	7	B	B		
4	3	9	7	B	B		

DOMINOES

Each one of the following diagrams uses the 28 dominoes of a domino set to make a table. The values of each domino are written down in numbers instead of in dots, but we have not identified the individual dominoes. That's exactly what you'll have to do. In the first tables, we have helped you with some of them.

Notice that each table contains the 28 dominoes and no tile appears twice in the same table. Below each table you will find a list of the 28 dominoes so that you can track what you have found and what you are still missing.

(Dominoes was created by Mr. Lech Pijanovsky, from Poland.)

65. TABLE 1

Find the 28 dominoes.

1	5	5	3	0	6	0	6
5	4	4	2	4	4	6	2
2	6	0	1	1	2	5	1
4	3	5	5	3	2	6	0
0	3	0	3	3	3	1	0
5	2	6	2	3	6	0	1
4	5	6	4	1	4	2	1

Here is a list of the 28 dominoes:

```
0-0
0-1   1-1
0-2   1-2   2-2
0-3   1-3   2-3   3-3
0-4   1-4   2-4   3-4   4-4
0-5   1-5   2-5   3-5   4-5   5-5
0-6   1-6   2-6   3-6   4-6   5-6   6-6
```

66. TABLE II

Find the 28 dominoes.

3	1	2	2	6	1	3	4
5	5	3	4	0	5	3	2
2	6	5	1	1	2	0	0
1	1	0	6	0	3	3	0
0	6	4	3	6	5	4	5
3	2	5	4	0	1	6	2
5	4	6	4	2	4	6	1

Here is a list of the 28 dominoes:
0-0
0-1   1-1
0-2   1-2   2-2
0-3   1-3   2-3   3-3
0-4   1-4   2-4   3-4   4-4
0-5   1-5   2-5   3-5   4-5   5-5
0-6   1-6   2-6   3-6   4-6   5-6   6-6

67. TABLE III

Find the 28 dominoes.

1	0	2	2	3	6	5
1	6	6	4	3	6	5
2	3	5	0	1	4	6
0	4	3	0	2	4	0
3	6	5	4	5	4	1
0	0	5	1	3	1	2
3	6	2	2	5	3	2
1	1	4	0	4	6	5

Here is a list of the 28 dominoes:

0-0						
0-1	1-1					
0-2	1-2	2-2				
0-3	1-3	2-3	3-3			
0-4	1-4	2-4	3-4	4-4		
0-5	1-5	2-5	3-5	4-5	5-5	
0-6	1-6	2-6	3-6	4-6	5-6	6-6

68. TABLE IV

Find the 28 dominoes.

5	4	2	3	6	3	4
4	6	5	5	0	6	3
4	6	2	3	4	1	2
6	0	6	3	0	4	1
0	6	0	2	3	4	2
5	5	6	1	4	5	3
5	1	3	2	2	1	1
1	5	2	0	1	0	0

Here is a list of the 28 dominoes:

0-0						
0-1	1-1					
0-2	1-2	2-2				
0-3	1-3	2-3	3-3			
0-4	1-4	2-4	3-4	4-4		
0-5	1-5	2-5	3-5	4-5	5-5	
0-6	1-6	2-6	3-6	4-6	5-6	6-6

69. TABLE V

Find the 28 dominoes.

4	0	0	1	1	1	0
5	2	3	5	6	5	6
3	5	4	4	3	4	2
2	0	0	5	6	5	3
2	2	1	5	6	0	1
2	4	4	3	2	6	4
5	6	0	3	2	3	6
1	1	3	6	4	1	0

Here is a list of the 28 dominoes:
0-0
0-1 1-1
0-2 1-2 2-2
0-3 1-3 2-3 3-3
0-4 1-4 2-4 3-4 4-4
0-5 1-5 2-5 3-5 4-5 5-5
0-6 1-6 2-6 3-6 4-6 5-6 6-6

70. TABLE VI

Find the 28 dominoes.

4	5	1	6	0	5	1
2	5	3	5	3	6	5
6	2	0	4	2	2	6
6	6	2	0	5	3	3
3	1	1	2	3	6	4
4	0	3	1	0	0	4
4	1	2	1	4	5	3
5	1	2	0	0	4	6

Here is a list of the 28 dominoes:
0-0						
0-1	1-1					
0-2	1-2	2-2				
0-3	1-3	2-3	3-3			
0-4	1-4	2-4	3-4	4-4		
0-5	1-5	2-5	3-5	4-5	5-5	
0-6	1-6	2-6	3-6	4-6	5-6	6-6

71. HOUND—I

A hound started on a square numbered 1, and moved from square to square numbering them in succession to the last one, numbered 20. The hound moved horizontally and vertically only, never entering any square twice. The numbers were then deleted. All we know is that the squares with circles had the numbers 5, 10, and 15, in some order. Figure out the path of the hound.

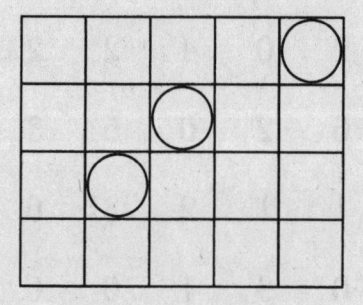

72. HOUND—II

A hound started on a square numbered 1, and moved from square to square numbering them in succession to the last one, numbered 35. The hound moved horizontally and vertically only, never entering any square twice. The numbers were then deleted. All we know is that the squares with circles had the numbers 7, 14, 21, 28, and 35, in some order. Figure out the path of the hound.

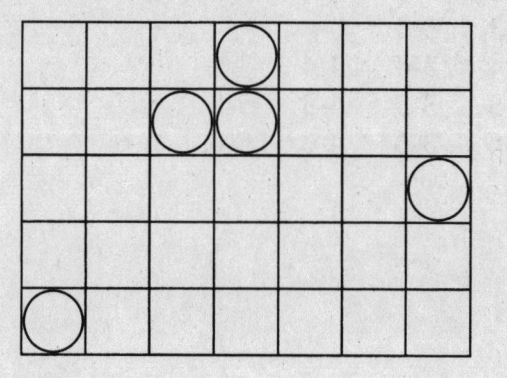

73. HOUND—III

A hound started on a square numbered 1, and moved from square to square numbering them in succession to the last one, numbered 25. The hound never entered any square twice and moved horizontally and vertically only, except for one diagonal move to a neighboring square. All the numbers except those shown were then deleted. Figure out the path of the hound.

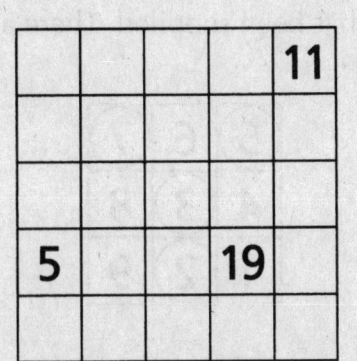

74. HOUND—IV

A hound started on a square numbered 1, and moved from square to square numbering them in succession to the last one, numbered 25. The hound never entered any square twice and moved horizontally and vertically only, except for one jump move like a chess knight, shown below left. All the numbers except those shown were then deleted. Figure out the path of the hound.

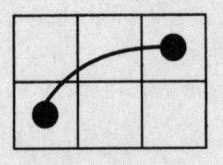

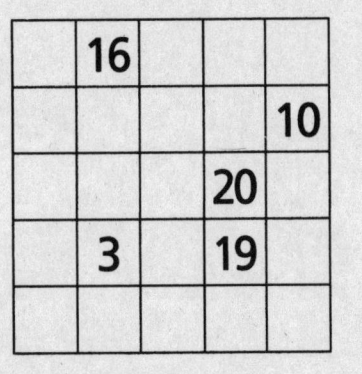

75. Hound—V

A hound started on a square numbered 1, and moved from square to square numbering them in succession to the last one, numbered 9. The hound never entered any square twice and moved horizontally and vertically only. The prime numbers in the grid formed a symmetric pattern. Figure out the path of the hound in the bigger board where the prime numbers (2, 3, 5, 7, 11, 13, 17, 19, and 23) form a symmetric pattern. One number has been supplied. There are two answers.

POKER

We have a set of 28 poker cards (with 8, 9, 10, J, Q, K, and A). We select 25 and make a five-by-five table, like in the drawings.

We then have twelve "hands" of five cards (five horizontally, five vertically, and two diagonally). Next to each "hand" we write its combination.

Pair: two cards of the same value.

Two pair: two pairs plus a fifth card.

Three of a kind: three cards of equal value.

Full house: three of a kind with a pair.

Four of a kind: four cards of the same value.

Straight: five cards of consecutive values. The ace can be high or low, so the possible combinations of a straight are: A-8-9-10-J, 8-9-10-J-Q, 9-10-J-Q-K, and 10-J-Q-K-A.

Straight flush: a straight where all the cards are of the same suit.

(We write "nothing" when we have none of these combinations.)

Important: The cards of each "hand" do not have to be in order. For example, the line containing the straight can have a 9, then an 8, then a J, then a 10, then an A.

Find the values (just the values, not the suits) of all cards left blank.

131

76. POKER—1

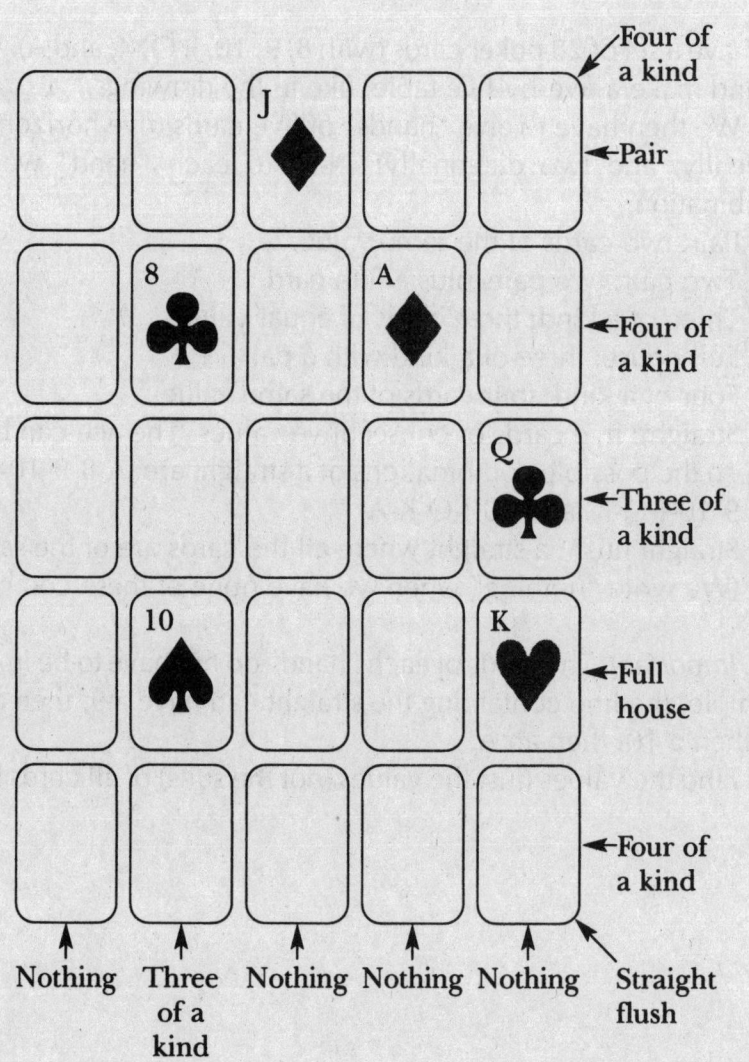

Find the values (just the values, not the suits) of all cards left blank.

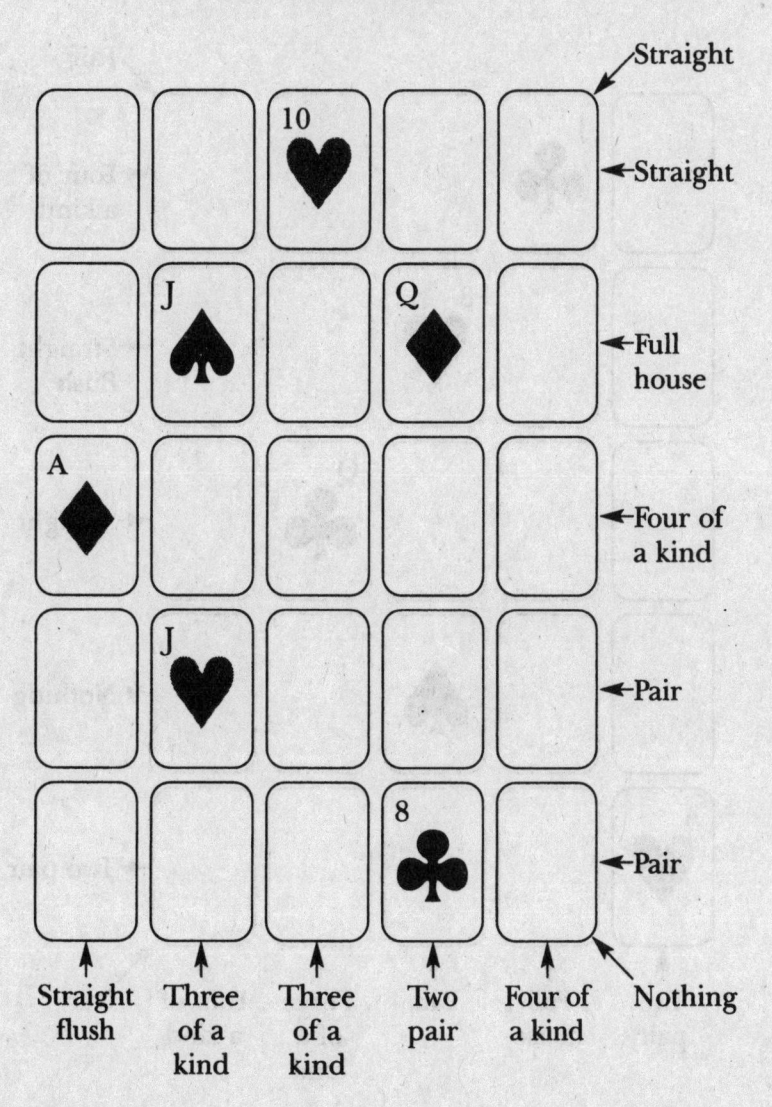

Find the values (just the values, not the suits) of all cards left blank.

78. POKER—III

Pair

J♣

Four of
a kind

8♥

Straight
flush

Q♣

Straight

9♠

Nothing

A♥

Two pair

Pair

Two
pair

Full
house

Pair

Three
of a
kind

Four of
a kind

Find the values (just the values, not the suits) of all cards left blank.

79. POKER—IV

Find the values (just the values, not the suits) of all cards left blank.

135

80. POKER—V

Find the values (just the values, not the suits) of all cards left blank.

81. POKER—VI

Find the values (just the values, not the suits) of all cards left blank.

137

HINTS

Here are clues to help solve the problems.

1. **Twins.** If a person always lies or always tells the truth, can he call himself a liar?

2. **Twin Statistics.** Imagine there are 100 births, with 3% being twin births. How many people are born?

3. **Place Your Cards.** Place the diamond by following the first clue given in the puzzle. You can now tell what the queen's suit is.

4. **The Professor and His Friend.** Did you notice that each player takes an odd number of matches?

5. **Irregular Circuit.** Why not take the first pass as a new starting point?

6. **Economical Progression.** The three digits are 1, 2, and 6.

7. **Skin and Shoes.** Look at one foot and count the rest.

8. **Up and Down.** The professor had an advantage of 11 steps and is climbing at twice my speed.

9. **What Month — I.** It must be a strange month, right?

10. **What Month — II.** Note that 38 is a very high number for the sum of the first Thursday of the month and of the last Monday of another month. What days could give such a high result?

11. **Eve's Enigma.** The snake tells Eve that today is Saturday and tomorrow is Wednesday. Isn't that odd? On what days of the week can the snake talk like that?

12. **Broken M.** It might be useful to draw three straight lines on a white piece of paper and then draw an M on top of them.

13. **Soccer Scores — I.** How many games were played in the tournament? How many points in total were there in the entire tournament?

14. **Soccer Scores—II.** What were the scores for the games played by the Lions? What were the scores for the Bears?

15-18. **What Time Is It.** Think of a time, say, 3 o'clock. Are the conditions of the problem true for the time you just thought of? In what area of the clock are we closer to the conditions of the puzzle?

19. **Prohibited Connection.** Notice that the number 1 can be connected with five other digits. This does not occur for 2, 3, 4, or 5.

20. **Concentric.** Move the figure. What happens when you rotate the small square?

21. **John Cash.** When John erased the first number, there was a two-digit number left. Think about it. If you remove the number in the tens column, this two-digit number is divided by five.

22. **Russian Roulette.** By the first answer you know that the snuff/salt pair is vertical. Can it be on the right side? Remember that a jar never contains the ingredient shown on the label.

23. **New Race.** Take A as the starting point.

24. **The Calculator Keys.** This puzzle has two solutions. Give it a try.

25. **Nice Discounts.** Buy all the books in just two days.

26. **Enigmatic Fares.** The tickets have consecutive numbers. The sum of the digits of both is 62, an even number. What is the last digit of the first ticket?

27. **Horoscope.** Without doubt, this is a very special date.

28. **Strangers in the Night.** There are exactly four true statements. Only one person is guilty. What does this mean about the "I'm innocent" statements?

29. **Monte Carlo.** Let's say that you start with $100. If you lose and win, what happens to your money?

30. **The Foreigners and the Menu.** Out of the five dishes they order each night, could it be that two of them are the same?

31-35. **Fort Knox Jumping Frogs.** Play with some coins.

36. **The Harem.** Try it. If the door had 3 locks, could the Great Tamerlan's system work?

37. **The Dividing End.** Let's call the ID number ABCDEFGHI. ABCDE can be divided evenly by 5, so we know what E is.

38. **The Island and the Englishmen.** Draw 4 circles that represent the clubs. Connect the clubs to the members.

39. **Logic Apples.** Alonso would not have asked the question if he had eaten 5 or more apples, because nobody could have eaten more than him.

40. **Added Corners.** Place the 8 first. Can it be in a corner?

41. **Rectangles.** Find a simple way to divide the figure.

42. **A Warm Farewell.** Add the number of handshakes and kisses. It comes to a total of 55. If each Porter said good-bye to each Robinson, the number of the Porter family members multiplied by the number of the Robinson family members must equal 55.

43. **Four Minus One is a Crime.** Go from A to B on the map. Try different routes. Count how many blocks you travel every time. Compare it with the suspects' statements.

44. **On The Route Of Marco Polo.** Each sign points to a different village. What can be said of the sum of the distances in each direction?

45. **On the Road.** From one sign to the next the tens' column must change.

46. **Touching Squares.** You'll need more than 10 squares.

47. **Equal Vision.** It can be done with three or four watchmen. Can you do it with more?

48. **Blood and Sand.** Why did the commissioner suspect Begonias? Put yourself in his shoes. You do not know that Begonias inverted the hourglass, but instead you believe that Lincoln Dustin did it when dying.

49. International Summit. Use the table below. B and C speak English. Put an X in rows B and C in the English column. D doesn't speak English. Put an O in the D row in the English column.

	Eng.	Sp.	Fr.	Port.	Ital.
A					
B	X				
C	X				
D	O				
E					

50. Mister Digit Face. Where can 9 go?

51. Digit Tree. With the nine digits we have to make 7 numbers. Two numbers will have two digits each. What is the highest number that could be at the top of the tree?

52. Figures to Cut in Two. Try several times. There is no definite way. It's a matter of eyesight.

53. Segments. The sum of all nine digits is 45.

54. Multiple Towers. Certain levels must have even numbers.

55. Earthlings. The second earthling had one answer in common with the first one and one in common with the third. Is this earthling honest, a liar, or both?

56. The Ant and the Clock. Draw a clock. Draw the path of the ant. Compare distances.

57-59. Hidden Word. Compare the words in column 0 with the others. If one letter appears in the same position in column 0 and also in another, you can cross it out in that column, since you know it will not be in the word in the rectangle.

60-64. Secret Number. When you know that a digit is not in the secret number, cross it out. If you discover that a digit is in the secret number, but don't know where, circle it. When you find its

correct position, mark it with a square. Do this for all lines. Make a list of the digits that are definitely in the secret number, another for those that are not in the secret number, and a third list for those you are not sure about.

65-70. **Dominoes.** Cross out the dominoes that are already placed in the list. Let's imagine that the domino 3-4 has already been placed. Separate every other instance of 3 and 4 together in the table (remember, dominoes only appear once). Then look for pairs of numbers that are together (like 5 and 6, for example) and do the same. As you go from one puzzle to the next, you will think of more strategies.

71. **Hound—I.** If you think of the distances between the marked squares you can place the number 10. Think of where the odd and even numbers go.

72. **Hound—II.** The lower left box is 21.

73. **Hound—III.** The lower left box is 25.

74. **Hound—IV.** The lower left box is 1.

75. **Hound—V.** We have 9 prime numbers. To obtain a symmetric figure, we must have the same quantity of prime numbers on the left as on the right.

If we paint the board like a checkerboard with a black diagonal, we will have 12 white squares and 13 black ones. Where do the prime numbers go?

76-81. **Poker.** The straight combinations are the most useful information for you at first, especially the straight flushes. Four of a kind is also useful. Remember that all straights must have a 10 and a J, and that a four of a kind has four cards of equal value. If for a certain card you have two possible values, consider each value individually until you find the solution.

ANSWERS

1. **Twins**

   I spoke to Peter. If a person always lies or, alternately, always tells the truth, he cannot admit that he is lying (if this person were a liar, he would be telling the truth, and if this person were honest, he would be lying). Therefore, Paul could not have answered my question. Peter could answer about Paul without contradicting himself. What we don't know is who the liar is.

2. **Twin Statistics**

   More than 3% of the population are twins. Out of 100 births, 97 are single and 3 are twins. That's 103 babies in total, six of which are twins, which represents 5.8% of the population.

3. **Place Your Cards**

   From left to right: queen of spades, six of diamonds, and ace of hearts.

4. **The Professor and His Friend**

   Professor Zizoloziz wins. Every player takes an odd number of matches per play. After the first player goes, there will always be an odd number of matches left. After the second player goes, there will always be an even number of matches left. Therefore, the second player is the winner.

5. **Irregular Circuit**

   300 yards from point A. The first passing point can be considered as a new starting point. Therefore, the new passing point will be 150 yards away.

6. **Economical Progression**

   1, 6, 11, 16, 21, 26. Other solutions are also possible.

7. **Skin and Shoes**

   It is enough to look at only one shoe. If, for example, the white man's right shoe is red, the left one has to be black. This means that the black man will have one left red shoe and one right white shoe, and so on.

8. Up and Down

22 steps. While Zizoloziz goes up the entire staircase, I descend the staircase except for 11 steps (7 at the top + 4 at the bottom). Since he goes twice as fast as me, the entire staircase is 2 X 11 steps.

9. What Month—I

February of a leap year. If a month starts and ends with the same day of the week, it must have a complete number of weeks plus one more day. The only possible month is a 29-day February.

10. What Month—II

August. In order to add up to 38, it can only be the highest possible number for the last Monday of a month (31) and the highest for the first Thursday of a month (7). Therefore, both last month and the current month must have 31 days. The only two 31-day months in a row in the same calendar year are July and August.

11. Eve's Enigma

Thursday. The snake is lying, because it says that today is Saturday and tomorrow is Wednesday. Therefore, today is one of the days when the snake lies (Tuesday, Thursday, and Saturday). It cannot be Saturday or else the snake would not be lying in one statement. Nor can it be Tuesday, for the same reason. It can only be Thursday.

12. Broken M

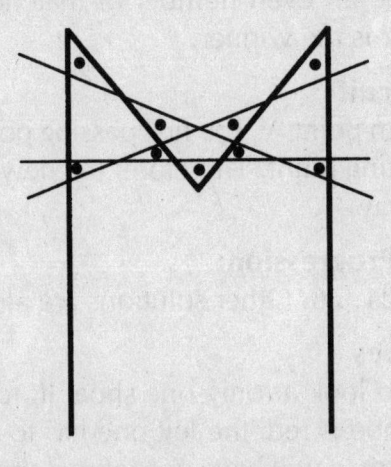

13. **Soccer Scores—I**

The Eagles had 5 points. There were 10 matches in the tournament with a total of 20 point to be won by the teams. The table already has 15 points assigned. Therefore, the remaining 5 points must belong to the Eagles.

14. **Soccer Scores—II**

Lions 0, Tigers 0. Lions 1, Bears 0. Tigers 1, Bears 1. The Lions could only win 3 points by winning one match and tying another. Since they only scored one goal, the results must be 1-0 and 0-0. The Bears tied one and lost the other match. The scores must have been 1-1 and 0-1. Their tied game must have been against the Tigers. So the Lions beat the Bears 1-0, and the Lions tied the Tigers 0-0.

15. **What Time Is It—I**

5:00. From here, the minute hand will take 30 minutes to reach 6, and the hour hand will take an entire hour.

16. **What Time Is It—II**

There are two possible times in this situation: 5:15 (the minute hand takes 15 minutes to read 6 and the hour hand takes 45) and 3:45 (the minute hand takes 45 minutes to reach 6 and the hour hand takes 2 hours and 15 minutes, which is 135 minutes).

17. **What Time Is It—III**

2:12. The hour hand is at the first minute mark after 2, and the minute hand is on the next minute mark.

18. **What Time Is It—IV**

9:48. The minute hand is on 48 minutes and the hour hand is on the next minute mark.

19. **Prohibited Connection** (Diagram next page)

Each middle digit (2, 3, 4, and 5) can only be connected to three others (for example, 2 can only be connected to 4, 5, and 6). There are two circles with four connections. We can only put 1 and 6 in them. Once you insert these, the rest is easy to figure out. Another solution exists where the order of the numbers is switched, so 1 and 6 switch, as do 2 and 5, and 3 and 4.

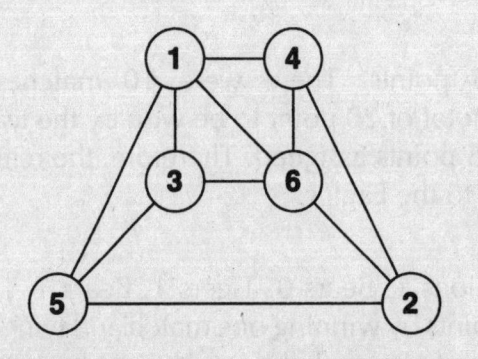

20. Concentric

30 square inches. We turn the small square as shown in the picture. We can see that it is half the size of the big one, as indicated by the dotted lines. These dotted lines divide the large square into 8 triangles, and the small square into 4 triangles.

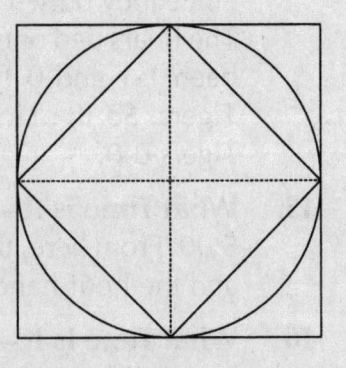

21. John Cash

The reward was 125 dollars. If you erase 1, you have 25 left, which is one-fifth the original amount. If you erase 2, you have 5 left, which is one-fifth of this amount.

To get 125, find a two-digit number in which you can take the first digit off and the result is one-fifth of the number. The only possible number is 25. 25 x 5 = 125.

22. Russian Roulette

The arsenic is in the jar labeled "SUGAR." We know that the snuff is above the salt. They cannot be on the right side, because then the salt would be in the jar labeled "SALT." They cannot be in the center either, because then the second answer would not be true since the coffee and sugar would not be next to each other. Therefore, they are on the left. So the coffee and sugar are in the jars marked "TEA" and "SALT," respectively, leaving arsenic for either the jar marked "ARSENIC" or "SUGAR." Since it's not in the correctly labeled jar, it must be in the jar marked "SUGAR," and the tea is in the jar marked "ARSENIC."

23. New Race

One car goes twice as fast as the other. The first crossing took place at point A. Consider A as a new starting point. Do the same for every crossing point. Since they drove at consistent speeds, the distances from A to B, B to C, and C to A are the same. After point A, one car must have driven twice the distance as the other to reach B at the same time. Therefore, one goes twice as fast as the other.

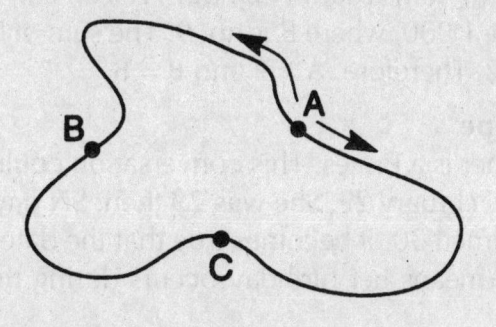

24. The Calculator Keys

There are two possibilities:

    1. Change the 4 with the 5 and the 2 with the 8.
729 - 546 = 183.

    2. Change the 3 with the 9 and the 4 with the 6.
783 - 654 = 129.

25. Nice Discounts

You first buy books for $80 and, the next day, for $70, which represents a discount of $70 x .08 = $5.60. (It will be the same result by inverting the order of the purchases, first the $70 purchase and the next day the $80 one.)

26. Enigmatic Fares

98999 and 99000. The tickets are consecutive in number. If the professor had answered "yes" to the question about the five digits of one ticket adding up to 35, the friend could have not figured out the numbers. There would have been several possibilities (78659 and 78660, 36989 and 36990, etc.), so the professor must have answered that indeed none of the tickets added up to 35.

Both tickets add up to 62 (an even number), which means that the first one must end in a 9. If it ended in only one 9, one ticket would add up to 35. Let's call the first ticket ABCD9 and the second one ABC(D + 1)0. The sum is A + B + C + D + 9 + A + B + C + D + 1 = 62, meaning that A + B + C + D + 9 = 35. If it ended in two 9s, the sum of both tickets would give us an odd number.

Therefore, the ticket must end in three 9s and no more than three, or the sum wouldn't be 62. We can call the tickets AB999 and A(B + 1)000, where B is not 9. The sum of both is 2 X (A + B) + 28 = 62. Therefore, A = 9 and B = 8.

27. Horoscope

The teacher is a Pisces. This conversation could have only taken place on February 29. She was 29 then. Six days later (March 6), having turned 30, it becomes true that the date is one fifth of her age. This means her birthday occurs during the six first days of March.

28. Strangers in the Night

The blonde woman killed Mr. Farnanski. There are only four true statements. Only one person is guilty. Therefore, three of the "I'm innocent" statements are true. Only one more statement can be true, and this must be the one made by the man in the dark suit or by the blond woman. Therefore, "The brunette killed him" and "One of the men killed him" are false statements, so the blonde woman is the killer.

29. Monte Carlo

He lost. Every time that Hystrix wins, his money increases 1.5 times (with 100, he bets $50 and if he wins, he has $150). When he loses, his money is reduced by half. So a win-loss combination results in a loss of one-quarter of his money. The more he plays, the more money he loses, even though he wins the same number of times as he loses.

30. The Foreigners and the Menu

They could have ordered ABCDD their first night (finding out what D is), AEFGG the second night (finding out what G is and what A is, since they had ordered it the previous night, too), and BEHII the third night, (finding out what I, B, and E are). This leaves C, F and H out, and since they had never ordered these dishes twice and each came on a different night, they should know what they are.

31. Fort Knox Jumping Frogs—I

Move 5 onto 2, 3 onto 7, 1 onto 4 and 6 onto 8.

32. Fort Knox Jumping Frogs—II

Move 5 onto 2, 3 onto 7, 4 onto 13, 6 onto 1, 12 onto 9, 11 onto 14, and 10 onto 8.

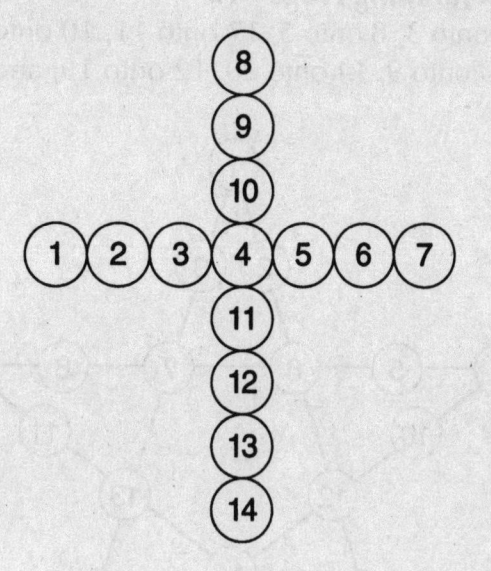

33. Fort Knox Jumping Frogs—III

Move 5 onto 12, 6 onto 4, 10 onto 11, 8 onto 1, 3 onto 2, and 9 onto 7.

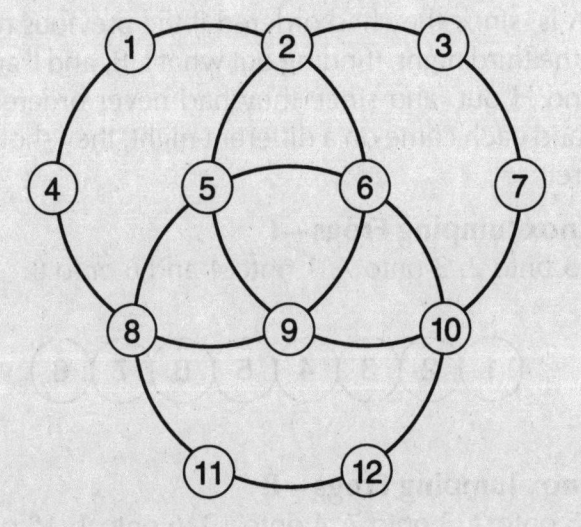

34. Fort Knox Jumping Frogs—IV

Move 16 onto 3, 8 onto 5, 17 onto 11, 10 onto 18, 2 onto 15, 7 onto 1, 13 onto 9, 14 onto 20, 12 onto 19, and 6 onto 4.

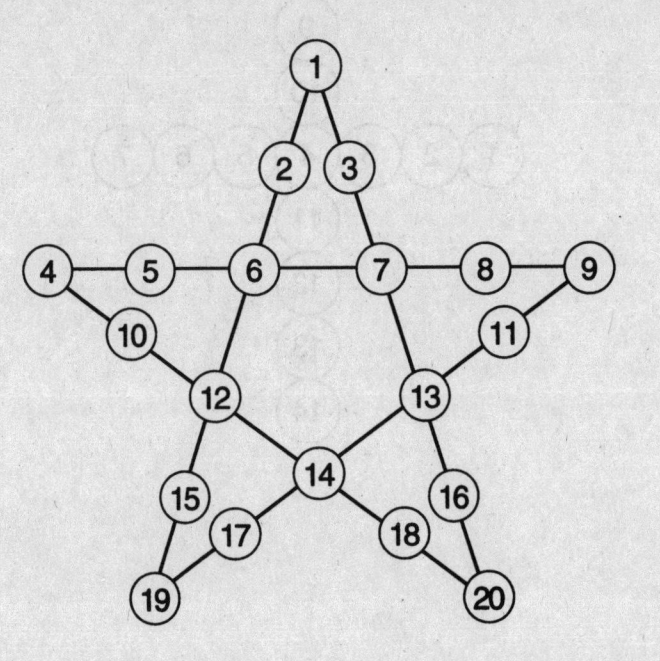

35. Fort Knox Jumping Frogs—V

Move 1 onto 4, 10 onto 7, 11 onto 14, 20 onto 17, 5 onto 3, 6 onto 8, 15 onto 13, 16 onto 18, 2 onto 12, and 19 onto 9.

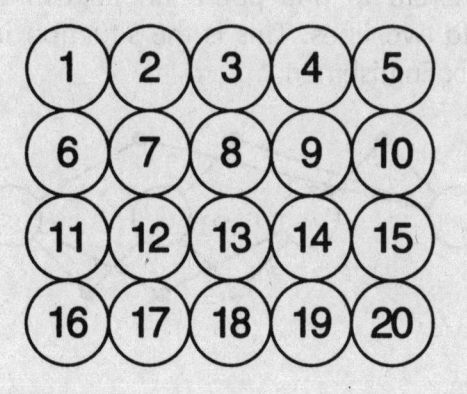

36. The Harem

There were seven locks. Let's name the locks A, B, C, D, E, F, and G. The visier had keys for A, B, C, D, E, and F. One of the slaves had the keys for A, B, C, and G. Another one, for A, D, E, and G. Another, for B, D, F, and G. And the last, for C, E, F, and G. With seven locks, the Great Tamerlan's system works—but not with fewer locks.

37. The Dividing End

The number is 381654729.

If the number is ABCDEFGHI, B, D, F, and H are even numbers. The rest are odd numbers. ABCDE can be divided evenly by 5, thus E = 5.

ABCD can be divided evenly by 4. Therefore, CD can also be divided evenly by 4, and since C is an odd number, D can only be 2 or 6.

ABCDEF can be divided evenly by 6 (by 2 and by 3). Since ABC can be divided by 3, DEF can be also. Consequently, DEF is 258 or 654.

You can deduce the rest from here.

38. The Island and the Englishmen

Six Englishmen. Let's draw four circles representing the clubs. Every two clubs have one member in common, so we draw a line from each circle to one point (an Englishman). Each dot is connected to two lines. This is the situation in the illustration, indicating six Englishmen.

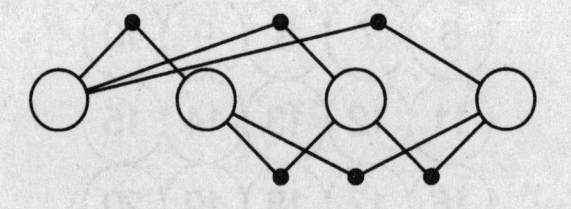

39. Logic Apples

Alonso 1, Bertrand 2, George 3, and Kurt 5.

Alonso could not have eaten 5 or more. Bertrand could not have eaten only one or he would have known that he hadn't eaten more than Alonso. Neither could he have eaten 5 or more. He could have eaten 2, 3, or 4. George figures this out, although he still doesn't know if he ate more than Bertrand. This means that George must have eaten 3 or 4. Kurt can only deduce the other amounts if he ate 5. And the rest, in order to add up to 11, must have eaten 1, 2, and 3.

40. Added Corners

The 8 cannot be in a corner, so we have to put it in a square. The 7 must go in a square too. This makes it easy to figure out the rest.

41.   Rectangles

Both rectangles have the same area, 40 square inches. If you draw the dotted line you will see that the line divides the inclined figure into two equal pairs of triangles on both sides.

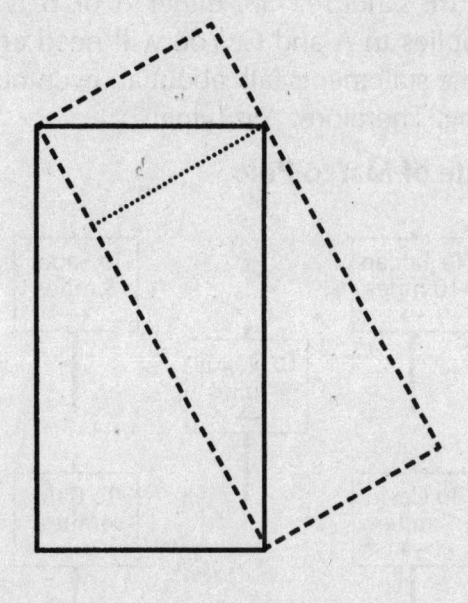

42.   A Warm Farewell

10 men and 6 women. The number of handshakes and kisses adds up to 55. Each Porter said good-bye to each Robinson. If we multiply the number of members of both families, the result should be 55. There are two possibilities: 55 = 11 X 5 (one family with 11 members and the other one with 5), or 55 = 55 X 1 (which could not be possible, since a family is not formed by only one person).

We now analyze the handshakes following the same procedure. There are two possibilities: 21 = 7 X 3 (7 men in one family and 3 in the other) or 21 = 21 X 1 (which could not be possible, because none of these families has so many members, as seen above). Therefore, one family is formed by 7 men and 4 women, and the other by 3 men and 2 women.

43. Four Minus One Is a Crime

The killer is Mr. A. To go from A to B you will always travel an even number of blocks. However, in the statements there is an odd number (13 blocks from A to the corner of the meeting and from there to B's house). So, either A or B is lying. A similar condition applies to A and C. You will need an odd number of blocks, but the statements talk about an even number. So, either A or C is lying. Therefore, A is lying.

44. On the Route of Marco Polo

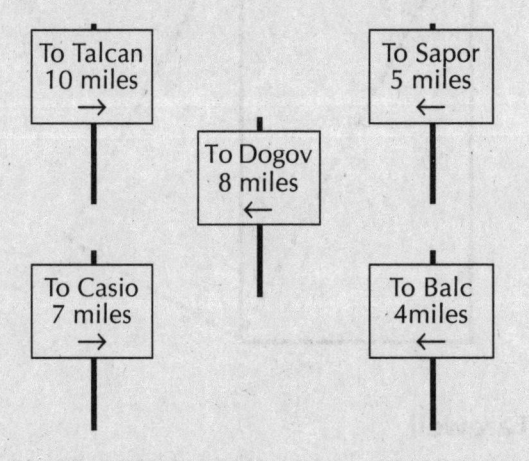

The road signs each point to a different village. The sum of distances in one direction and the sum in the opposite direction must be equal. This can only be achieved with $10 + 7 = 8 + 5 + 4$. Therefore, the signs with 10 and 7 point in one direction and the three others point in the opposite direction.

45. On the Road

10 miles from Philadelphia.

The five signs indicate the following distances: 98, 76, 54, 32, 10.

Other possible sequences include: 90, 81, 72, 63, 54 and 90, 72, 54, 36, 18. However, in all cases the distance from the final sign to Philadelphia is greater.

46. Touching Squares
14 squares.

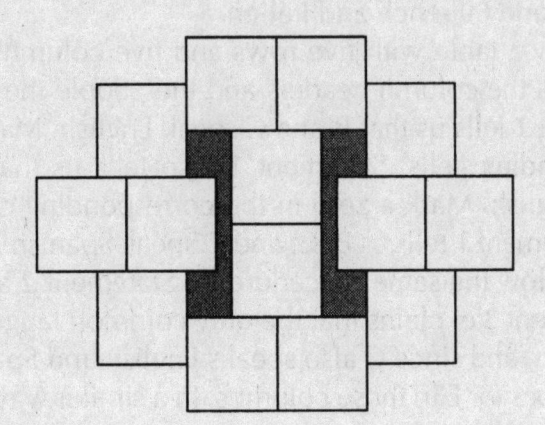

47. Equal Vision
Six watchmen. One way to do it is shown below.

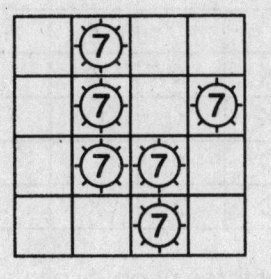

48. Blood and Sand
Lincoln Dustin died at 5:30. At first the commissioner thought that Mr. Dustin had inverted the hourglass at 7:30 (which would account for the 15 hours that the hourglass took to finish). The evident suspect is Begonias, who was at the mansion at the time. Then Begonias told him that he had inverted the hourglass. This made the commissioner think that Mr. Dustin had inverted the hourglass and then Begonias did as well, which means that the time between both inversions counted twice toward the total amount of time. Since the total time was 3 hours, Begonias inverted the hourglass one and a half hours after Mr. Dustin had. If Begonias said that he had inverted it at 7 P.M., this means that Mr. Dustin inverted it at 5:30.

49. International Summit

A-Spanish, French, Portuguese; B-all; C-all except French; D-Spanish; and E-French and Italian.

Draw a table with five rows and five columns, making the languages the column headers and the people the row headers. Statement 1 tells us that B and C speak English. Mark an X in the corresponding cells. Statement 1 also tells us that D does not speak English. Mark a zero in the corresponding cell. Additionally, Statement 1 tells us B, C, and D speak Spanish. Mark it in the table. Follow the same procedure for Statement 2 and Statement 3. Statement 3 explains that the only common language to C and E is Italian, and since C also speaks English and Spanish, we can write zeroes for E in those columns. In a similar way, write a zero for French in C.

This is how the table will look at this point:

	Eng.	Sp.	Fr.	Port.	Ital.
A			X		
B	X	X	X		
C	X	X	O		X
D	O	X			
E	O	O	X		X

We can see that three people speak Spanish and French. Add another X for Spanish, since it is the most common language.

From Statement 6 we need one person who speaks only one language. The only possibility is D. Complete the row with zeroes. From Statement 4 we look for the three people who speak Portuguese. They cannot be C and E, since their common language was Italian. Therefore, two of the Portuguese speakers must be A and B. From Statement 6 we need a person who speaks only two languages. It can only be E, so we write a zero for E in Portuguese. The third person who speaks Portuguese must be C, so we mark an X in the corresponding cell. We look now for the person who speaks three languages, and it can only be A. Fill in the row with zeroes. So, the person who speaks five languages is B. The table is now complete.

50. Mister Digit Face

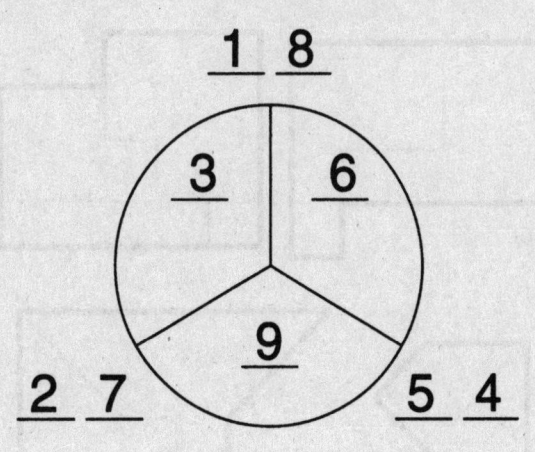

The 9 must be inside the circle, because no product can be 9_ or _9. The 1, 2, and 5 must be outside the circle. From here on you can find the solution. (Other answers can be made by flipping or rotating the circle.)

51. Digit Tree

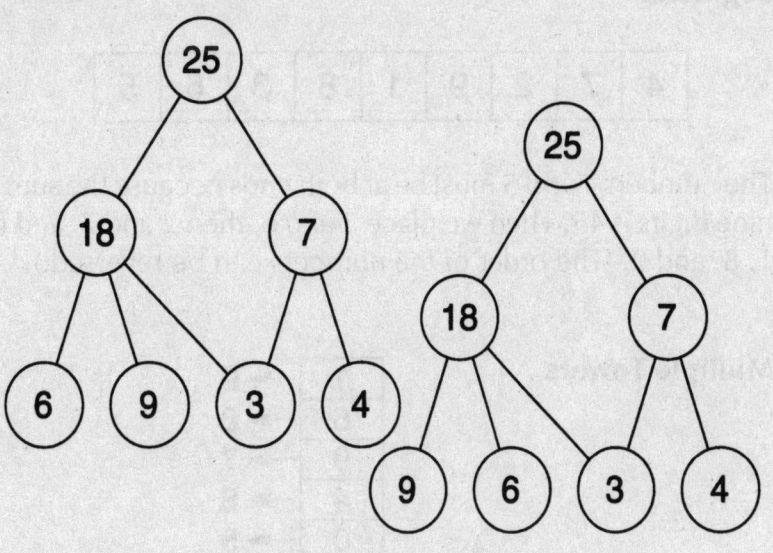

52. Figures to Cut in Two

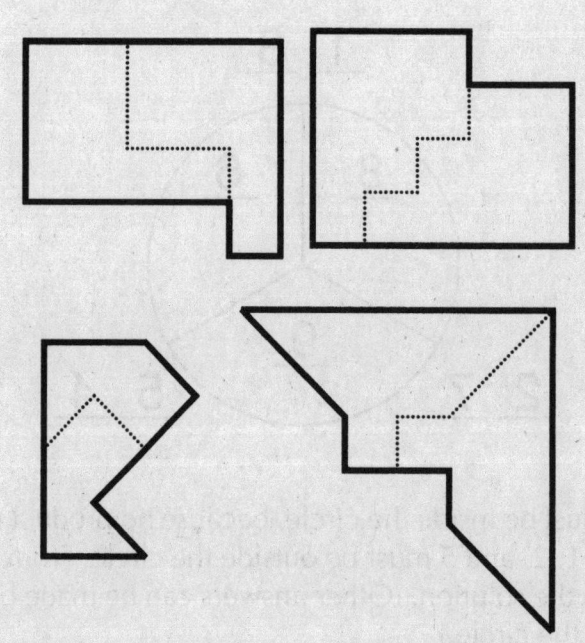

53. Segments

4	7	2	9	1	8	3	6	5

The numbers 4 and 5 must be at both ends because the sum of the nine digits is 45. Then we place 3 and 6, then 2 and 7, and finally 1, 8, and 9. (The order of the numbers can be reversed.)

54. Multiple Towers

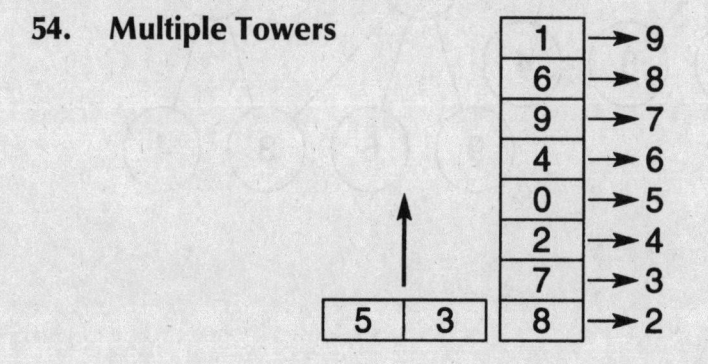

55. Earthlings

Uruguay came in first, Spain second, Zaire third. The second earthling has one answer in common with the first one and one in common with the third one. In which category is the second earthling, then? He cannot always be telling the truth, because he has something in common with a liar, and he cannot always be lying because he has something in common with the honest one. If his first answer were true, then the third one would also be true, and they would be the same as the first and third answers from the honest man. There is no match, however, so this is not the case.

Therefore, the first answer from the man that alternately lies and tells the truth must be a lie. The second is true and the third a lie, so the third man is the honest one, and thus his answers are the results of the soccer championship.

56. The Ant and the Clock

The ant walked 54 minutes. From the first meeting to the second, the minute hand traveled 45 minutes and the ant a distance in minute marks of 105 minutes (45 + a complete 60-minute lap). The illustration below shows the path followed by the ant. The speed ratio is 45/105 = 3/7. From the start to the first meeting, the minute hand traveled a distance X and the ant (30 - X). Using the speed ratio, this would be X/ (30 - X) = 3/7. X=9 minutes. If we add these to the 45 minutes that it took the ant to get to the second meeting, we come to 54 minutes for the ant's trip.

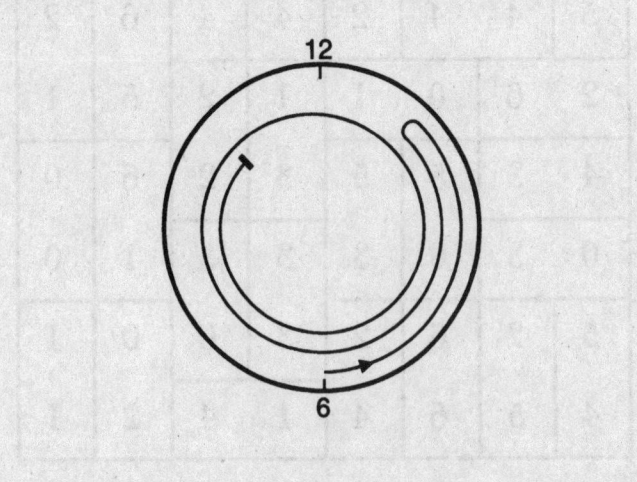

57. Hidden Word—I
VISE

58. Hidden Word—II
SOB

59. Hidden Word—III
PITHY

60. Secret Number—I
3719

61. Secret Number—II
9381

62. Secret Number—III
2754

63. Secret Number—IV
2739

64. Secret Number—V
8327

65. Dominoes Table I

1	5	5	3	0	6	0	6
5	4	4	2	4	4	6	2
2	6	0	1	1	2	5	1
4	3	5	5	3	2	6	0
0	3	0	3	3	3	1	0
5	2	6	2	3	6	0	1
4	5	6	4	1	4	2	1

66. Dominoes Table II

3	1	2	2	6	1	3	4
5	5	3	4	0	5	3	2
2	6	5	1	1	2	0	0
1	1	0	6	0	3	3	0
0	6	4	3	6	5	4	5
3	2	5	4	0	1	6	2
5	4	6	4	2	4	6	1

67. Dominoes Table III

1	0	2	2	3	6	5
1	6	6	4	3	6	5
2	3	5	0	1	4	6
0	4	3	0	2	4	0
3	6	5	4	5	4	1
0	0	5	1	3	1	2
3	6	2	2	5	3	2
1	1	4	0	4	6	5

163

68.   Dominoes Table IV

5	4	2	3	6	3	4
4	6	5	5	0	6	3
4	6	2	3	4	1	2
6	0	6	3	0	4	1
0	6	0	2	3	4	2
5	5	6	1	4	5	3
5	1	3	2	2	1	1
1	5	2	0	1	0	0

69.   Dominoes Table V

4	0	0	1	1	1	0
5	2	3	5	6	5	6
3	5	4	4	3	4	2
2	0	0	5	6	5	3
2	2	1	5	6	0	1
2	4	4	3	2	6	4
5	6	0	3	2	3	6
1	1	3	6	4	1	0

70.   Dominoes Table VI

4	5	1	6	0	5	1
2	5	3	5	3	6	5
6	2	0	4	2	2	6
6	6	2	0	5	3	3
3	1	1	2	3	6	4
4	0	3	1	0	0	4
4	1	2	1	4	5	3
5	1	2	0	0	4	6

71.   Hound—I

20	13	12	11	(10)
19	14	(5)	6	9
18	(15)	4	7	8
17	16	3	2	1

72.   Hound—II

25	26	27	(28)	29	30	31
24	15	(14)	(35)	34	33	32
23	16	13	12	11	8	(7)
22	17	18	1	10	9	6
(21)	20	19	2	3	4	5

73. Hound—III

2	1	9	10	11
3	8	16	15	12
4	7	17	14	13
5	6	18	19	20
25	24	23	22	21

74. Hound—IV

25	16	15	12	11
24	17	14	13	10
23	22	21	20	9
2	3	18	19	8
1	4	5	6	7

75. Hound—V

There are two possible solutions.

⑬	12	⑪	8	⑦
14	15	10	9	6
⑰	16	③	4	⑤
18	1	②	25	24
⑲	20	21	22	㉓

⑰	16	③	4	⑤
18	15	②	1	6
⑲	14	⑬	12	⑦
20	㉓	24	⑪	8
21	22	25	10	9

76. Poker—I

J	10	J	K	A
8	8	8	A	8
Q	10	A	Q	Q
K	10	K	10	K
A	9	9	9	9

77. Poker—II

9	J	10	Q	K
J	J	Q	Q	Q
A	A	A	A	K
8	J	10	8	K
10	9	10	8	K

78. Poker—III

K	J	K	K	K
9	J	8	Q	10
9	8	J	Q	10
A	J	9	Q	10
A	8	8	A	10

79. Poker—IV

10	Q	K	J	A
8	8	K	8	8
J	10	K	Q	A
Q	J	K	10	A
9	9	9	9	A

81. Poker—VI

80. Poker—V

NEARLY IMPOSSIBLE BRAIN BAFFLERS

Are you impossibly smart? If you answer all of these tricky number, word, chess, logic, and spatial puzzles, you must be!

Along the way you'll try to decipher a Top Forty song chart, decide whether you'd rather a tiger chase you or a zebra, and give three boys' names that are anagrams of one another.

Fortunately, the answers are provided—but don't look unless you must!

The **answers** for this section can be found on **pages 225** through **251**.

1

What word, expression, or name is depicted below?

FAREDCE

2

Find a ten-digit number containing each digit once, so that the number formed by the first n digits is divisible by n for each value of n between 1 and 10.

3

When the examination results were published, one college found that all 32 of its students were successful in at least one of the three exams that each of them had taken. Of the students who did not pass Exam One, the number who passed Exam Two was exactly half of the number who passed Exam Three. The number who passed only Exam One was the same as the number who passed only one of the other two exams, and three more than the number who passed Exam One and at least one of the other two exams.

How many students passed more than one exam?

4

If 89 players enter a single elimination tennis tournament, how many matches would it take to decide the winner, excluding byes?

5

Using exactly two 2s and any of the standard mathematical symbols, write down an expression whose value is five.

6

What word, expression, or name is depicted below?

7

This puzzle was devised by Dr. Karl Fabel and published in 1949 in "T.R.D.'s Diamond Jubilee" issue of the *Fairy Chess Review*.

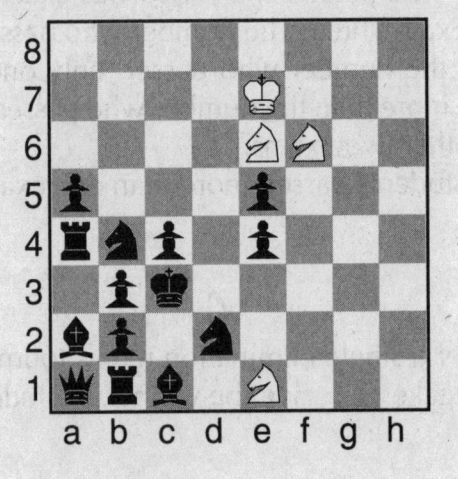

White to play and mate in sixty.

8

What word, expression, or name is depicted below?

T RN

9

Find a ten-digit number whose first digit is the number of ones in the number, whose second digit is the number of twos in the number, whose third digit is the number of threes in the number, and so on up to the tenth digit, which is the number of zeros in the number.

10

Without using a calculator, guess which is bigger: e^π or π^e?

11

A selection of eight cards is dealt with every second card being returned to the bottom of the pack. Thus the top card goes to the table, card two goes to the bottom of the pack, card three goes to the table, card four to the bottom of the pack, and so on. This procedure continues until all the cards are dealt.

The order in which the cards appear on the table is:

A K A K A K A K

How were the cards originally stacked?

12

Gambler A chooses a series of three possible outcomes from successive throws of a die, depending simply on whether the number thrown each time is odd (O) or even (E). Gambler B then chooses a different series of three successive possible outcomes. The die is then thrown as often as necessary until either gambler's chosen series of outcomes occurs.

For example, Gambler A might choose the series EOE and B might choose OEE. If successive throws gave, say, EEOOEOE, then A would win the game after the seventh throw. Had the sixth throw been E rather than O, then B would have won.

A has chosen the series EEE and B, who was thinking of choosing OEE, changes his mind to OOO. Has B reduced his chance of winning the game or is it still the same?

13

What word, expression, or name is depicted below?

R I
D N
S K
HOUSE

14

Find three different two-digit primes where the average of any two is a prime, and the average of all three is a prime.

15

Each letter in the sum below represents a different digit. Can you crack the code and discover the uncoded sum?

```
    T  W  E  L  V  E
    T  W  E  L  V  E
    T  W  E  L  V  E
    T  W  E  L  V  E
+   T  W  E  L  V  E
    N  I  N  E  T  Y
```

16

A spider is in a rectangular warehouse measuring 40 x 10 x 10 meters. The spider is on the 10-by-10-meter wall, 5 meters from the sides and 1 meter above the ground. The proverbial fly is on the opposite wall 5 meters from the sides and 1 meter below the ceiling. What is the shortest route for the spider to walk to the fly?

17

What word, expression, or name is depicted below?

amUous

18

In a game of table tennis, 24 of the 37 points played were won by the player serving, and Smith beat Jones 21-16. Remembering in table tennis that service alternates every five points, who served first?

19

This chess puzzle by C.S. Kipping was published in the *Manchester City News* in 1911.

White to play and mate in three.

20

What word, expression, or name is depicted below?

EVER
EVER
EVER
EVER
EVER

21

In the three envelopes shown, the statements on one of the three are both true, the statements on another are both false, and the remaining envelope has one statement that is true and one that is false.

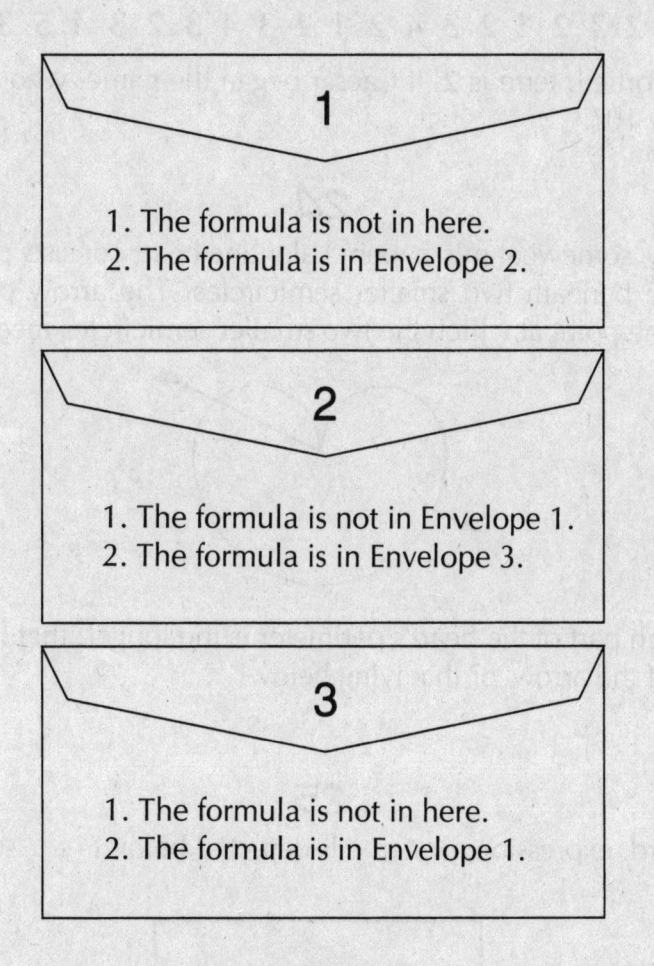

1

1. The formula is not in here.
2. The formula is in Envelope 2.

2

1. The formula is not in Envelope 1.
2. The formula is in Envelope 3.

3

1. The formula is not in here.
2. The formula is in Envelope 1.

Which envelope contains the formula?

22

How can eleven matches make nine, nine matches make ten, and ten matches make five?

23

Caesar and Brutus are playing a game in which each says the next number from a well-known sequence. The first 20 terms of the sequence are given below:

1 2 3 2 1 2 3 4 2 1 2 3 4 3 2 3 4 5 3 2

The fortieth term is 2. If Caesar began the game, who will be the first to say 10?

24

This (okay, somewhat misshapen) Valentine heart consists of one large semicircle beneath two smaller semicircles. The arrow passes right through the point at which the two smaller semicircles meet.

Which part of the heart's perimeter is the longer: that lying above the line of the arrow, or that lying below?

25

What word, expression, or name is depicted below?

**BEND
DRAW
DRAW
DRAW**

26

This week's chart of the top 40 pop songs has just been published. The song that was at number 35 in last week's chart has dropped out, and there is a new entry at number 32. There are also five non-movers, at positions 1, 23, 29, 31 and 37. Of the other 34 songs in the new chart, 18 have moved up and 16 down, but in every instance the number of positions moved, whether up or down, was a factor (greater than one, but possibly equal to the number itself) of the song's position in last week's chart.

The titles of last week's top 40 are shown below. Complete this week's chart.

Last week		This week	Last week		This week
Atomic	1	Atomic	Valentine	21	
Blockbuster	2		What	22	
Classic	3		Xanadu	23	Xanadu
Dizzy	4		YMCA	24	
Emma	5		Zabadak!	25	
Footloose	6		Autumn Almanac	26	
Gaye	7		Angie Baby	27	
Hello	8		Another Day	28	
Intuition	9		Angel Eyes	29	Angel Eyes
Jesamine	10		Angel Fingers	30	
Kayleigh	11		Amateur Hour	31	Amateur Hour
Lamplight	12		Angela Jones	32	New entry
Mickey	13		Ain't Nobody	33	
Night	14		American Pie	34	
Obsession	15		Ant Rap	35	
Perfect	16		Alphabet Street	36	
Question	17		Alternate Title	37	Alternate Title
Reward	18		As Usual	38	
Sandy	19		Adoration Waltz	39	
True	20		Always Yours	40	

27

What word, expression, or name is depicted below?

agb

28

The following was originally a list of five-letter words, but in each case two consecutive letters (though never the first two) have been removed. The 26 missing letters are all different. What was the original list?

```
A   N   T
A   S   S
B   A   Y
C   O   Y
D   I   M
E   E   L
F   A   R
M   A   R
P   I   E
S   E   E
T   I   E
T   O   P
W   I   N
```

29

There is one in a minute and two in a moment, but only one in a million years. What are we talking about?

30

Find nine different integers from 1 to 20 inclusive such that no combination of any three of the nine integers form an arithmetic progression. For example, if two of the integers chosen were 7 and 13, then that would preclude 1, 10, and 19 from being included.

31

This puzzle was composed by Hans August and Dr. Karl Fabel, and was published in 1949 in *Romana de Sah.*

White has just made his seventeenth move. What was Black's ninth move, and what were the moves that followed it?

32

Two travelers set out at the same time to travel opposite ways round a circular railway. Trains start each way every 15 minutes, on the hour, 15 minutes past, half past, and 45 minutes past. Clockwise trains take two hours for the journey, counterclockwise trains take three hours. Including trains seen at the starting point and the ones they are traveling on, how many trains did each traveler see on his journey?

33

The Roman numerals still in use are I = 1, V = 5, X = 10, L = 50, C = 100, D = 500, and M = 1000. Examples of four Roman numbers are VIII = 8, LXXVI = 76, CXXXVI = 136, and MDCCCLXII = 1862.

Today, the Roman numbers IIII, VIIII, and DCCCC are usually abbreviated as IV, IX, and CM, respectively, a numeral to the left of a higher numeral denoting subtraction. Where there is an opportunity, these abbreviations are used in this cross-number, together with CD for CCCC, XC for LXXXX, and XL for XXXX. Thus 1904 would be written as MCMIV and 49 as XLIX. Note that the logical extension of this method of abbreviation, such as IL for 49, for example, was never fully developed and so is not used here. All that is used, where there is an opportunity, are the six usual abbreviations already mentioned.

In the grid below all answers are Roman numerals and, when converted to Arabic (normal) numbers, are palindromes (none starting with zero) of two digits or more. One number occurs twice, the rest are all different.

34

We place in a box 13 white marbles and 15 black. We also have 28 black marbles outside the box.

We remove two marbles from the box. If they have a different color, we put the white one back in the box. If they have the same color, we put a black marble in the box. We continue doing this until only one marble is left in the box. What is its color?

35

What word, expression, or name is depicted below?

at
the
•
of
on

36

A drawer contains a number of red and blue socks. If I pull two out at random, then the chance of them being a red pair is a half and the chance of them being a blue pair is a twelfth. How many socks are in the drawer?

37

A long time ago, you could buy eight hens for a dollar or one sheep for a dollar, and cows were ten dollars each. A farmer buying animals of each type bought a hundred animals for a hundred dollars. What animals did he buy?

38

Are 1997 nickels worth more than 1992 nickels?

39

What word, expression, or name is depicted below?

N

I

P

40

Insert the missing letter:

J ? M A M J J A

41

In a league of four soccer teams, each team played the other three teams. Two points were awarded for a win and one point for a tie. After all six games were played, a final league table was prepared, as shown below:

Team	Won	Tied	Lost	Goals for	Goals against	Points
A	3	0	0	6	1	6
B	1	1	1	2	4	3
C	1	0	2	2	2	2
D	0	1	2	2	5	1

What was the score in each of the six games?

42

Lynsey is a biology student. Her project for this term is measuring the effect of an increase in vitamin C in the diet of 25 laboratory mice. Each mouse will have a different diet supplement of between 1 to 50 units. Fractions of a unit are not possible.

Although the university pays for the mouse food, Lynsey has to buy the vitamin C supplement herself. The first consideration in designing this experiment was therefore to minimize the total number of supplements.

The second consideration was that no mouse should have an exact multiple of another mouse's supplement. Thus, if one mouse was on a supplement of 14 units, then this would preclude supplements of 1, 2, 7, 28, and 42 units.

What supplements should Lynsey use?

43

Find two ten-digit numbers, each containing the digits from 0 to 9 once and once only, with the property that successive pairs of digits, from left to right, are divisible in turn by 2, 3, 4, 5, 6, 7, 8, 9, and 10.

44

What word, expression, or name is depicted below?

STEP
PETS
PETS

45

What are the numbers in the tenth line of the following pyramid?

```
            1
           1 1
          2 1
         1 2 1 1
        1 1 1 2 2 1
       3 1 2 2 1 1
      1 3 1 1 2 2 2 1
     1 1 1 3 2 1 3 2 1 1
    3 1 1 3 1 2 1 1 1 3 1 2 2 1
```

46

What word, expression, or name is depicted below?

READING

47

What digit does each letter represent in the multiplication below, given that no two letters stand for the same digit?

LAGER
x 4
REGAL

48

The order of the clues has been muddled up, but 21-Across is correct.

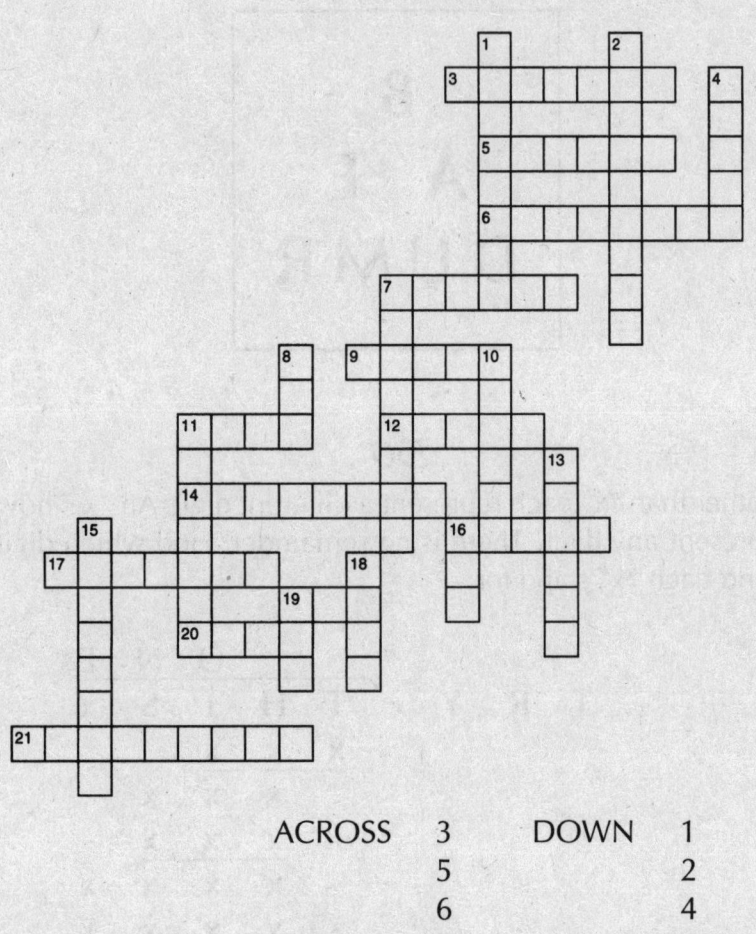

ACROSS	3	DOWN	1
	5		2
	6		4
	7		7
	9		8
	11		10
	12		11
	14		13
	16		15
	17		16
	19		18
	20		19
	21		

49

What word, expression, or name is depicted below?

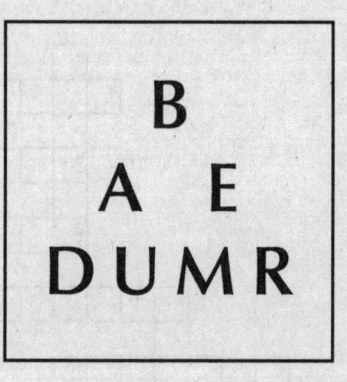

B
A   E
D U M R

50

Letters other than "x" each represent a different digit. An "x," however, may represent any digit. There is no remainder. Find which digits the letters and each "x" stand for:

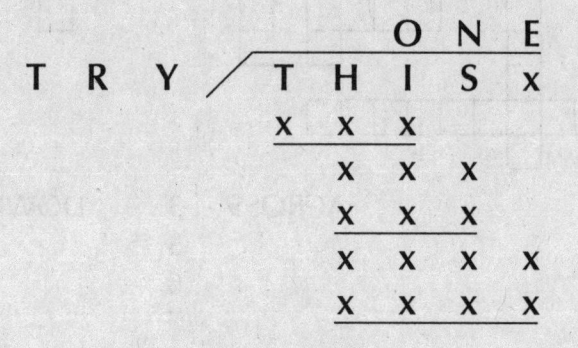

```
                    O N E
T R Y / T H I S x
        x  x  x
           x  x  x
           x  x  x
           x  x  x  x
           x  x  x  x
```

51

The number 6 has factors (not counting itself) of 1, 2, and 3, which add up to 6. The number 28 has the same property, since its factors, 1, 2, 4, 7, and 14, add up to 28. What four-digit number has this property?

52

Between noon and midnight, but not counting these times, how often will the minute hand and hour hand of a clock overlap?

53

What word, expression, or name is depicted below?

54

A set of building blocks contains a number of wooden cubes. The six faces of each cube are painted, each with a single color, in such a way that no two adjacent faces have the same color. Given that only five different colors have been used and that no two of the blocks are identical in their colorings, what is the maximum number of blocks there can be in the set?

55

The Bowls Club has fewer than 100 members. To the nearest whole number, 28% of the members are former committee members, 29% are current committee members, and 42% have never been on the committee. Again to the nearest whole number, 35% of the former committee members are women. What is the total membership of the club?

56

The pars for a nine-hole golf course designed by a mathematician are:

3 3 5 4 4 3 5 5 4

On which very well-known series (as well-known as one, two, three, etc.) are the pars based?

57

This may seem self-contradictory, but find three integers in arithmetic progression (that is, with equal differences, such as 230, 236, and 242) whose product is prime.

58

What is the next term in this series:

1248 1632 6412 8256 ?

59

What word, expression, or name is depicted below?

ONE
T
S

60

The ages of Old and Young total 48. Old is twice as old as Young was when Old was half as old as Young will be when Young is three times as old as Old was when Old was three times as old as Young. How old is Old?

61

Consider a five-by-five version of a chessboard with one player having five queens and the other player three queens. There are no other pieces. Can you place the queens on the board so that neither player's queens can capture one of his or her opponent's queens?

62

ACROSS

1. Starting piece between 3 and 4
3. 2-Down minus a perfect square
5 Three!

DOWN

2. A perfect square
4. 1.5 times 5-Across (or two-thirds of 5-Across)

63

What word, expression, or name is depicted below?

NE14
10S?

64

A full set of dominoes (0-0 to 6-6) has been laid out in a rectangular array. The numbers in the diagram represent the spots on the dominoes, and the puzzle is to identify the position of each domino within the pattern.

12616345
33643254
30603122
05546502
02515001
64344111
22645036

65

At the end of the soccer season, every player had scored a prime number of goals and the average for the eleven players was also a prime number. No player's tally was the same as anyone else's, and neither was it the same as the average.

Given that nobody had scored more than 45 goals, how many goals did each player score?

66

What word, expression, or name is depicted below?

timing

tim   ing

67

Allwyn, Aitkins, and Arthur are to fight a three-way duel. The order in which they shoot will be determined by lot and they will continue to shoot until two are dead. Allwyn never misses, Aitkins is eighty percent accurate, and Arthur, the cleverest of the three, hits his target just half of the time. Who has the best chance of surviving?

68

What word, expression, or name is depicted below?

GR12"AVE

69

Can you subdivide a square measuring eleven by eleven into five rectangles such that the five lengths and five widths of the rectangles are all different and integral? There are two solutions.

70

What are the missing numbers?

31   62   __   25   56   __   19

71

Find three different positive integers whose factorials are each one less than a perfect square, and whose factorials sum to a perfect square.

72

I recently overheard a conversation that went roughly as follows:

Bob: "Here's a problem that might interest you. On my bus this morning there were only three other passengers, all of whom I knew. We discovered that the product of their ages was 2,450, and that the sum was exactly twice your age. How old are they?"

Jim: "Hang on. You haven't given me enough info."

Bob: "Oh, sorry. I forgot to mention that one of the passengers on the bus was someone older than me, and I am—"

Jim: "I know how old you are. And I now know the passengers' ages, too."

How old are Jim, Bob, and each of the three other passengers?

73

This puzzle is based on a theme by W.A. Shinkman, and the mate-in-three was first solved by Sam Loyd. The puzzle below was published in the *Leeds Mercury Supplement* in 1895.

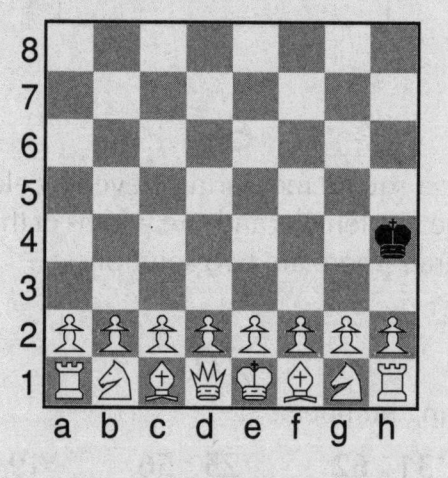

White to play and mate in three.

74

Construct a game that will leave the position shown for Puzzle 73 after Black's sixteenth move.

75

In a game of poker, one of the hands of five cards had the following features:

- There was no card above a 10 (an ace is above a 10 in poker).
- No two cards were of the same value.
- All four suits were represented.
- The total values of the odd and even cards were equal.
- No three cards were in sequence.
- The black cards totaled 10 in value.
- The hearts totaled 14.
- The lowest card was a spade.

What was the hand?

76

What word, expression, or name is depicted below?

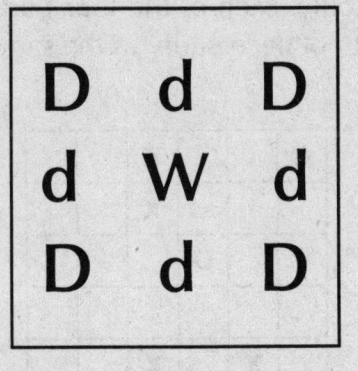

77

"Bookkeeper" has three consecutive double letters. What common two-word phrase, if you remove the space, also has three consecutive double letters?

78

What word, expression, or name is depicted below?

ON
THE THE

79

Divide the following figure into four identical parts, with each part made up of whole squares only. Each of the four parts should also contain one O and one X, but not necessarily in the same relative positions.

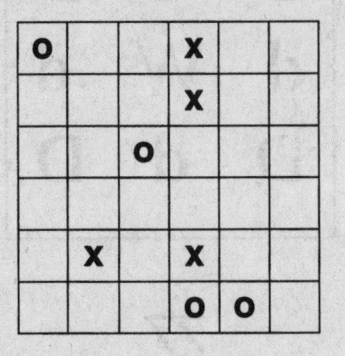

80

Using each of the numbers 1, 5, 6, and 7 once and once only, parentheses as required, and any combination and any number of the following symbols: + - x /

find an expression that equals 21.

81

P and Q are integers that between them contain each of the digits from 0 to 9 once and once only. What is the maximum value of P x Q?

82

What word, expression, or name is depicted below?

COTAXME

83

A total of five triangles can be seen in the diagram on the left.

How many triangles can be found in the diagram on the right?

84

Both my father and my father's grandfather were born in years that can be expressed as $m^n - n^m$, where m and n are both integers. In which years were they born?

85

What word, expression, or name is depicted below?

86

In this long division, each "x" represents a digit. Find which digits each "x" stands for:

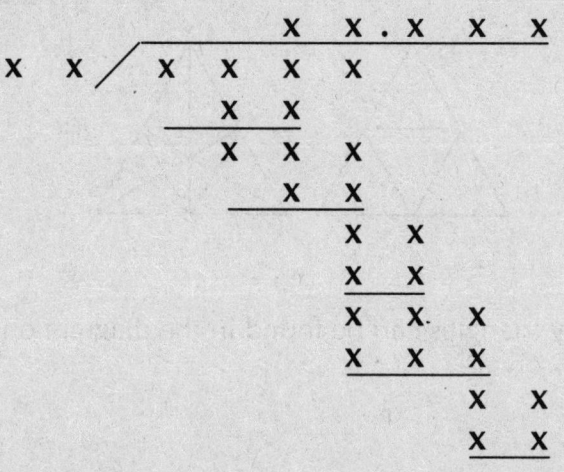

198

87

What are the two missing numbers in the series below?

_ _ 3 3 7 7 2 3 6 5

88

Five soccer teams, United, County, Rovers, Albion, and Thistle, took part in a league tournament. Their colors were white, yellow, green, red, and blue, though not necessarily in that order. No teams were tied in the standings at the end of the tournament. From the following information, determine for each team its captain, colors, and position in which it finished in the league.

- Rovers did not win the league, but finished higher than fourth.
- Neither Albion nor the team in green finished in the top three.
- Evans captained the team in yellow.
- Cooke's team finished ahead of County, which was captained by Dixon.
- Allen's team finished second and Boyle's team finished last.
- The team in white finished lower than both United and the team in blue, but above Evans's team.
- Albion was not the green team and United was not the blue team.

89

What word, expression, or name is depicted below?

Symphon

90

Arrange the digits from 1 to 9 in a 3 x 3 array in such a way that the sum of a number's immediate neighbors (including diagonals) is a multiple of that number.

9	5	1
6	7	2
4	3	8

The example shows an unsatisfactory attempt. The three numbers bordering 9 add to 18, which is a multiple of 9 as required, and the numbers bordering 1, 2, 3, 4, and 5 also meet the condition specified. The numbers bordering 6, 7, and 8, however, do not meet the required condition.

91

What word, expression, or name is depicted below?

GIVE GET

GIVE GET

GIVE GET

GIVE GET

92

What is the minimum difference between two integers that between them contain each digit once?

93

This position was created by F. Amelung and published in *Düna Zeitung* in 1897. It is a puzzle that has since defeated many good chess players, and one cannot but wonder whether it has ever occurred naturally in a real game. If it did, and you were White and about to play, how could you force mate in two?

White to play and mate in two.

94

Arrange the digits from one to nine in a three by three square in such a way that each of the three-digit numbers reading across, and the three-digit number on the diagonal from top left to bottom right, are all perfect squares.

95

The digital root of a number is obtained by summing its digits and then repeating this process until the answer is a single digit. For example, the digital root of 8777 is 2.

Noting that any number divisible by nine has a digital root of nine, what is the digital root of $(9^{6130} + 2)^{4875}$?

96

If six equilateral triangles, each of one unit in area, are joined edge-to-edge, twelve different shapes each of six units in area can be constructed as shown below:

    Show that it is impossible to form any six of these shapes into a six-by-six-by-six equilateral triangle of 36 units in area.

97

Which of the following poker hands is stronger?

    A♣ A♦ A♥ K♣ K♥ or A♣ A♥ K♣ K♦ K♠

Think about it!

98

Continue the sequence:

       202 122 232 425 262 728 ? ?

99

What word, expression, or name is depicted below?

VAD ERS

100

The third and fourth powers of this integer contain between them exactly one of each digit. What is the integer?

101

Complete the eight words using each letter of the alphabet once and once only.

```
_ A _ E R I _ _
_ U _ _ _ E
_ I _ _ E
_ _ L _ E R
_ I _ _
_ _ A P
B R _ _ _ N
_ O L _ _ A _
```

102

Is the tenth root of ten
A little bit more
Than the root of the square
Of the sixth root of four?

103

This cross-number uses Roman numbers only and yes, every clue is the same! If you are struggling to remember what the Roman numerals are and how they are used, a description is given in Puzzle 33 on page 182.

ACROSS

1 A perfect square
7 A perfect square
8 A perfect square
9 A perfect square
10 A perfect square
13 A perfect square
14 A perfect square
17 A perfect square
19 A perfect square
20 A perfect square

DOWN

1 A perfect square
2 A perfect square
3 A perfect square
4 A perfect square
5 A perfect square
6 A perfect square
7 A perfect square
11 A perfect square
12 A perfect square
15 A perfect square
16 A perfect square
18 A perfect square
19 A perfect square

104

What word, expression, or name is depicted below?

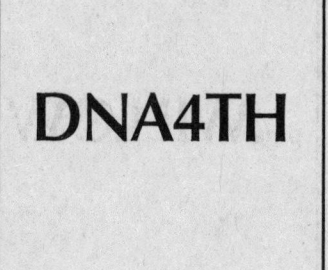

DNA4TH

105

A horizontal line from the top of the inside edge of a bicycle tire to the two outside edges of the tire measures 24 centimeters as shown in the side view below:

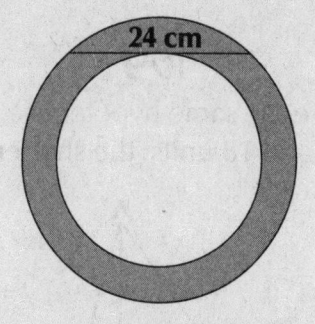

24 cm

What is the area of the bicycle tire visible from this view?

106

In the following line, cross out six letters so that the remaining letters, without altering their sequence, will spell a familiar English word.

B S A I N X L E A T N T E A R S

107

What word, expression, or name is depicted below?

ping WILLOW

108

What is the smallest integer that can be expressed as the sum of two squares in three different ways? The answer is less than 500.

109

Two right triangles share the same hypotenuse AB. The shorter sides of the first triangle are 13 and 18 units; the shorter sides of the second are 7 and 20 units.

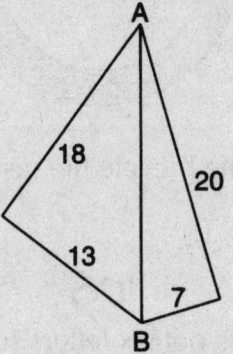

Clearly we are not measuring in base ten. What base is being used, and how long is the hypotenuse?

110

A ball with a diameter of 40 centimeters is lying on the ground, tight against a wall:

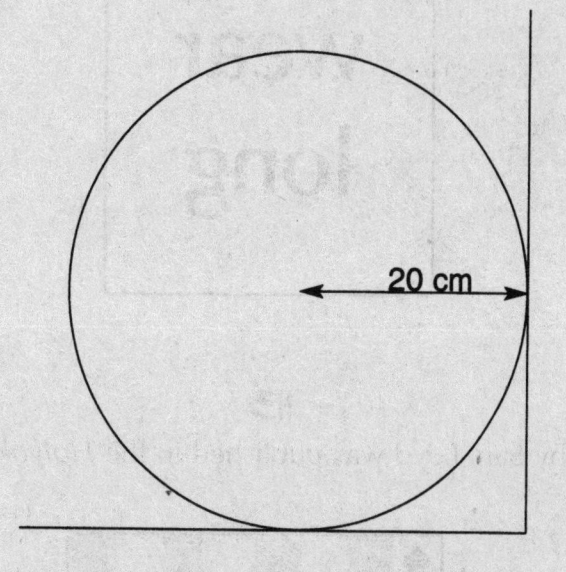

20 cm

Can a ball with a diameter of seven centimeters pass through the gap between the ball, ground, and wall?

111

What word, expression, or name is depicted below?

1D 5U
2R 6L
3A 7A
4C

112

What word, expression, or name is depicted below?

wear
long

113

This puzzle by Sam Loyd was published in the *Holyoke Transcript* in 1876.

White to play and mate in three.

114

"Strength" is an eight-letter word with only one vowel. What's an eight-letter word with five vowels in a row?

115

The array of blocks shown below spells the word "PUZZLE." Could we be looking at six different views of the same block, or is one or more of the views inconsistent with the others?

116

What word, expression, or name is depicted below?

117

Using the digits one to nine in ascending order and no more than three standard arithmetical signs, find an expression that equals 100. An example that uses six standard arithmetical signs is shown below:

$$1 + (2 \times 3) - 4 + (56 \div 7) + 89 = 100$$

118

If the integers that contain each digit once were arranged in ascending order, which would be the millionth? (Numbers can't start with 0.)

119

A Christmas decoration comprises a symmetrical four-pointed star supported by three threads. The decoration hangs in the center of a small circular window:

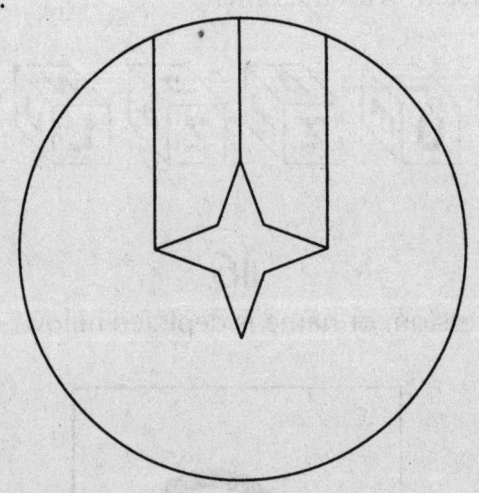

  The central thread is 4 centimeters long, and the outer two are each 6 centimeters long. What is the width of the star?

120

What word, expression, or name is depicted below?

79 S 34 A 92
F 185 E 376
7 T 27 Y 12

121

One for the children: Would you rather a tiger chased you or a zebra?

122

In the expression below, do the three letters represent three different digits?

$$(ANNE)_{base\ 8} - (ANNE)_{base\ 5} = (ANNE)_{base\ 7}$$

123

Eric the Halibut is swimming to the right. Move three sticks (and his eye, smile, and bubbles) so that he is swimming to the left.

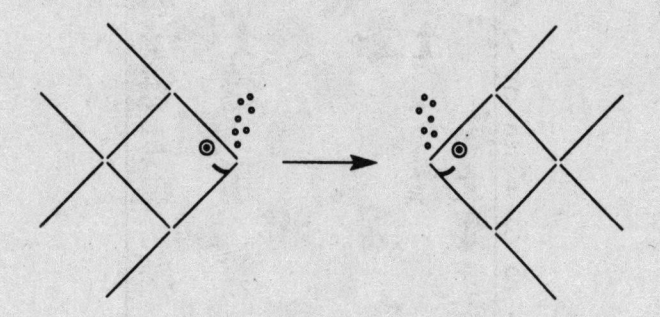

124

What word, expression, or name is depicted below?

```
        R
        O
        D
      ROADS
        D
        S
```

125

Losers' Chess is a fun game that often turns in a surprise result. To play it, ignore checks and checkmates, for the object is either to lose all of one's men, king included, or be stalemated (unable to play a move). Players must capture an opponent's man if they can, but where there is a choice, can choose which. All other rules are the same as for ordinary chess.

   Puzzles in Losers' Chess are rare, and ones with an unusual twist like the one below even rarer. This one, by T.R. Dawson, was first published in 1925 in *Das Wochenschach*. In the first analysis it looks like Black can force White to stalemate him, but White, who is playing up the board, can play and win by forcing Black to cause the stalemate. How?

White to play and win (Losers' Chess rules).

126

 A ladder 5 meters long leans against a wall. A box measuring 1 x 1 x 1 meters just fits in the gap. If the base of the ladder is nearer to the wall than the top of the ladder is to the ground, how far is the base of the ladder from the wall?

127

No answer begins with a zero.

1	2	3	4	5	6	7
8			9			
10				11		12
13		14			15	
16	17		18	19		
20				21		
22					23	

ACROSS

1 See 3-Down
3 A multiple of 3
8 3 x 17-Down
9 2 x 15-Down
10 See 14-Down
11 See 6-Down
13 2 x 4-Down
16 Not 3-Down
18 See 5-Down
20 2 x 2-Down
21 Not 6-Down
22 See 1-Down
23 Same as 20-Down

DOWN

1 2 x 22-Across
2 See 20-Across
3 2 x 1-Across
4 See 13-Across
5 2 x 18-Across
6 3 x 11-Across
7 Same as 23-Across
12 2 x 3-Across
14 2 x 10-Across + 4
15 See 9-Across
17 See 8-Across
19 Square of 23-Across
20 See 23-Across

128

What number, when spelled out, has no repeated letters and has each of the vowels (not including Y) once?

129

What word, expression, or name is depicted below?

130

Shown below are six numbered pool balls arranged in a triangular pattern such that each number in the pattern is equal to the difference between the two numbers above:

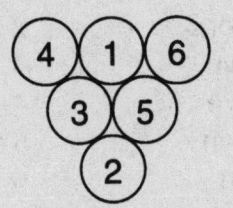

Find a similar triangular pattern for fifteen pool balls numbered 1 to 15.

131

What is the next term in this series?

100 121 144 202 244 400 ____

132

What are the next two letters in the following series and why?

W A T N T L I T F S __ __

133

The diagram shows a regular pentagram:

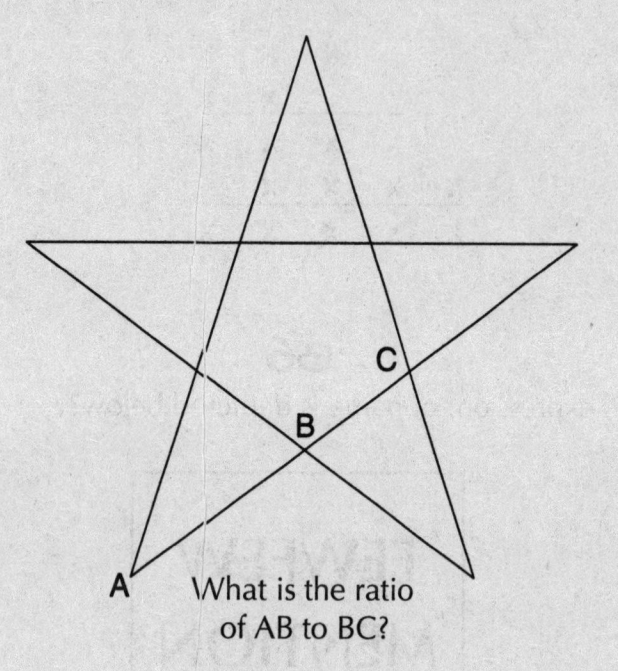

What is the ratio
of AB to BC?

134

If B is two A,
C three A plus B,
And A is "eleven eleven,"
Is B to the C
Plus C to the B
Divisible by seven?

"Eleven eleven,"
So you won't be confused,
Has nothing to do with odd bases.
It's simply ten thou
That's multiplied by
One ninth to four decimal places.

135

Reconstruct the following multiplication, using the digits 2, 3, 5, and 7 only.

```
        x  x  x
           x  x
     x  x  x  x
  x  x  x  x
  x  x  x  x  x
```

136

What word, expression, or name is depicted below?

FEWFEW

MENTION

MENTION

137

Find a three-digit number containing three different digits where the first digit plus the number formed by the second and third digits, the first digit multiplied by the number formed by the second and third digits, and the sum of the three digits are all perfect squares.

138

Which three boys' names are anagrams of one another?

139

Five checks by White in four moves (including a double check) followed by a checkmate to solve a puzzle that is more than 500 years old! It was first published by Lucena in 1496.

White to play and mate in five.

140

Two equal squares, ABCD and DEFG, have the vertex D in common. The angle between the two squares is 60°:

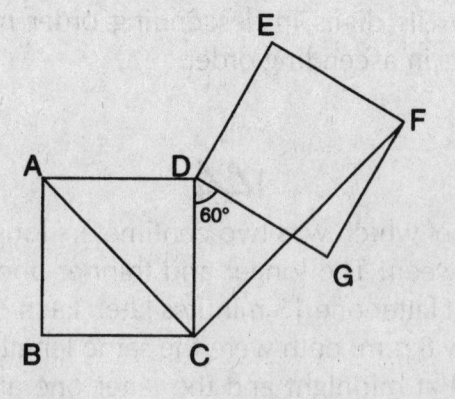

What is the angle ACF?

217

141

Heather left her hotel room between 7 and 8 p.m. and glanced at her watch. When she next looked at her watch it appeared as if the hour and minute hands had changed places. In fact, it was now between 10 and 11 p.m. Exactly how long ago had she left her room?

142

What word, expression, or name is depicted below?

143

Find a four-digit number, with four different digits, that is equal to the number formed by its digits in descending order minus the number formed by its digits in ascending order.

144

Two candles, one of which was two centimeters longer than the other, were lit for Halloween. The longer and thinner one was lit at 4 p.m. and the shorter but fatter one 15 minutes later. Each candle burned at a steady rate, and by 8 p.m. both were the same length. The thinner one finally burned out at midnight and the fatter one an hour later. How long was each candle originally?

145

What word, expression, or name is depicted below?

house
PRAIRIE

146

The following eight numbers can be grouped into four pairs such that the higher of each pair divided by the lower is a number (to an average of five decimal places) of particular mathematical significance.

113 323 355 408 577 610 878 987

What are the four pairs?

147

The following relationships hold among the ages of the members of a family of four. All ages are integral.

The mother is three times as old as the daughter was when the father was the same age as the mother is now. When the daughter reaches half the age the mother is now, the son will be half as old as the father was when the mother was twice the age the daughter is now. When the father reaches twice the age the mother was when the daughter was the same age as the son is now, the daughter will be four times as old as the son is now. Given that one of their ages is a perfect square, what are the four ages?

148

What word, expression, or name is depicted below?

LE
VEL

149

Find a three-by-three magic square in which the following properties
are true:
- The sum of each row, column, and long diagonal is 111.
- Each cell has a number with no factors other than one and itself.
- Each cell is different.
    As a hint, you should start by figuring out the center square.

150

Twice eight are ten of us, and ten but three.
Three of us are five. What can we be?
If this is not enough, I'll tell you more.
Twelve of us are six, and nine but four.

151

In the expression below, each letter represents a different digit:

$$A^5 + B^5 + C^5 + D^5 + E^5 = ABCDE$$

What is ABCDE?

152

This self-mate in four was first published by William Shinkman in the *Chess Player's Chronicle* in 1883.

In a fit of kindness, White decides she wants Black to win and offers her resignation. Black turns down White's offer by announcing that he thinks the game should be played to the finish.

White then forced Black to mate her in four moves anyway.
How does White do this?

153

What word, expression, or name is depicted below?

B
O
B

154

A professor asked four students how long each of them had been studying. One of the students replied: "We have all been studying a whole number of years, the sum of our years of studying is equal to the number of years you have been teaching, and the product of our years of studying is 180."

"I'm sorry," replied the professor after some thought, "but that doesn't give me enough information."

"Yes, you're right," agreed another of the students. "But if we told you whether any of us were into double figures in our years of study, then you could answer your question."

How long had each of the four been studying?

155

In how many different ways can the 16 chess pieces be arranged on one side of a chess board for the start of a game of chess? For example, the two rooks can switch places, and any two of the eight pawns can be swapped and still leave the standard starting position.

156

What word, expression, or name is depicted below?

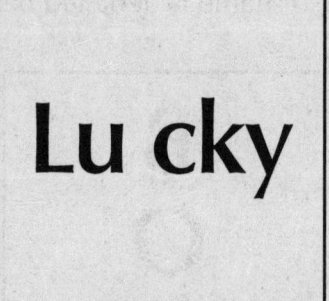

157

In an athletics contest between the army, the navy, and the air force, each team entered three athletes in a particular race. The winning athlete scored eight points, the runner-up seven, third place six, and so on down to none for last place.

Once the race was run, the judges needed a photograph to separate the first two army men to finish. A member of the navy's team finished last. When the points were totaled, all three teams were found to have the same score.

Find by team the order in which the nine athletes finished.

158

What word, expression, or name is depicted below?

159

In a game of chess, Black has agreed to mirror White's first three moves. White promptly mates Black on the fourth move. What were White's moves?

160

Which day of the week has an anagram?

161

What word, expression, or name is depicted below?

OWHER

162

What word, expression, or name is depicted below?

HOROBOD

224

ANSWERS

1. Red in the face.

2. 3,816,547,290.

3. Eleven students passed Exam One only, three passed Exam Two only, and eight passed Exam Three only. Thus ten students passed more than one exam.

4. Each match will eliminate one player, so starting with 89 players will require 88 matches to decide the winner.

5. $\overline{.2^{-2}}$, which shows that two twos can make five!

6. Square meal.

7. For White to win, he has to force one of Black's knights to move. Then, provided White's king is safe from unwanted checks and White has not moved his own knights, White wins with Ne4 mate or Nd5 mate. The actual winning move will depend upon which knight Black eventually moves.

   Black can delay moving a knight for 59 moves! His tactic is to shunt the rook at a4 to and fro to a3 whenever he can. Accordingly, and taking the route that avoids unwanted checks, White uses his king to inhibit the shunting rook by timing the arrival of his king at b5 to follow Black's move Ra3.

   On the first four occasions White does this, Black keeps his rook out of danger by moving a pawn on the e file. On the fifth occasion, to avoid moving a knight and to save his rook, Black must block his rook in with a5-a4. On his next move Black is compelled to move a knight and expose himself to an instant checkmate. Note that if Black moves his pawns before he has to, then the mate is simply speeded up. With Black's best defense as shown below, White will mate in sixty.

   White's first move can be either Ke8 or Kd6. White's king then proceeds d7, c8, b7, b6, b5. By moving to d7 via e8 or d6, the White king arrives at b5 after an even number of moves. Thus, for move six, Black's shunting rook will be at a3 and Black must

move a pawn, lose his rook, or be mated. To defer mate as long as possible, Black must play e4-e3.

   After Black's move, e4-e3, White moves his king away from b5 and Black can continue with the shunting of his rook. White must now move his king back to b5 in an odd number of moves in order to catch the shunting rook at a3. The shortest route for White to achieve this that avoids unwanted checks is b6, b7, c8, d7, e8, f8, f7, e8, d7, c8, b7, b6, b5, and this he repeats four times. On moves 19, 32, and 45 Black takes a break from shunting his rook and moves a pawn on the e file. On move 58, however, Black can do no better than to block his rook in with a5-a4. White then plays a waiting move, Kb6. If Black moves the knight at b4, then White mates with Nd5, and if Black moves the knight at d2, then White mates with Ne4. This gives White mate in sixty.

8. No U-Turn.

9. 2,100,010,006.

10. e^π is greater than π^e. To two decimal places, e^π = 23.14 and π^e = 22.46.

11. AAKAAKKK.

12. By changing his mind, B reduced his chance of winning the game.

   The only way in which EEE can appear before OEE is if the first three throws of the die are EEE. Otherwise the sequence EEE must be preceded by an O. The probability of the first three throws being E is $(1/2)^3$, so if B chooses OEE when A has chosen EEE, then B wins with probability $7/8$. If B chooses OOO in response to A's choice of EEE, then B's chance of winning is $1/2$.

13. Round of drinks on the house.

14. 11, 47, and 71.

15. TWELVE = 130760, THIRTY = 194215, and NINETY = 848015.

16. A straight-line route that takes the spider one meter down to the floor, forty meters across the floor, and nine meters up toward the ceiling is fifty meters.

   Two quicker straight-line routes, found by drawing straight

lines from the spider to the fly on a flattened plan of the warehouse, are shown below. The first of these sees the spider heading up the side wall, crossing the ceiling, and finally approaching the fly from above. The distance of this route is $\overline{(14^2 + 46^2)}$ = 48.08 meters.

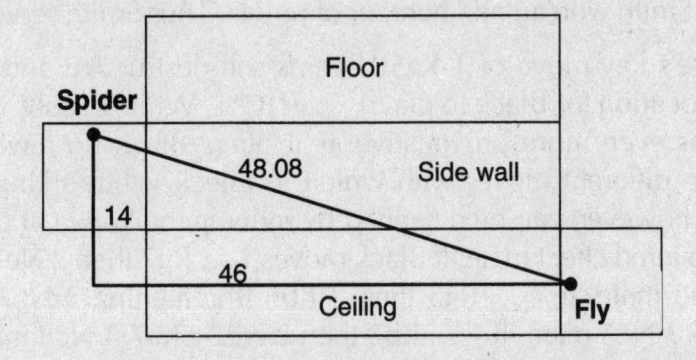

The third straight-line route sees the spider heading diagonally to the floor, then up the side wall, crossing the corner of the ceiling and again at the end approaching the fly from above. The distance of this route is $\overline{(20^2 + 42^2)}$ = 46.52 meters.

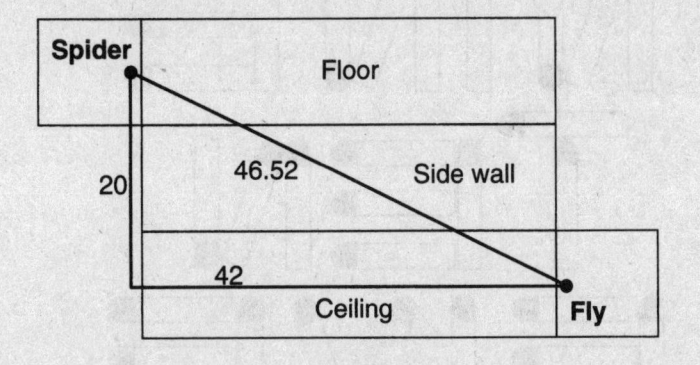

The shortest route is 46.52 meters.

17. Ambiguous.

18. Smith served first. One possible proof is as follows:
Whoever served first would have served on 20 of the points played and the other player would have served on 17 of them. Suppose the first player won x of the points on which he served

and y of the points served by his opponent. The total number of points lost by the player who served them is then 20 − x + y. This must equal 13, since we are told that 24 of the 37 points were won by the player serving. Thus x = 7 + y, and the first server won (7 + y) + y = 7 + 2y points in total. This is an odd number, and only Smith won an odd number of points. Thus Smith served first.

19. White's key move of 1 Ka5!! seems self-destructive and a sure provocation for Black to play 1 … e1(Q)+. White's reply, 2 Kb6!, seems even more provocative as it offers Black no fewer than seven different moves with which to check White's king. Each one, however, can be defended by moving the knight at c6 for a discovered checkmate. If Black moves 1 … Rg7 then 2 Ne7+ Ka7 3 Nc8 mate. If 1 … Rg5 then 2 Kb6 (threatening 3 Ne7 mate) Rxd5 3 Nc7 mate. If 1 … Kb7 then 2 Ne7+ Ka7 3 Nc8 mate.

20. Forever and ever.

21. The envelope with the formula is Envelope 3.

22.

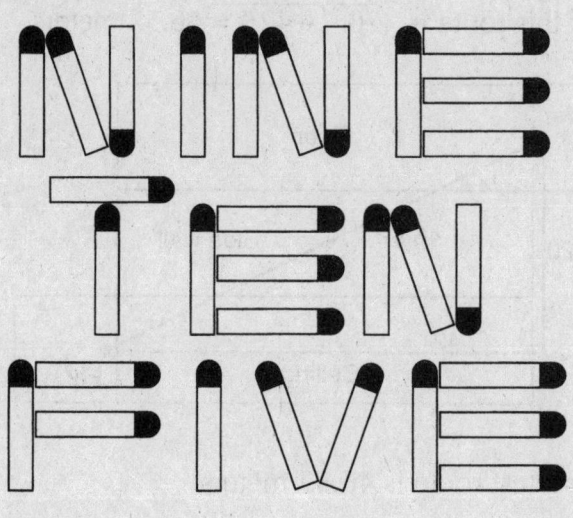

23. The series is generated by counting the number of characters in the corresponding Roman numeral, as shown for the first ten numbers below:

I	II	III	IV	V	VI	VII	VIII	IX	X
1	2	3	2	1	2	3	4	2	1

The first term to equal 10 is the 288th in the series: CCLXXXVIII. Thus the answer to the question is Brutus.

24. To show the perimeter is divided into two equal lengths, whatever the angle of the arrow, let the diameter of each of the smaller semicircles (and thus the radius of the large semicircle) be d and let the arrow lie at an angle of a radians to the horizontal.

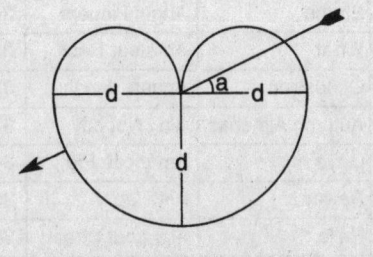

The perimeter length lying above the horizontal line is $^d/_2 + ^d/_2 = d$, which is the perimeter length lying below the horizontal line. Therefore, to prove the heart's perimeter is divided into two equal lengths, we need to show that the part of the perimeter above the horizontal line and below the arrow is equal in length to the part of the perimeter that is below the horizontal line and above the arrow.

Begin by letting C be the center of the smaller semicircle on the right as shown below:

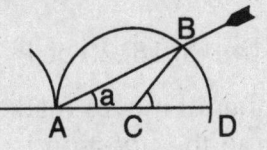

Since triangle ABC is isosceles, angle BCD is 2a radians. Thus the length of arc BD is $^{2a}/_2$ multiplied by the perimeter of the small circle = $^{2a}/_2$ x d = ad. This is also the length of the arc of the big semicircle that is below the horizontal line and above the arrow and so the result is proven.

25. Bend over backwards.

26. The new chart is shown below:

Last week		This week	Last week		This week
Atomic	1	Atomic	Valentine	21	Another Day
Blockbuster	2	Dizzy	What	22	Kayleigh
Classic	3	Footloose	Xanadu	23	Xanadu
Dizzy	4	Blockbuster	YMCA	24	Angie Baby
Emma	5	Jesamine	Zabadak!	25	True
Footloose	6	Classic	Autumn Almanac	26	Mickey
Gaye	7	Night	Angie Baby	27	YMCA
Hello	8	Perfect	Another Day	28	Valentine
Intuition	9	Lamplight	Angel Eyes	29	Angel Eyes
Jesamine	10	Emma	Angel Fingers	30	Ain't Nobody
Kayleigh	11	What	Amateur Hour	31	Amateur Hour
Lamplight	12	Obsession	Angela Jones	32	New entry
Mickey	13	Autumn Almanac	Ain't Nobody	33	Angel Fingers
Night	14	Gaye	American Pie	34	Question
Obsession	15	Reward	Ant Rap	35	Always Yours
Perfect	16	Hello	Alphabet Street	36	Adoration Waltz
Question	17	American Pie	Alternate Title	37	Alternate Title
Reward	18	Intuition	As Usual	38	Sandy
Sandy	19	As Usual	Adoration Waltz	39	Alphabet Street
True	20	Zabadak!	Always Yours	40	Angela Jones

27. Mixed bag.

28. ANGST, ABYSS, BAWDY, COMFY, DENIM, EXPEL, FAKIR, MA-JOR, PIQUE, SERVE, TITLE, TOPAZ, WINCH.

29. The letter m.

30. Either 1, 2, 6, 7, 9, 14, 15, 18, 20 or 1, 3, 6, 7, 12, 14, 15, 19, 20.

31. The minimum number of moves made by White's men to reach the position shown in the question is: queen's pawn 5 (d4, c5, b6, a7, a8), new queen 2 (a7, e3), queen's knight 2 (c3, a4), king's knight 2 (f3, h2), king's rook 2 (h3, g3), king's rook's pawn 2 (h3, g4), king's bishop's pawn 1 (f3) and king 1 (f2). These total seventeen and therefore account for all of White's moves. Noting that Black's missing pieces were captured on c5, b6, a7, and g4, the

position after White's ninth move would have been as follows:

The game from White's ninth move was:

9	...	Ra7
10	bxa7	h4
11	a8(Q)	h3
12	Qa7	h2
13	Qe3	h1(B)
14	Nh2	a5
15	f3	a4
16	Kf2	a3
17	Na4	

32. The traveler on the fast train sees all the trains going the other way around that left up to three hours ago or that will leave in the next two hours. The traveler on the slow train sees all the trains going the other way around that left up to two hours ago or that will leave in the next three hours. In five hours, including the beginning and end, 21 trains depart in each direction. Including the train they are traveling on, each traveler therefore sees 22 trains on his journey.

231

33.

C	D	X	C	I	V	D
L	V	M	M	I	I	L
X	C	I	X	D	X	V
I	C	C	X	C	I	I
C	M	L	X	X	I	X
X	I	I	I	V	C	I
I	X	X	X	I	I	I

34. White marbles can only be removed from the box in pairs. There is an odd number of white marbles to start with, so the last marble in the box will be white.

35. At the point of no return.

36. There are 120 socks in the drawer: 85 red ones and 35 blue ones.

37. 72 hens, 21 sheep, 7 cows.

38. The value of 1,997 nickels is $99.85, 25 cents more than 1,992 nickels (worth $99.60).

39. Pin-up.

40. F for February. The letters are the initials of the first eight months of the year.

41. A won against B, C, and D with scores of 3-0, 1-0, and 2-1 respectively. B won against C with a score of 1-0 and tied D with a score of 1-1. C won against D with a score of 2-0.

42. Supplements to use are: 8, 12, 14, 17, 18, 19, 20, 21, 22, 23, 25, 26, 27, 29, 30, 31, 33, 35, 37, 39, 41, 43, 45, 47, and 49. They total 711.

43. The solutions are 1,872,549,630 and 7,812,549,630, and are derived as follows: The 5 and 0 can be placed immediately. The sixth digit must be 4. The seventh digit is odd (since every second digit must be even), so it must be 9. The eighth digit must be 6. The ninth digit must be 3. The third digit is 1 or 7, so the fourth digit must be 2. The first three digits are therefore 187 or 781.

44. One step forward, two steps back.

45. Each line describes the line above. For example, since line five is 1 1 1 2 2 1, which can be expressed as three ones (3 1), two twos (2 2), and one one (1 1), line six is 3 1 2 2 1 1.

     The tenth line in the pyramid is therefore:
1 3 2 1 1 3 1 1 1 2 3 1 1 3 1 1 2 2 1 1.

46. Reading between the lines.

47. The solution to LAGER x 4 = REGAL is 21978 x 4 = 87912.

48. This puzzle is designed so that most people who see it will think (falsely) that the clues are missing. They think this because they mistake the clues for clue numbers. The clues cannot be the clue numbers, however, since for one thing the puzzle would not then be solvable, and for another the order of the clues has been muddled up.

    Clue 21-Across is 21 or, in letters, TWENTY-ONE. Once this clue has been solved the rest are easy. The answer is shown below:

```
                        N           S
                  S I X T E E N     S
                        N     V     E
                  E L E V E N       V
                        T     N     E
                  E I G H T E E N
                        E     E
              T W E N T Y       N
                  H
          O   E I G H T
          N   R       W
      F I V E     T H R E E
      I       E       L     E
      F O U R T E E N V     L
  N   T           N   S E V E N
  S I X T E E N     F   I     V
      N       T W O   U   X   E
      E   N I N E     R       N
      E           N   R
      T
  T W E N T Y O N E
      N
```

49. Bermuda Triangle.

50.

```
              1   4   5
    2  0  6 / 2  9  8  7  0
              2  0  6
              9  2  7
              8  2  4
              1  0  3  0
              1  0  3  0
```

51. 8128.

52. Not eleven, but ten times. The times are between 1 and 2, between 2 and 3, and so on, ending with once between 10 and 11. It does not happen between 11 and 12, since it happens at exactly 12 (noon and midnight). The question excludes noon and midnight, so that occurrence doesn't count.

53. Just between you and me.

54. The maximum number of blocks in the set is 55.

If only three of the five available colors are used, then opposite faces of a block must have the same color. Thus by symmetry there is only one way in which a block can be painted with any three given colors, and there are 10 different ways in which three colors can be chosen.

If four colors are used, then two pairs of opposite faces must each have the same color. By symmetry it doesn't matter which way around the other two faces are painted. The colors for the two pairs of matching faces can be chosen in ten different ways, and the other two colors can then be chosen in three ways, giving an overall total of 30 combinations.

Finally, if five colors are used then just one pair of opposite faces will have the same color. The remaining four colors can be arranged in three different ways, so using five colors gives a total of 5 x 3 = 15 combinations.

The maximum number of blocks in the set is therefore 10 + 30 + 15 = 55.

55. There are 26 former committee members (9 of whom are women), 27 committee members, and 39 members who have never been on the committee. This gives a total of 92 members.

56. The series consists of the numbers of letters in the words one, two, three, etc.

57. The integers are −3, −1, and 1.

58. Regrouping the series as 1, 2, 4, 8, 16, 32, 64, 128, and 256, the next two terms in this series are 512 and 1024. The answer to the question is 5121.

59. Cornerstone.

60. Old is 30 and Young is 18.

61.

62. Five across is three factorial, which is SIX. Two-thirds of SIX or, more precisely, the last two-thirds of the word SIX, is IX, which is the Roman numeral nine.

63. Anyone for tennis?

64. Noting that the 3-5 domino can be placed uniquely, the full array is soon easily figured out, as shown.

1	2	6	1	6	3	4	5
3	3	6	4	3	2	5	4
3	0	6	0	3	1	2	2
0	5	5	4	6	5	0	2
0	2	5	1	5	0	0	1
6	4	3	4	4	1	1	1
2	2	6	4	5	0	3	6

65. The players scored 5, 7, 11, 13, 17, 19, 29, 31, 37, 41, and 43 goals. Their average was 23 goals.

66. Split-¡second timing.

67. Despite being the worst shot of the three, Arthur has the best chance of surviving, with a probability of .5222. Allwyn has the next best chance of surviving at .3 and Aitkins the least chance at .1778.

Arthur's tactic will be to aim to miss if the other two are alive. This is because the other two, if they get the choice, will fire at each other rather than Arthur. This will leave Arthur with the first shot at the survivor. The reason that Allwyn would choose to fire at Aitkins rather than Arthur is that he would rather have Arthur shooting at him with a 50% hit rate than Aitkins with an 80% success rate. The decision for Aitkins to fire at Allwyn rather than Arthur, if he gets the choice, is because for Aitkins to fire successfully at Arthur would be to sign his own death warrant.

68. One foot in the grave.

69. The two possible ways of dividing the square are shown below:

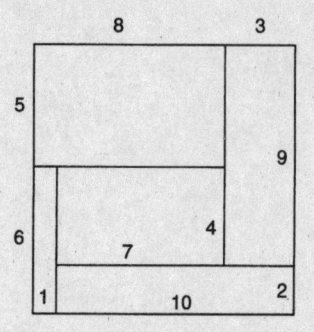 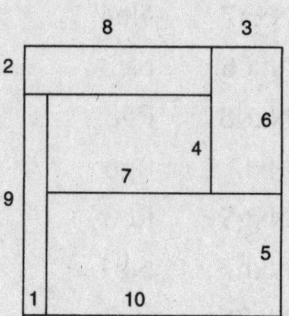

70. 93 and 87. When the digits in each number of the sequence are reversed, the sequence is the multiples of 13; that is, 13, 26, 39, 52, 65, 78, and 91.

71. $4! + 5! + 7! = 24 + 120 + 5040 = (5^2 - 1) + (11^2 - 1) + (71^2 - 1) = 72^2$.

72. By factorizing 2,450 and then compiling a list of the age groups with the desired product, it is found that only two have the same sum, namely 64. Thus Jim is 32, and the three passengers are either 50, 7, and 7 or 49, 10, and 5.

When he was told there was someone older than Bob on the bus, Jim was able to determine the passengers' ages. Obviously Bob cannot be older than 49, and if he were younger than this then both groups would still have been acceptable. Thus, knowing Bob was 49, Jim was able to determine the three passengers were aged 50, 7, and 7.

73. Mate in three can be forced only by 1 d4.

If 1 … Kh5 then 2 Qd3 Kg4 (or Kh4) 3 Qh3 mate.

If 1 … Kg4 then 2 e4+ Kh4 3 g3 mate.

74. This is H.E. Dudeney's solution:

1	Nc3	d5
2	Nxd5	Nc6
3	Nxe7	g5

4	Nxc8	Nf6
5	Nxa7	Ne4
6	Nxc6	Nc3
7	Nxd8	Rg8
8	Nxf7	Rg6
9	Nxg5	Re6
10	Nxh7	Nb1
11	Nxf8	Ra3
12	Nxe6	b5
13	Nxc7+	Kf7
14	Nxb5	Kg6
15	Nxa3	Kh5
16	Nxb1	Kh4

75. ♠2, ♥9, ♥5, ♦4, ♣8.

76. West Indies.

77. Sweet tooth.

78. On the double.

79.

80. $6 / (1 - \frac{5}{7}) = 21.$

81. 96,420 x 87,531 = 8,439,739,020.

82. Income tax.

83. The diagram contains 47 triangles in total, as below:

1 triangle of full size   6 triangles of $\frac{1}{2}$ size

3 triangles of $\frac{1}{3}$ size   10 triangles of $\frac{1}{4}$ size

6 triangles of $\frac{1}{6}$ size   12 triangles of $\frac{1}{8}$ size

3 triangles of $\frac{1}{12}$ size   6 triangles of $\frac{1}{24}$ size

84. My father was born in 1927 (2^{11} - 11^2), and his grandfather in 1844 (3^7 - 7^3).

85. Receding hairline.

86.

```
                6 6 . 3 7 5
      16 / 1 0 6 2
            9 6
            1 0 2
              9 6
                6 0
                4 8
                1 2 0
                1 1 2
                    8 0
                    8 0
```

87. Four and three. The numbers are the numbers of letters in the words of the question.

88.

Position	Team	Captain	Color
1	United	Cooke	Red
2	Rovers	Allen	Blue
3	County	Dixon	White
4	Albion	Evans	Yellow
5	Thistle	Boyle	Green

89. Unfinished Symphony.

90. Other than rotations and reflections there is only one solution. The best way to start is with the central number, which must be a factor of 45, the sum of all nine numbers.

5	1	4
6	3	8
2	7	9

91. Forgive and forget.

92. $50,123 - 49,876 = 247$.

93. If this position had occurred in a real game, then Black's last move must have been g7-g5. Therefore, White can force mate in two with **1** hxg6 e.p. Kh5 **2** Rxh7 mate.

94.

3	6	1
5	2	9
7	8	4

95. Digital Root $(9^{6130} + 2)^{4875}$

= Digital Root $(2^{4875} + 9 \times (\text{large number}))$

= Digital Root $(8^{1625} + 9)$

= Digital Root ((9 − 1)^{1625} + 9)

= Digital Root ((9 x (large number) − 1) + 9)

= Digital Root (9 − 1 + 9)

= 8

96. To prove this, color the large triangle of 36 units in area as shown, giving 21 light and 15 dark unit triangles.

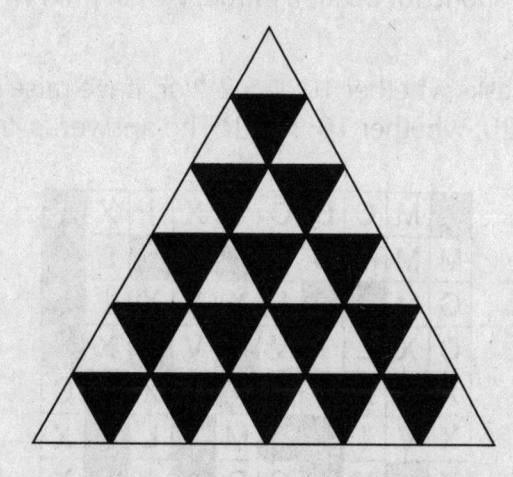

If the twelve available shapes are colored in a similar manner, ten are found to have an equal number of light and dark unit triangles. In the remaining two cases, there are four light and two dark (or vice versa). However, to tile the shape above requires at least three pieces where the difference between the numbers of light and dark triangles is two. Since there are only two such pieces, no solution is possible.

97. The two hands clearly cannot occur in the same deal, so we compare the number of hands that beat these two. They are both beaten by the same number of four-of-a-kinds, but the first hand is beaten by 32 straight flushes, the second by 31. Hence the full house with the three kings is the stronger hand.

98. Regrouping the sequence as 20, 21, 22, 23, 24, 25, 26, 27, 28, it is obvious the next three terms in this more normal format are 29, 30, and 31. Using the question's format, the required answer is 293 and 031.

99. Space Invaders.

100. 18, since $18^3 = 5,832$ and $18^4 = 104,976$.

101. Maverick, subtle (or bustle), pique, golfer, jinx, wrap, brazen, and holiday.

102. The verse asks whether $10^{1/10} > 2^{1/3}$ or, if we raise each side to the power of 30, whether $10^3 > 2^{10}$? The answer is "no."

103.

104. Back and forth.

105. Let the radii of the larger and smaller circles be R and r respectively. The desired area is then $R^2 - r^2 = (R^2 - r^2)$.

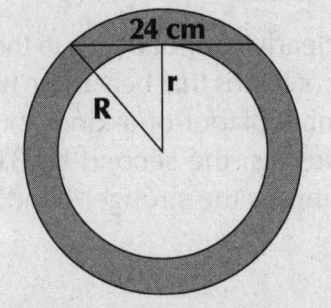

24 cm

Using the Pythagorean theorem, it can be seen that $R^2 - r^2 = (^{24}/_2)^2 = 144$, so the desired area is $144 = 452.4$ sq. cm.

106. By crossing out "SIX LETTERS," we are left with the word "BA-NANA."

107. Weeping willow.

108. $325 = 1^2 + 18^2 = 6^2 + 17^2 = 10^2 + 15^2$.

109. The base n of the measurements can be found using the Pythagorean theorem, which gives the following decimal equation: $7^2 + (2n)^2 = (n + 3)^2 + (n + 8)^2$, from which n = 12. Thus the base being used in the question is 12, and using this base, the hypotenuse measures 21. In base ten the sides are 7, 24, and 25, and 15, 20, and 25.

110. Let the radius of the largest ball that will fit in the gap be r, and let the distance from the corner to the center of the smaller ball be y.

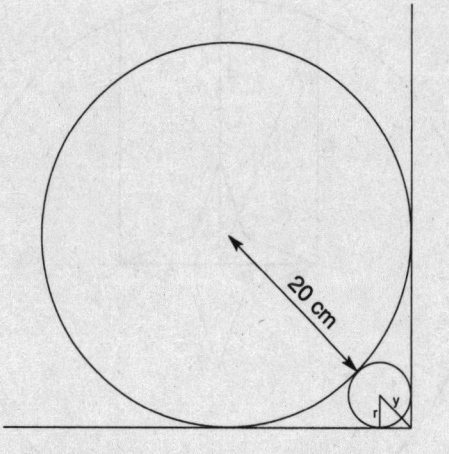

The distance from the corner to the center of the big ball is $20 + r + y = \overline{(20^2 + 20^2)}$, so $r + y = \overline{800} - 20 = 8.28$ cm. Since $y = \overline{(r^2 + r^2)}$, $2r^2 = (8.28 - r)^2$, from which $r^2 + 16.57r - 68.63 = 0$ and r = 3.43 cm. This means that the largest ball that can fit in the gap has diameter 2 x 3.43 = 6.86 cm, so the answer to the original question is no.

111. Count Dracula.

112. Long underwear.

113. **1** bxa8(N) Kxg2 **2** Nb6 any **3** a8(B or Q) mate. Note that White's second move prevents **2** … Bxa7.

114. Queueing.

115. At least two blocks are featured. The first five views are all consistent with each other, but the sixth is not. The "Z" on the upper face would have to be a "U" (with its base at the edge adjoining the face with the "E") for this block to match the others.

116. See-through blouse.

117. $123 - 45 - 67 + 89 = 100$.

118. 3,782,915,460.

119. Let the width of the star be 2a, and construct a line from the center of the star (and circle) to where one of the two outer threads meets the circle.

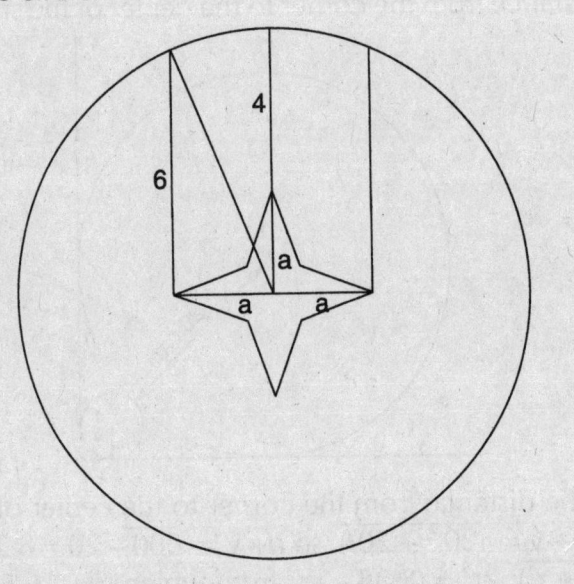

Clearly, the radius of the circle is 4 + a. The diagonal line is a radius, but it is also the hypotenuse of a right-angled triangle with sides of length 6 and a. Thus by the Pythagorean theorem we have $6^2 + a^2 = (4 + a)^2$, so a equals 2.5 cm and the width of the star is 5 cm.

120. Safety in numbers.

121. I would not want a tiger to chase me or a zebra to chase me. Given the choice, I'd rather a tiger chased a zebra, not me.

122. Rewriting each ANNE in base ten, we have:

$A(8^3 - 5^3 - 7^3) + N(8^2 + 8 - 5^2 - 5 - 7^2 - 7) + E(1 - 1 - 1) = 0$

That is, $44A - 14N - E = 0$. Noting that A, N, and E are all digits of a number written in base five, so A, N, and E are all less than five, A = 1, N = 3, and E = 2 is the unique solution. Thus the three letters do represent three different digits.

123.

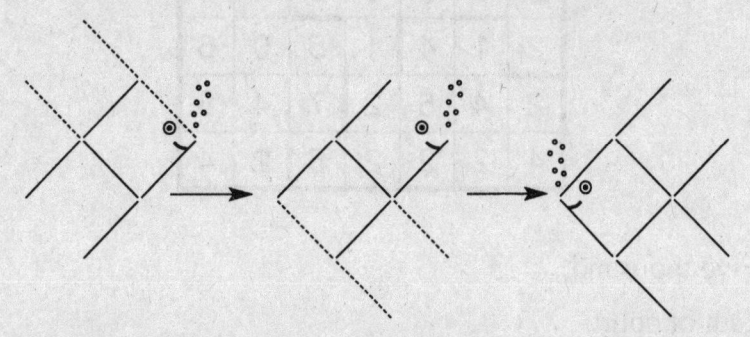

124. Crossroads.

125. Black's last move was a7-a5. It could not have been a6-a5 since a pawn at a6 would have had to capture White's pawn. Neither could it have been b6xa5 since this would imply, given the position of Black's other pawns, that Black had made nine captures (which is impossible since White still has eight pieces on the board). Thus White plays **1** bxa6 e.p.

White wins by being stalemated as follows: **1** ... bxa6 **2** b5 axb5 **3** f5 any, and White is stalemated.

126. In the diagram below, the two smaller triangles are similar, which means the ratio of their sides is constant and more particularly, that $^y/_1 = ^1/_x$.

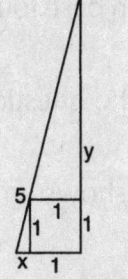

By the Pythagorean theorem
$(x + 1)^2 + (y + 1)^2 = (x + 1)^2 + (^1/_x + 1)^2 = 25$ so
$x^4 + 2x^3 + 2x^2 + 2x + 1 = 25x^2$ from which
$(x^2 + x + 1)^2 = 26x^2$ so
$x^2 + (1 - \overline{26})x + 1 = 0$ and x = 0.2605 meters.

The base of the ladder is 1.2605 meters from the wall.

127.

8	1	1	2	3	4	2
4	2	6	8	0	8	4
4	2	2	4	1	6	2
5	6	8	0	2	4	4
2	1	4	1	5	0	6
2	4	5	2	7	4	8
4	2	2	2	6	2	4

128. Five thousand.

129. Out of court.

130.

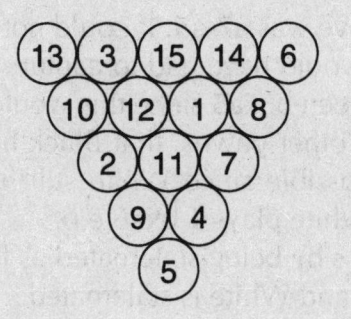

131. The terms in the series are one hundred in base ten, one hundred in base nine, one hundred in base eight, …, one hundred in base five. The next term in the series is one hundred in base four, which is 1210.

132. The letters are the first letters of the words in the question. Thus the next two letters are A and W.

133. Construct another regular five-pointed star as shown in the diagram. Since both are regular stars, $^{AB}/_{BC} = {}^{AD}/_{DB}$.

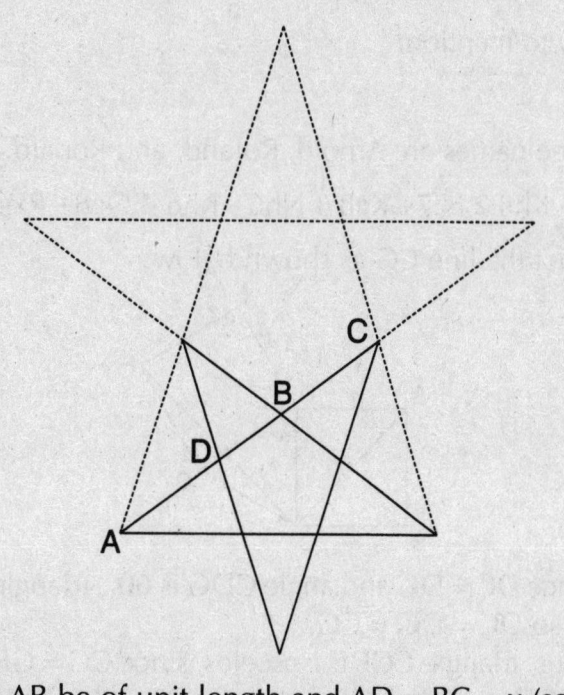

Let AB be of unit length and AD = BC = x (so DB = 1 – x). Then: $^{AB}/_{BC} = {}^{AD}/_{DB}$ so $^1/_x = {}^x/_{(1-x)}$.

So $x^2 + x - 1 = 0$, $x = -\frac{1}{2} + \frac{1}{2}\sqrt{5} = 0.618034$, and the ratio of AB to BC is the reciprocal of 0.618034, which is 1.618034.

134. The values of A, B, and C are 1111, 2222, and 5555, respectively, and the question is whether $B^C + C^B$ is divisible by seven.

$$B^C + C^B = (B^C + C^B) + (4^C - 4^B) - (4^C - 4^B)$$
$$= (B^C + 4^C) + (C^B - 4^B) - 4^B(64^A - 1^A)$$

Since C is odd, $(B^C + 4^C)$ is divisible by $(B + 4)$, which is divisible by seven. $(C^B - 4^B)$ is divisible by $(C - 4)$, which is divisible by seven. Lastly, $4^B(64^A - 1^A)$ is divisible by $(64 - 1)$, which is divisible by seven. Thus $B^C + C^B$ is divisible by seven.

135.

		7	7	5
			3	3
	2	3	2	5
2	3	2	5	
2	5	5	7	5

136. Too few to mention.

137. 916.

138. The three names are Arnold, Roland, and Ronald.

139. **1** Qe6+ Kh8 **2** Nf7+ Kg8 **3** Nh6+ Kh8 **4** Qg8+ Rxg8 **5** Nf7 mate.

140. Construct the line CG as shown below:

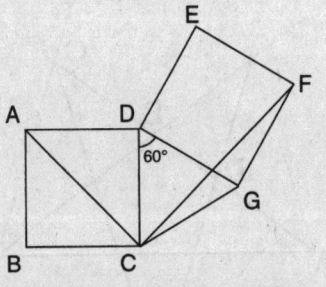

Since DC = DG and angle CDG is 60°, triangle CDG is equilateral, so DC = DG = CG.

Thus, triangle CGF is isosceles, since CG = GF. Angle CGF is angle CGD + angle DGF, which is 60° + 90°, or 150°. So angles GCF and GFC are both 15°.

Since angle DCG is 60° and angle GCF is 15°, angle FCD is 45°. Angle ACD is also 45°, so angle ACF is the sum of FCD and ACD, or 45° + 45°, which is 90°.

141. The hands on the clock face show roughly when Heather left her room. The hour hand has moved (x – 35) minutes since 7 p.m., and the minute hand y minutes. Since the minute hand moves twelve times faster than the hour hand, y = 12(x – 35).

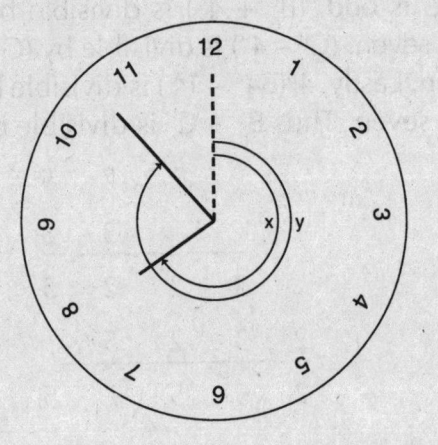

Now consider the position when the hands have changed places. The hour hand will have moved (y – 50) minutes since 10 p.m., and the minute hand x minutes. Hence x = 12(y – 50).

Solving these equations, $x = 39^{63}/_{143}$ and $y = 53^{41}/_{143}$. Thus the time elapsed since Heather left her room was 2 hours 46 minutes $9^{3}/_{13}$ seconds.

142. Laid back.

143. 6174.

144. Let the longer candle burn at L $^{cm}/_{hr}$ and the shorter candle at S $^{cm}/_{hr}$. Then the longer candle was 8L cm, the shorter candle 8.75S cm, and 8L = 8.75S + 2.

At 8 p.m. the candles were the same length, so 4L = 5S. Solving with the above, $S = {}^{8}/_{5}$ and L = 2, so the longer candle was 16 cm and the shorter candle was 14 cm.

145. *Little House on the Prairie.*

146. The pairs are:

$^{355}/_{113}$ = 3.1415929…   (= 3.1415926…)

$^{577}/_{408}$ = 1.414215…   ($\overline{2}$ = 1.414213…)

$^{878}/_{323}$ = 2.71826…   (e = 2.71828…)

$^{987}/_{610}$ = 1.618032…   (φ = 1.618033…)

where   is the area of a circle of unit radius, e is the base for natural logarithms, and φ is the golden ratio. Interesting properties of φ include its relationship with its square (which equals φ + 1) and its reciprocal (which equals φ – 1). φ = (1 + $\overline{5}$) / 2.

147. The four ages are 12, 16, 42, and 44.

148. Split level.

149. The number at the center of any three-by-three magic square is always one-third of the magic square's constant. Thus the center square must be 37. The rest then follows. (Reflected and rotated answers are also possible.)

43	1	67
61	37	13
7	73	31

150. "We" are the number of letters in each word. Thus "twelve" is six, "nine" is four, etc.

151. ABCDE is 93084.

152. The key move is 1 Bh3, to which Black must reply with a queen move. If Black plays **1** … Qa8 or **1** … Qe8, then **2** Qd4+ Qe4 **3** Qf6+ Qf5 **4** Qg5+ Qxg5 mate.

   If Black keeps his queen on the same rank, say **1** … Qd4, then **2** g3+ Kf3+ **3** Bg4+ Qxg4 mate.

   If Black plays any other queen move, then White plays either **2** Qb4+ or **2** Qc4+ or **2** Qd4+ forcing Black to reply with either **2** … Qxb4 or **2** … Qxc4 or **2** … Qxd4 and then White forces Black to win as above. For example, **1** Bh3 Qa6 **2** Qc4+ Qxc4 **3** g3+ Kf3+ **4** Bg4+ Qxg4 mate.

153. Bob up and down.

154. Of all possible sets of four whole numbers whose product is 180, the only sets with sums that are not unique are those with sums of 18 and 22. Thus the professor must have been teaching for one of those two periods.

   If it is 18 years, then the four lengths of study could be 1, 5, 6, and 6 years; 2, 2, 5, and 9 years; or 2, 3, 3, and 10 years. If it is 22 years, then the possible combinations are 1, 2, 9, and 10 years, or 2, 2, 3, and 15 years.

   We are told that knowing whether any of the students were into double figures would enable the professor to determine the four periods, so a length of teaching of 22 years is ruled out. Of the three sets whose sum is 18 years, two contain no double-digit numbers, which leaves the third set as the only possibility.

   Thus the four students had been studying for 2, 3, 3, and 10 years.

155. There is no choice regarding the queen and king; each has only one square on which to be placed. The rooks, knights, and bishops can each be positioned in two ways, giving a total of $2^3 = 8$ different combinations. The eight pawns can be positioned in 8! = 40,320 ways. Thus for the pieces of one color there are a total of 8 x 40,320 = 322,560 possibilities.

156. Lucky break.

157. The positions were first, fifth, and ninth for the navy; second, sixth, and seventh for the air force; and third, fourth, and eighth for the army.

158. Three wise men.

159. **1** d4 d5 **2** Qd3 Qd6 **3** Qh3 Qh6 **4** Qxc8 mate.

160. Monday is an anagram of dynamo.

161. The middle of nowhere.

162. Robin Hood.

INDEX

All puzzles are indexed by page number.